NEW PARADIGMS IN PUBLIC POLICY

NEW PARADIGMS IN PUBLIC POLICY

Edited by
Peter Taylor-Gooby

Published *for* THE BRITISH ACADEMY
by OXFORD UNIVERSITY PRESS

Oxford University Press, Great Clarendon Street, Oxford OX2 6DP

© *The British Academy 2013*
Database right The British Academy (maker)

First edition published in 2013

British Library Cataloguing in Publication Data
Data available

Library of Congress Cataloging in Publication Data
Data available

Typeset by New Leaf Design, Scarborough, North Yorkshire
Printed and bound in Great Britain by TJ International Ltd

ISBN 978-0-19-726493-5

Contents

Figures and Tables

Figures

Tables

Notes on contributors

Andrew Gamble

Andrew Gamble is Professor of Politics at the Department of Political and International Studies at the University of Cambridge, and a Fellow of Queens' College. He was a founding member and later Director of the Political Economy Research Centre at the University of Sheffield. His research interests include the British political economy and the ideologies, institutions and histories that have shaped it, the relationship between doctrines of political economy and modern ideologies, and a range of applied and theoretical issues in political economy. He was elected a Fellow of the British Academy in 2000, and received the Sir Isaiah Berlin Prize for Lifetime Contribution to Political Studies from the UK Political Studies Association in 2005. His recent publications include *The Spectre at the Feast: Capitalist crisis and the politics of recession* (2009.

Ian Gough

Ian Gough is Professorial Research Fellow at the Centre for Analysis of Social Exclusion at the London School of Economics and Political Science, an Associate at the Grantham Research Institute on Climate Change at the LSE, and Emeritus Professor of Social Policy at the University of Bath. Ian Gough has published work on a range of issues including human needs and well-being, welfare regimes and social change, and the political economy of welfare states. He is now researching climate change and social policy.

Tariq Modood

Tariq Modood is Professor of Sociology, Politics and Public Policy at the University of Bristol and is also the founding Director of the Centre for the Study of Ethnicity and Citizenship. He is a regular contributor to the media and policy debates in Britain. He was awarded an MBE for services to social sciences and ethnic relations in 2001 and was elected a member of the Academy of Social Sciences in 2004. Professor Tariq Modood served on the Commission on the Future of Multi-Ethnic Britain, the IPPR Commission on National Security and on the National Equality Panel, which reported to the UK Deputy Prime Minister in 2010. His recent publications include *Multiculturalism: A Civic Idea*, 2nd edition (2013); and as co-editor, *Global Migration, Ethnicity and Britishness* (2011) and *European Multiculturalisms* (2012).

Anne Power

Anne Power is Professor of Social Policy at the London School of Economics and Head of LSE Housing and Communities, a research group based within the Centre for Analysis of Social Exclusion. Her areas of expertise include cities and sustainable development, disadvantaged and run-down neighbourhoods, race relations and international and UK housing and social change. She was awarded an MBE in 1983 for work in Brixton, and a CBE in June 2000 for services to regeneration and resident participation. She is a Senior Fellow of the Brookings Institution and an Honorary Fellow of the Royal Institute for British Architects. She is author and co-author of many books, reports and articles on housing, cities and low-income communities, including *Phoenix Cities: The fall and rise of great industrial cities* (with Jörg Plöger and Astrid Winkler, 2010), *Family Futures: Childhood and poverty in urban neighbourhoods* (with Helen Willmot and Rosemary Davidson, 2011) and *Cities for a Small Country* (with Richard Rogers, 2000).

Gerry Stoker

Gerry Stoker is Professor of Politics and Governance at the University of Southampton. His research interests include democratic politics, public participation, public service reform, local and regional governance, and urban politics. He is the author or editor of more than twenty books, including *Why Politics Matters: Making democracy work* (2006) and *Governance Theory and Practice* (with Vasudha Chhotray, 2008). Professor Stoker was the founding chair of the New Local Government Network, has advised governments in the UK, Europe and further afield, and has won prestigious awards from the Political Studies Association for his work and its impact.

Peter Taylor-Gooby
Peter Taylor-Gooby is Professor of Social Policy at the University of Kent. He was elected a Fellow of the British Academy in 2009. His publications include: *Reframing Social Citizenship,* (2009); *New Risks, New Welfare* (2009); *Risk in Social Science* (2006, with Jens Zinn). He chairs the 2014 REF Social Work and Social Policy sub-panel. Current research, supported by a Leverhulme Fellowship, examines social cohesion.

Pat Thane
Pat Thane is Research Professor in Contemporary History at King's College, London. She co-manages the History and Policy project (http://www.historyandpolicy.org). Her most recent publications are: *Sinners? Scroungers? Saints? Unmarried Mothers in Twentieth Century England* (with Tanya Evans, 2012); *Unequal Britain: Equalities in Britain since 1945* (ed. 2010); *Women and Citizenship in Great Britain and Ireland in the Twentieth Century* (co-edited with Esther Breitenbach, 2010).

Preface and Acknowledgements

In 2010 the British Academy Policy Centre launched 'New Paradigms in Public Policy', a project to consider future directions in public policy in the UK and the framework of ideas that surround policymaking. The project published a series of reports in 2011 and 2012 which considered some particularly difficult issues in public policy: climate change, multiculturalism, recession and recovery, population ageing, neighbourhood problems and the Third Sector, rebuilding democratic engagement, and managing the demands of an increasingly assertive public. These have now been revised and are brought together in one volume. The chapters deal with the specifics of each area. The common thread is the need for new approaches which call into question some of the assumptions that guide current policies in order to address the problems we face more effectively.

The British Academy Policy Centre oversees a programme of activity aimed at stimulating dialogue and engagement between leading researchers, parliamentarians and policymakers in the UK and abroad. It aims to shed light on matters of public interest and concern, drawing on insights derived from the best available research in the humanities and social sciences.

Acknowledgements

The members of the project team are grateful to the staff of the British Academy, in particular Emma McKay, Helen Haggart and Brigid Hamilton-Jones, for their help and support in the series of meetings and seminars that led up to the reports. More generally, their thanks are due to all those members of the social science communities who have helped shape their thinking on the issues discussed in the volume.

1

Introduction: public policy at a crossroads

PETER TAYLOR-GOOBY

Public policy in Britain, as in other developed countries, faces severe challenges from many directions. The continuing economic crisis and its aftermath bring these issues to the forefront of public debate, but risk obscuring the underlying issues behind immediate political tussles over the recovery programme, constitutional reform, bankers' bonuses and other pressing questions.

This book tackles the basic questions that confront twenty-first century policy-making in seven substantive chapters, each written by a leading expert in the field: finding a way forward for the British economy; the dilemma of coping with rising demand in the context of limited resources; how to respond to climate change; managing ethnic diversity as multi-culturalism appears to have lost its way; whether demographic change equates with a growing burden of dependency; under what circumstances localism helps resolve concentrated neighbourhood problems; and how to overcome public disaffection with politics. A concluding chapter considers the more practical issue of developments in social science that might help it make a more forceful contribution to public policy.

The chapters analyse the contribution of social science to understanding the issues in each of these areas. They go on to review the range of possible developments in the medium-term future We will first set out the contents of the individual chapters and then discuss the notion of policy paradigm that underlies the approach to the relationship between ideas and policy-making contained in them. We will move on to examine emerging themes in the relationship between government and other agencies bound up in policy-making, individual citizens, market actors and community activity, and conclude by reviewing the relationship between social science and public policy.

The chapters

The first substantive chapter, by Professor Andrew Gamble, is written as the British economy emerges unsteadily from the most serious recession since the 1930s. Professor Gamble argues that a political economy perspective is necessary to understand the debates surrounding economic growth. He reviews the way in which commentators have analysed the challenges facing public policy. He then examines debates about the crash and the deficit, the role and size of the state and the appropriate growth model. The major alternative approaches to growth currently under discussion lie between a return to the liberal financial model, dominant since the 1980s and sometimes termed 'privatised Keynesianism', and greater government intervention to restore the role of the manufacturing sector, possibly involving a shift to a more European-style corporatism. The chapter concludes by considering three scenarios: a return to growth; a shift in the international environment that renders austerity permanent; and the imposition of radical changes to curb expansion and cut back carbon emissions to sustainable levels.

Current demands to reduce the level of public debt draw attention to the insistent pressures on public spending. Population ageing and rising public expectations demand increases. The exigencies of international competitiveness, and now the economic crisis, require cutbacks. In the next chapter Professor Peter Taylor-Gooby reviews the range of strategies that have been developed to manage the dilemma between maintaining services and constraint including shifts in responsibility in various areas towards the market and the individual or voluntary sector, target-setting, manifold attempts to manage and restrain public provision, and attempts to change people's behaviour to cut demand. None of these approaches is entirely acceptable to public opinion and none has been markedly successful in solving the problem. This suggests that the dilemma of spending versus cutting will continue to underlie policy-making, that future policies must combine a range of approaches, and that greater attention to fostering a more informed and genuinely democratic debate is necessary so that new policy directions will be able to gain public support.

The challenge to current economic and social policies posed by climate change is more severe than in any other area. Chapter 4 by Professor Ian Gough reviews evidence on the nature of the problem, focusing particularly on debates about the impact on economic growth. He reviews current responses: that capitalist economies will find ways to cope with growing carbon emissions as they expand; that growth strategies compatible with environmental futures are possible; and that it is impossible to maintain growth rates and address the problem. He concludes that adequate and practicable responses cannot be generated within current policy frameworks. Current policies place too great an emphasis on economic incentives and fail to exploit the additional opportunities to reduce emissions through direct regulation or stronger leadership in cultural change.

The non-white population of European countries is small, rapidly growing and heavily concentrated, so that in many cities ethnic minority populations will grow rapidly towards 40 or 50 per cent within 40 years. This development poses major political and cultural challenges. In chapter 5 Professor Tariq Modood reviews the chief current policy responses—assimilation, integration and multiculturalism—in the context of claims by politicians in Germany, France and the UK that 'multiculturalism is dead'. He distinguishes between two multicultural approaches: a valuing of diversity which accords full recognition to differences between cultural groups within a liberal democratic framework; and a multiculturalism which values cultural interaction and social mixing but withholds institutional recognition from groups, especially religious ones. The first approach may unintentionally strengthen barriers between groups and foster segregation, whilst the second may marginalise certain cultural orientations and communities. Progressive policy-making must uphold individual rights and freedom to belong or not belong but it must not stigmatise or exclude groups from full participation in public life. The chapter concludes by analysing the emerging ethnic fault lines across Europe and stresses the significance of a shift from colour to religion as the foundation of group identity, with major implications for the relationship between religon and politics.

In chapter 6, Professor Pat Thane examines debates about future demographic patterns. She shows that the case for immediate cutbacks in spending and for the restructuring of pensions, health and social care to defuse a presumed 'demographic time-bomb' is not compelling. She goes on to examine alternative demographic scenarios and sets out some guidelines for policies to cope with future demographic change, recognising the contributions that older citizens can make to society.

Building a 'Big Society' in which citizens would be empowered to deal with local issues is high on the political agenda. In chapter 7 Professor Anne Power stands back from current debates in this field. She traces the origins of community politics in the co-operative institutions that people set up to manage the pressures and problems of eighteenth- and nineteenth-century industrialisation. Post-war debates in this country have been heavily influenced by US experience in the struggles for civil rights and in the Great Society programme. These led to the implementation of neighbourhood policies under both Labour and Conservative governments from the 1970s onwards. The key theme in all these developments has been the support and involvement of the state in enabling citizen's groups to operate effectively and in providing resources for them. Professor Power's analysis shows that Big Society is not an alternative to government but that, to be effective, the two must operate within a framework of mutual support.

The problems outlined in this book require new directions in policy-making if they are to be tackled effectively. Chapter 8 by Professor Gerry Stoker sets out changes in UK political systems that will help to build public support for reforms. The current context is one of growing popular disaffection with politics. Professor Stoker reviews explanations of how this has come about: declining trust in politicians; the discrediting of political processes; and disappointment with the output in terms of policies and policy-thinking. He then considers solutions proposed by those who seek to reinvigorate representative institutions through such changes as greater use of proportional representation and more devolution of powers to local government, and those who wish to go further in supporting citizen activism and creating new opportunities for participation. He suggests that both approaches need to be combined.

The final chapter, by Professors Gerry Stoker and Peter Taylor-Gooby, returns to the question of how best social scientists can contribute to public policy. It discusses how both the policy-making process and the professional organisation of social science, as currently structured, militate against helpful interchange. This leads in two directions. First, it is desirable to open up the range of approaches and orientations available to policy-making, by ensuring that those involved are recruited from a wide range of communities, by analysing how policy objectives are selected and defined and by promoting greater interplay at different career stages between government and academic life.

Secondly, it is difficult to envisage radical changes in the operation of a system driven by the immediate and imperative demands of day-to-day government and by the concern of many politicians to gain and retain power through election. These issues take the centre of policy-making outside the remit of most academic work. For these reasons more weight must be placed on possible changes within social science. We suggest that social science needs to develop, alongside the academic research which is at its heart, a 'design arm' directed to practical issues and concerned with the application of research findings in improving policy outcomes.

The issues with which this book deals are fiercely debated across the policy community by academics, think-tanks, politicians and policy-makers. The objective is to stand back from the immediate debate and map out what social science has to offer to policy-makers and how best it may make that contribution. The analysis uses the notion of policy paradigm to understand how the range of viewpoints and approaches developed by academic commentators relate to the more concrete and focused conceptions of those engaged in practical policy-making.

Paradigms and policy discourse

A paradigm links together normative and descriptive elements, the former subject to dispute, the latter in principle empirically based, to provide a way of approaching a particular issue and of justifying that approach. Peter Hall explains the core idea in an influential paper as follows:

> policy-makers customarily work within a framework of ideas and standards that specifies not only the goals of policy and the kind of instruments that can be used to attain them, but also the very nature of the problems they are meant to be addressing. Like a Gestalt, this framework is embedded in the very terminology through which policymakers communicate about their work, and it is influential precisely because so much of it is taken for granted and unamenable to scrutiny as a whole (Hall 1993, 279).

This perspective is widely used in the study of public policy-making.

The paradigm approach draws on the Kuhnian idea that progress in natural science takes place within paradigms in order to exploit the idea of paradigm revolution. Kuhn argued that scientists work within a para-digm—a framework of ideas that defines what is known, highlights areas for future work and explains why they are important (1962). So long as the paradigm proves fruitful, science develops within the framework. If research findings fail to fit the paradigm, it will be modified to accommodate the new material. Finally, it breaks down. A period of confusion follows. If alternative paradigms emerge, debates between them will provide an unstable structure. Eventually one will succeed, and 'normal' science, framed within a fresh paradigm, progress. Standard examples would be the Copernican revolution in astronomy or the Einsteinian revolution in physics.

Policy-making is not natural science and the term is used by analogy. Policy paradigms provide a framework of ideas that links together descriptive statements about the area of policy with normative statements about the goals of policy. They explain why some policies will achieve desired goals and others will not. Normal policy continues within the framework until it appears unsuccessful. There follow modification, confusion and opportunities for a new paradigm to emerge. Policy entrepreneurs within political parties, the world of think-tanks and lobby groups and the Whitehall community compete to offer one. Hall explains the shift between neo-Keynesian economic management and monetarism in the 1980s as a paradigm shift. The experience of stagflation in the 1970s demonstrated the failure of interventionism. The government was unable to manage the economy successfully by using the available regulatory mechanisms. As a result a new approach was introduced, linked to the ideas associated with the radically reforming Conservative government elected in 1979 (see chapter 2).

In the social world, in contrast to that of natural science, paradigm change is a political process. Different paradigms compete to explain developments and justify responses. For example, in the late 1970s, the Labour party pursued a reflationary state-centred alternative economic policy; other commentators promoted the European corporatist approach and the Conservative party spearheaded the monetarist paradigm. It is always possible that no new paradigm may emerge or that a paradigm shift may take place that does not enable policy to achieve the specified goals, so that the country fails to find a plausible route towards its economic goals, as in Japan during the 'lost decade' of the 1990s.

Disputes between proponents of different policy approaches are not easy to resolve. The political process tends to foreground particular paradigms that fit the prior assumptions of policy-makers and treat others as irrelevant. The paradigms dominant in each area frame policy thinking and delimit the range of possible solutions.

The first step in linking social science to policy-making is to recognise this point. In this book we review the policy paradigms that could be constructed on the basis of available social science knowledge and theory-building in the fields we discuss. We consider the relationship between these paradigms and public policies, and point out that many potential social science contributions fail to enter the policy arena. We call for openness to a wider range of viewpoints in tackling the problems that confront public policy. We also suggest that social scientists should develop a more consciously policy-oriented approach alongside their academic research, which would examine how this work might be applied to more practical issues. In each chapter we can identify a dominant paradigm that drives current policy, and also a range of available alternatives discussed by others. To summarise:

- The first substantive chapter discusses the range of approaches to the current economic crisis. It argues that a liberal financial paradigm, emphasising the role of private market actors, tends to predominate in current policy-making. It discusses the range of alternatives that posit a stronger role of government intervention or lean towards a more corporatist approach. These would rest on a broader political economy.

- In the second, on dilemmas facing public policy-makers, the dominant theme in current policy is of continuing austerity, following the evidence of increased demographic and other pressures on public spending and the likelihood that these will continue. A wide range of approaches to managing public provision exist, drawing on developments in management science, public administration, behavioural psychology and micro-sociology. Since none appears capable of solving the problem by itself and any new departures will require strong public support, future policies will require more open and serious public debate about the services government can offer.

- The third policy chapter, dealing with climate change, shows how current attempts to control carbon emissions rest heavily on economic incentives, following a rational actor model. Too little attention is paid to alternatives such as direct state regulation or changing behaviour by offering leadership in public opinion. These would rest on a broader political economy approach to the issue and require a more interventionist role from the state.

- The analysis of multiculturalism in the next chapter suggests that current approaches combine a degree of hostility to group-based multiculturalism with a certain degree of pragmatic corporatism in policies towards minorities with strong group identities. It argues that a more sophisticated approach to identity will not be based on an exclusively individualist paradigm but will prize individual agency as well as group belonging and embrace measures to promote individual as well as group rights.

- The discussion of demographic shifts in the following chapter analyses how policy-making tends to rest on the assumption that population ageing is problematic on the grounds that a growing proportion of dependent older people will require extra public spending so that current services become unsustainable. The chapter seeks to move beyond the economics of spending to include a broader and more sociological account of the contributions that older people make to society and of how these might be enhanced by a more supportive approach from government, mitigating the problem.

- Much of the debate about neighbourhood problems and the 'Big Society' conceives community activities as an alternative to government. This fails to take seriously the fact that the activities of individuals in communities have developed alongside the growth of the modern welfare state and how government intervention and support is essential to maintain successful local initiatives. An alternative approach requires a more complex model of community politics and of how actions at the individual and local level relate to the more top-down activities of government.

- Evidence of a growing mistrust of the political class, expressed in political disengagement (chapter 8) has led commentators to offer a range of solutions. The chapter argues that these address different aspects of the problem and that it is necessary to combine them and to give a stronger role to citizen activism to develop a more engaged politics in the UK. The approach to understanding the issues needs to embrace the full range of factors underlying the problem.

- In the final chapter, the relationship between social science and public policy is examined. The chapter argues for greater two-way engagement requiring more interplay between policy-makers and academics, and also greater willingness on the part of academics to consider the practical relevance of what they do.

Since the issues covered in the different chapters vary it is hard to generalise across them. Some common themes emerge, concerning the relationship between government and the other actors in public policy, individual citizens, the community and the market, and the way in which social science relates to public policy issues.

State and civil society

The chapters show how the dominant paradigms in each area may neglect evidence and theories so that policy debate passes over alternative approaches to the issues at stake. We suggest that more prominent state interventions are necessary to address many of the problems we discuss. A shift to a more liberal political economy offers a limited approach to the problem of restoring stable growth in the UK. There is no comprehensive solution to the problem of financing adequate public services under permanent austerity. A range of options must be combined and must also be acceptable to voters, which requires greater efforts to involve the public in the issues. Market policies such as carbon pricing have had little success in containing emissions at acceptable levels. A holistic and inclusive multiculturalism will not see the support of individuals and of communities as an either/or but will seek to promote an open social environment in which individuals can flourish in the kinds of communities that are meaningful to them. Government can manage population change in a more positive manner by enabling different generations to contribute. Localism and democratic empowerment depend on policies to address inequalities and to enable groups to contribute to the public good in the same way that multicultural policies as they are practised seek to do. Nudge economics can only succeed outside a limited area if government restrains the private commercial interests that are seeking to shape 'choice architecture'.

An emphasis on the role of government does not imply that these issues can be entirely resolved by central direction. Top-down interventions face limits to what they can achieve, and must be reinforced by bottom-up approaches resting on commitments in civil society. The relationship between state and individual citizen or local community is not a zero-sum game in which a loss of power by one automatically generates an equivalent gain by the other. Community initiatives and engaged citizenship require government support, especially for more vulnerable groups, and regulation to ensure that commercial interests are constrained.

These problems cut across many aspects of society. Just as social science must draw on the resources of a number of academic disciplines to understand them fully, so must policy-making integrate activities across agencies and across areas of government. The chapters review the contributions of political economy, social psychology, political sociology, demography, political science, social policy and historical studies to paradigm-building. They also show how adequate policy responses cannot be confined to the macro-level, but involve changes at the level of local government and in the way individuals and communities manage such issues as cultural difference, carbon footprints, the status of older people and their engagement with the political system.

Social science and public policy

The book demonstrates the twofold contribution of social science to public policy-making. Academic work can chart out the available viewpoints and show that it often contains a range of perspectives that is broader and richer than that dominant in policy debate. It can also contribute to identifying the policies that are likely to be most fruitful in managing the issues that confront us. Social scientists can also develop work consciously directed at policy design as well as analytic understanding in order to contribute to public policy-making.

We show how collaborative use of the repertoire of disciplinary approaches available across social science is essential in understanding issues that impact on different areas of social life and different aspects of policy. Corresponding to interdisciplinarity at the practical level, many of the issues require policy responses that link up different government departments, challenging existing structures at both central and local levels.

The final chapter considers the changes needed for social science to realise its contribution to practical policy-making: what are the implications for social science practice in developing a 'design arm' alongside the established academic focus? Scientific approaches foreground analysis, relate instances to more general categories and construct causal accounts. A design approach focuses more on synthetic thinking, cutting across different contexts. It is centrally concerned with achieving a given goal. The problem we identify is that a paradigm-driven political process risks neglecting some of the most valuable potential contributions of academic work when these are not included within the dominant paradigm.

Social science in the UK is excellent in its analytic and theoretical activities (by international comparisons), but less well directed to inform policy-making. One reason is that the current structure of social science as a professional activity does not highlight policy relevance. Another is that policy-making is not well adapted to survey the range of possible contributions that academic work could support. If social scientists wish their work to have greater impact in 'speaking truth to power', the onus is on the scientific community: it is necessary to produce additional work that draws on established research to engage more directly with the issues that confront policy-making.

Conclusion

In this book we set out arguments for an approach that indicates the range of ways of understanding the apparently intractable problems we currently face. We argue that those debating policy should pay much more attention to alternative paradigms than those currently dominant for thinking about many of these problems and should think through the implications of different approaches. The paradigms currently informing policy-making often fail to embrace the full range of evidence and understandings so that the problems are addressed from a limited range of perspectives.

The clearest example of this process is the way in which current approaches often diminish the role of government and conceptualise it as a simple alternative to that of civil society or of the individual citizen. The most influential paradigm presents government and non-government as alternatives, so that state activity is seen to crowd out the private sector or community provision or individual resourcefulness. The possibility that under appropriate circumstances state and civil society may walk in step, government stimulating and supporting initiatives in the community and in the private sector, receives limited attention. The possibilities for generating economic progress through more substantial government interventions receive scant attention. At the same time the potential for citizens and community to contribute to resolving problems is diminished because the capacity of top-down policy-making to support, interact with and strengthen bottom-up initiatives is ignored. The chapters show that the contribution of citizens in responding to diversity, in reducing carbon production, in improving community health and in tackling neighbour-hood problems is potentially substantial, but that these benefits can only be fully realised with active government support.

This book deals with some of the most pressing issues in public policy. We hope it will help draw attention to the contribution that social science has to make to current debates. It shows how a range of approaches from different disciplinary backgrounds can be combined to understand the way in which the issues under consideration will develop. It suggests that policy-makers need to consider a broader range of approaches in their work and to do so at the highest level, at the level of the policy paradigms that define their objectives, and also pick out particular aspects of what research has to offer. The book also argues that social science itself needs to develop to strengthen its policy contribution, by paying greater attention to the bounded and practical issues of policy design.

References

Hall, P. (1993) 'Policy Paradigms, Social Learning, and the State: The Case of Economic Policymaking in Britain', *Comparative Politics* 25(3): 275–296.

Kuhn, T. (1962) *The Structure of Scientific Revolutions* (Chicago: University of Chicago Press).

2

Economic Futures

ANDREW GAMBLE

Introduction

The future of the British economy has an impact on many aspects of public policy. It is a vital concern for government. Yet our intellectual resources for thinking about it often appear limited. The Queen's reproach to the economics profession in 2008 after the financial crash ('If these things were so large how come everyone missed them' (Pierce 2008)) reflected a widespread scepticism about economic forecasting. It is often seen as unreliable, inconsistent, able to detect trees, but not woods. Yet such a view mistakes the kind of knowledge that economic forecasting can provide (Lawson 1997). Forecasting the future of the economy is only superficially similar to forecasting the weather or volcanic eruptions. There is a reasonable prospect that with greater understanding, better techniques and more sophisticated models, the accuracy of forecasts of natural events will improve. Economics, however, is different. There is no such prospect because the nature of what is being studied is fundamentally different.

One reason for this lies in the distinction between risk and uncertainty (Knight 1921). Some forms of uncertainty are measurable—these are what we call risks—but others are not. Economic forecasting seeks to establish probabilities about future events and trends in the economy and, in doing so, to assess the risks attached to different courses of action, and the costs and benefits associated with them. Cost–benefit analysis has, as a result, become a standard technique in government in the evaluation of policy programmes (Sunstein 2002). But although all modern societies have put enormous effort into the management of risk (Bernstein 1996), in order to narrow down the scope of uncertainty, they cannot eliminate it. There is radical uncertainty at the heart of social systems because decision-making never takes place with full information. Knowledge is fragmented and dispersed (Hayek 1949). A priori reasoning cannot eliminate indeterminacy from the future, neither can using the past as a guide. History does not repeat itself, because social events are unique.

Predicting the future of the British economy is complex, not just because it is made up of many different sectors, but because it is also part of networks and relationships that are regional, international and global—it is not a self-contained unit. The very concept of a national economy which can be managed by policy-makers is contested, and although during the twentieth century government came increasingly to think in terms of the 'national economy', it is an artificial construction, even if a necessary one. This is also true of many of the terms which litter debate on the economy, such as the concepts of the public and the private sector. The state is involved in so many different ways in the economy that attempts to define the boundaries of the state or policies to expand or to shrink the state are often highly ambiguous. Many of the simple frames used by politicians and the media to discuss economic policy often obfuscate rather than illuminate, because of the categories they persist in employing. Social science provides more sophisticated understanding of how government works, or how markets work, and the interdependence of the two (Lindblom 1977), but popular and public discourse rarely reflects it. This makes a political economy approach the most appropriate one for thinking about different futures for the British economy and the ideas which frame major issues in economic policy for the medium-term future.

The crash and the deficit

The financial crash of 2007–8 brought to an end a long period of growth and stability in the British economy. After the forced exit of sterling from the Exchange Rate Mechanism in 1992 and the spending cuts and tax increases which that made necessary, the British economy grew steadily and uninterruptedly for the next 15 years, allowing politicians to proclaim incautiously the end of boom and bust (Brown 2004). The growth was not just a British phenomenon, although for other countries it was at times interrupted by recessions and the collapse of financial bubbles, such as the Asian financial crash of 1997 and the dot.com crash of 2000. Yet no sooner had one bubble burst, than another was found to take its place. The general movement of the markets was upwards and the general sentiment was optimistic. Underlying this buoyancy was the impact of the entry of China and other rising powers into the global economy. The flood of cheap imports which they made possible, helped to keep inflation at low levels, and sustained the consumer boom, as well as encouraging the development of ever more sophisticated financial instruments to finance it (Glyn 2006; Frieden 2006).

The boom ended in the crash of 2007–8 and many parts of the international economy, including Britain and the United States, were plunged into recession, although China and the other rising powers continued to grow. The severity of the financial collapse has produced a flood of analysis of its causes and its implications. Is this crisis comparable to those in the 1930s and 1970s, or is it primarily a financial crisis created by asset bubbles, similar to the Asian financial crisis and the dot.com crisis, but having little long-term significance for the real economy? Was the crisis caused by too much or too little regulation? Much commentary blamed the banks for the crisis, and in particular the lending practices and the culture which many of the investment banks had developed during the boom (Tett 2009; Shiller 2008; Schwartz 2009; Turner 2008; Sorkin 2010). This was encouraged by the enthusiasm for the deregulation of finance, which was such a hallmark of the new financial regime established on Wall Street and in the City of London from the 1980s onwards. In this way, the crash has been depicted as the nemesis of the neo-liberal doctrines which had gained such ascendancy over economic policy (Wade 2008). But others have argued that the primary failing was the regulatory system for not restraining the increasingly dubious lending practices of some parts of the banking sector (Davies 2010), and that governments and regulators were complicit in the bubbles and in promoting the euphoria and the feeling that the boom could go on forever (Thompson 2009).

One interesting question is whether the regulators could have possessed greater foresight, or whether the nature of modern financial markets makes this impossible (Roubini 2010). Even if they had possessed the information that a crisis in the financial markets was fast approaching, would they have possessed the political capacity to do anything about it? It seems that many market agents were aware of the risks that were being run, and took steps to protect themselves, but the knowledge that is available to market agents, and which is sufficient for them to take action, is different from the knowledge which is available to regulators who are responsible for the whole system. Market agents only need to consult their own interests, but regulators must take a view of the interest of the system as a whole. Econometric models proved ineffective in anticipating the crash, but there were other theoretical models, for example the work of Hyman Minsky, first developed in the 1970s, which did anticipate the general form of the crisis, even though it could not predict its timing or its precise details (Minsky 1982). Minsky charts the nature and pattern of financial crises in the modern economy in ways which made the events of 2007–8 instantly recognisable within his framework. There is also a great deal of historical work on past crises (Kindleberger 1978) and since the recent crisis much of this work has been helpfully compiled by Carmen Reinhart and Kenneth Rogoff (Reinhart and Rogoff 2008). One of the things this literature demonstrates is how much the latest financial crash fits into a familiar pattern of financial and economic behaviour which has become established over the last 300 years, and how forgetful each new generation of politicians and regulators are of history. But that is different from saying that there are 'lessons of history' which, had policy-makers learnt, would have helped them avoid this latest crisis. The problem for regulators is that even when armed with the knowledge that all financial booms eventually collapse, it is still not possible to know the timing of the collapse and, given the competitive nature of financial jurisdictions, no regulatory authority will want to put its own financial sector at a disadvantage. So this becomes a collective action problem. It is the dispersed character of regulation which can lead to the toleration of unsafe practices, even when it is known that a financial collapse will take place. It is also true that certain kinds of economic reasoning persuaded some regulators, notably Alan Greenspan, that although regulators did not understand the complexity of the financial markets, the financial markets themselves possessed a higher intelligence than the regulators and therefore could be trusted to solve any problems that arose spontaneously. Greenspan has since acknowledged that he was mistaken (Greenspan 2008).

There is also a lively literature over whether it would have been possible to contain this bubble in the way in which some previous bubbles had been contained and safely deflated. Those who think it should have been possible point in particular to major mistakes which they believe were committed by politicians and regulators, notably the decision of the US secretary of the treasury, Henry Paulson, not to bail out Lehman Brothers (Kaletsky 2010; Williams 2010; McDonald and Robinson 2009). Others are more sceptical, believing that by 2008 the crisis was unavoidable, and any number of particular triggers could have set it off (Harvey 2011; Mason 2009). The significance of this debate for policy is the extent to which the regulatory regime can be blamed for the crash and whether a regulatory regime can be devised which could avoid the same mistakes in the future. Different kinds of regulation are involved, however. One argument has been that changing the responsibilities of some of the key players—the Bank of England, the Financial Services Authority and the Treasury—is sufficient because the fundamental problem was that no one was taking responsibility for ensuring that banking was being conducted safely. This approach argues for keeping regulation 'light-touch' and in the background so as not to damage the vitality and competitiveness of the financial sector in London, but making sure that the authorities are more alert to the dangers of a financial meltdown than they proved to be in the run-up to 2008. A more radical argument has focused on the character of financial services themselves and has argued that regulation is needed to reconstruct the nature of these services, for example, by imposing much higher capital ratios or splitting investment from retail banking, in effect breaking up the larger banks, and removing the possibility that in future any bank is too large to fail (Hutton 2010; Arestis and Sobreira 2010). This kind of regulation would be intrusive and interventionist, reshaping the way banks were organised and the way they operate.

In the UK the coalition government established the Independent Commission on Banking under Sir John Vickers to report on regulatory reform for the banks. The Commission issued an interim report in April 2011, pending its full report in September 2011. Parallel discussions have been going on at the international level about changing the Basel Accords, and moving to Basel III (Wolf 2009; Goodhart 2010b). The G20 document of 2009 under the British Presidency set out an ambitious vision for a new international regulatory order (HM Government 2009). However, expectations in 2010 and 2011 were not high that international agreement on a radically different set of rules for finance could be agreed. Without agreement, national jurisdictions with large financial sectors will be wary of imposing tougher regulation than is being imposed elsewhere, for fear of damaging their own status as a leading centre. There was a widespread international consensus immediately after the crash that a similar crisis should not be allowed to happen again, but three years on, that enthusiasm had abated and there were strong pressures for going back to business as usual. Attention had shifted from the problems of the banking system to the problems of sovereign debt. Critics argued that if the underlying causes of the banking crisis of 2007–8 were not addressed, the international economy could suffer further financial crashes in the years ahead (Hutton 2010; Roubini 2010; Eatwell and Milgate 2011). The sovereign debt crisis of 2011 on both sides of the Atlantic appeared to confirm those fears.

A second important debate arises from the many attempts to analyse the nature of the crash of 2007–8, to determine what kind of economic event it was, and what the implications are for policy. It has been argued that this crisis is of the same magnitude and potential significance as the crises in the 1930s and 1970s (Reinhart and Rogoff 2008). Both decades were characterised by a long period of political and economic restructuring and, in policy terms, both former crises are said to have facilitated a 'paradigm shift' in economic policy-making, in the first case from classical liberal political economy to Keynesianism, and in the second case from Keynesianism to monetarism. This interpretation was applied to the British case by Peter Hall in his theory of policy paradigms and social learning (Hall 1993). Hall distinguished between first order change, affecting the settings of the policy instruments, but leaving the overall goals the same; second order change, affecting the instruments of policy as well as their settings; and third order change, in which the goals as well as the instruments of policy and their settings are changed. In this third case the whole framework of policy discourse shifts.

Is the crisis of 2007–8 a third order change of the kind Hall describes, or might it lead to such a change in the future? Some are already suggesting that it will not, and therefore that it is wrong to label the events of 2008 a crisis at all (Hay 2010). On this view a crisis is only a crisis if it leads to a paradigm shift—if it makes it impossible to carry on in the old way. As argued above, in the area of financial regulation there is not yet much evidence that the shock of the events in 2008 by themselves will lead to significant policy change, certainly not of a third order kind; at most there will be some change to settings and to instruments. The dominant market liberal paradigm has not been displaced and this is partly because, as yet, there is no very convincing intellectual or political alternative to it (Wilson 2012).

Paradigm shifts take place when the breakdown in the existing system is so severe that something else must be put in place. New circumstances are often more compelling than new ideas. The ideas come later. The economic and financial collapse between 1929 and 1932, which included the end of the gold standard, forced radical policies of adjustment—such as the New Deal—to the fore. But the responses varied considerably between countries and were justified differently.

In the debates considered here, the issue of whether the crisis of 2008 requires a rethinking of the policy paradigm which has dominated British politics since 1976 is often implicit or explicit. Paradigm shifts in policy-making are rare since whenever there is an external shock, the normal reaction is to find ways of responding as effectively as possible but then returning to the way in which things were being done before. Adaptation is generally easier for human organisations than radical breaks. But sometimes the latter occur despite the best efforts of those seeking to keep the ship afloat. One difficulty faced by national policy-makers is that they may think that after a crisis they can restore policy at a national level to where it was before. It may be much harder to do so at an international level, but the international level may be critical for the success of the national policy (Thompson 2008, 2010). Some of the uncertainty arises because of the number of national jurisdictions and their different aims and interests, and the difficulty of finding coordinated ways to address common problems and dangers. This is particularly evident in long-term threats, such as the response to climate change.

Much of the political debate in the UK since the crisis has been dominated by the issue of public sector deficits which were created both by the collapse of economic activity following the crash and by the way governments responded by lowering interest rates, nationalising banks and pumping money into the economy though fiscal stimulus and quantitative easing. The banking crisis of 2008 quickly mutated into a fiscal crisis and then for many states became a sovereign debt crisis. A number of positions have emerged in these debates, between market fundamentalists and market realists and between deflationists and inflationists. There are technical issues involved but the more interesting questions in relation to different economic futures, are whether deficits are bad or good in themselves, and what they imply about the size of the state, the functions it should perform, and possible models of economic growth.

The first question can be framed in traditional terms as a dispute between Keynesian and Hayekian modes of economic reasoning. This way of thinking about the choices on offer makes little sense to many contemporary economists, but it retains its force in public debate. Hayekians argue that in a recession deficits are a barrier to recovery and must be removed as quickly as possible. The Keynesians argue that in a recession governments should be prepared to run deficits in order to make recovery happen. Immediately after the crash Keynesian arguments were in the ascendancy, developed by Paul Krugman, Joseph Stiglitz, Paul Davidson and David Blanchflower among others (Krugman 2008; Stiglitz 2010; Davidson 2009; Blanchflower 2009). There was a brief flurry of speculation about 'the return of Keynes' (Skidelsky 2009), but Hayekian arguments were soon in the ascendancy in the policy debate in the countries of the European Union, including the United Kingdom. The main disagreement in the British policy debate was over timing and the period over which the budget deficit should be eliminated—whether in the lifetime of one Parliament, or longer.

As Robert Skidelsky has pointed out (Skidelsky 2010), there is at present no party in Britain that is advocating a classical Keynesian approach to the deficit. A Keynesian approach would involve taking no steps to reduce it until the recovery was firmly established. Skidelsky argues that there is a fundamental divergence between the Keynesian and Hayekian arguments in their assumptions about how the economy works, and in particular whether public spending crowds out private spending. The Keynesian argument is that it only does so when there is full employment of resources, the Hayekian argument is that it does so at all times (Eatwell and Milgate 2011). Hayekian arguments have been buttressed by academic arguments claiming that debt over 90 per cent of national income reduced economic growth (Reinhart and Rogoff 2008), and that reducing deficits by cutting spending rather than increasing taxes was much more beneficial to recovery (Alesina and Ardagna 2010).

Economists are right in arguing that the Keynesian/Hayekian dichotomy is in many ways too simple. The current position is very different from 1930–1 because all governments since then have accepted the automatic stabilisers associated with Keynesianism as well as the extension of the state which rules out a pure Hayekian stance to the deficit. The actual policy positions adopted by the main political parties in the UK are nuanced, and quite close together. They reflect the mainstream approach in the

Treasury and the Bank of England, which has been criticised for being too focused on macroeconomic management, and insufficiently sensitive to the role of financial markets in the economy (Goodhart 2010a). Despite all the adversary rhetoric between the parties, the policy stance of the coalition government is only marginally tougher than the one to which Alastair Darling committed Labour before the election. The headline figures of 20–25 per cent cuts in many departments, rising to 40 per cent in some departments because of the protection afforded to others, are misleading because the cuts will be spread over a number of years. Public spending in real terms is planned to go on increasing over the course of the current Parliament. What changes is that it falls back as a percentage of gross domestic product (GDP) (although only to 40 or 41 per cent) because of the assumptions made about economic growth and inflation in the government forecasts. The headline figures of cuts and the displays of public anger towards some of them (such as the withdrawal of child benefit for higher earners) seem to have been sufficient to reassure the markets that the government's stance was tough enough. Yet, despite appearances, the markets did not regard the UK in 2009 and 2010 as a high credit risk, because of the way the UK debt was structured, with low bond yields on long-term loans. This position may change in the future, particularly if the growth forecasts underpinning the coalition government's deficit reduction plan are not met, but in the immediate aftermath of the crash the UK could in principle have afforded to borrow a great deal more and let the exchange rate take the strain (Wolf 2011). The market constraint is often invoked, but as in the case of the supposed constraint in 1976, the real reason for the decisions on public spending lies with policy decisions by the government rather than external pressure. The academic literature on the 1976 IMF crisis using the public records now available has made that clear (Ludlam 1992; Rogers 2010), and the same is likely to be true in future research on the current budget cuts. The reassertion of fiscal conservatism as the default position of the Treasury in the response to the recent crisis reflects both deep-seated preferences of state managers, and also the popular understandings of political economy to which politicians habitually appeal, in particular by comparing the national budget to the budget of an ordinary household, and the national 'credit card' to an individual's credit card.

There is a large literature showing the cyclical nature of many public spending programmes, as well as the long-term trend for public expenditure to increase (Peacock and Wiseman 1961; Mullard 1993). Periodic cuts in public spending form an essential part of this cycle. They slow the upward rise of public spending, but studies show that they do not reverse it. At best they contain it. The pressures making for higher public spending are highly resilient, and even the most radical governments have not actually succeeded in altering the level of public spending. What they can affect is the distribution of public spending between different programmes and the balance between tax increases and spending cuts. Even here, however, appearances can be deceptive. Sometimes the difference between a spending cut and a tax increase is a rather tenuous one. Cuts in child benefit or the trebling of student fees are presented as spending cuts, but in their impact on individuals are experienced much more like tax increases. So are other cuts in subsidies which lead to price increases. The final balance of a cuts package between spending cuts and tax increases can only be analysed retrospectively. The intention of the coalition for the balance to be 78 per cent spending cuts and 22 per cent tax increases is likely in practice to involve a higher percentage of tax increases, or to result in high borrowing and a higher deficit (NIESR 2011). The government has already retreated on a number of cost-cutting measures, including high-profile (although low expenditure) issues such as its plans for selling off the forests still in public hands, and it is in trouble on several other fronts, including public procurement, libraries, the National Health Service, and reducing the prison population.

An interesting question for social science is why it is so difficult even for governments that are ideologically committed to cut public spending to do so in a way that delivers a permanently smaller state (Pierson 1994). The state shrinks periodically but then grows back. This is because the popular way of understanding public spending in terms of a constant battle between an unproductive public sector and a wealth-creating private sector misrepresents the relationship between the two. A large part of the public sector active is centrally involved in wealth creation, but preserving the fiction of the unproductive state helps make periodic cuts legitimate. In terms of economic futures what is of interest is how different states have public sectors which are fixed within fairly narrow bands. Some advanced economies have much higher public spending and higher taxation than others. The political economy of these welfare states has long been a major subject for analysis, probing the extent to which the different levels of spending arise from political choices or from deep-rooted structural biases (Gough 1979; Esping-Andersen 1990).

Despite the persistence of very clear patterns of spending in different economies, this does not stop major changes taking place over time. The contraction of British defence spending through a series of major defence reviews in the last 70 years is one such example. Another is the decision of the coalition government to change radically the balance of the cost of higher education between the state and the student. An earlier British example was the sale of council houses. Decisions by governments as to what constitutes the 'agenda and the non-agenda of government' can be extremely important in framing public policy debates, and incremental decisions can have very large subsequent impacts as spending programmes contract or expand (Mullard 1993).

The size of the state

The debate on the deficit and how it should be handled focuses on an immediate problem, but it also raises much larger issues about what size of state is desirable and achievable. The question is relevant to economic futures since in the past, the British state was much smaller than it is today. By the GDP measure (which includes transfer payments) it was below 10 per cent before 1914, between 20 per cent and 30 per cent between the wars, and has averaged 38–41 per cent since 1945. The two periods in which there was a step change in the size of the state came during the two world wars. It rose to 56 per cent during the First World War and 70 per cent during the Second World War (Peacock and Wiseman 1961). It fell back once the war ended but in each case not to the level at which it had been before the war. There was a permanent upward ratchet in state spending. There have been periods in peacetime when public spending has also shown an upward secular trend, notably in the 1960s and in the 2000s. During recessions in 1974–5 and 2008–9 public spending ballooned as output and tax receipts collapsed, but these were strictly temporary. What is noticeable is that overall the secular trend for public spending to increase as a share of GDP has not been sustained. It has tended to fall back, often in response to a crisis in the public finances. On the other hand the share of spending and taxation in GDP has been very resilient, and has tended to rise in line with economic growth.

Governments disposed to favour a smaller state have not been successful in pushing the percentage lower.

Despite this history, the present debate over the deficit reveals three clearly articulated positions on the size and role of the state. There are those who advocate a larger state, funded by increased taxation to support existing services and to improve and extend them, with the level of provision in Scandinavian countries the main model (Toynbee and Walker 2010; Hutton 2010). Tony Blair's pledge in 2000 to raise spending on health to the European average was an example of this aim, and it had been substantially realised by 2007. The arguments for moving to a Scandinavian-style welfare state are partly about internal redistribution and social justice, but they also reflect a desire to build a strong, dynamic economy. One of the conditions for this is held to be a society with high levels of trust and social cohesion and low inequality (Rothstein 1998; Wilkinson and Pickett 2009; Arestis and Sobreira 2010).

The second position in the debate favours maintaining public spending in a steady state; not seeking to roll back public provision, but not seeking to increase it. This still allows for considerable reshaping and reordering of priorities, but no radical overall shifts. The political economy of this model is fairly clear. Support for maintaining public provision comes from users and public sector workers, while support for limiting its increase comes from taxpayers and consumers, many of them the same people. The political judgement that the limits of taxation have been reached plainly varies from country to country, but the politicians treat it as a real constraint rather than an imagined one. This position is politically difficult because, as cost inflation tends to be higher in public service provision than elsewhere in the economy, constant economies are needed, even in good times, simply to keep a lid on spending. This risks lowering the quality of service provision, which is politically unpopular.

The third position in the debate argues for a much smaller state, between 25 per cent or 35 per cent of GDP. This could not be achieved by spending restraint and economies; it requires the suppression of major programmes, the cutting out, or at least drastic reduction, of whole areas of public provision. This has become the explicit aim of sections of libertarian opinion in the United States, particularly those associated with the Tea Party, and the cap, cut and balance deficit reduction plan. Specific reductions are clearly possible, as the Thatcher government showed in the area of public housing, and as the coalition government is planning with higher education. The problem is that other programmes of public expenditure are often expanded to fill the gap, so that no net contraction is delivered. The defence budget has been steadily reduced over a long period, but a smaller state has not been the outcome. The argument for a smaller state, like the argument for a larger state, is associated with certain core values of justice and liberty and also with a model of growth. An economy with a substantially smaller state, and therefore substantially lower taxation, it is suggested, might be more unequal but would be more dynamic, more entrepreneurial, and would achieve a faster rate of growth if that is what its citizens chose. As a result there would be more resources ultimately to pay for a social minimum, or for the arts, or for environmental protection, or for whatever other public goods were thought desirable (Pennington 2011). There have always been Conservatives attracted by the prospect of a much smaller state (Redwood 1993), and some of them are influential within the coalition government. In political economy terms the idea of the Big Society can be interpreted as implying a much smaller state, with much lower spending and taxation, and a much larger role for the voluntary sector in providing public services and raising funding directly from the citizens rather than spending tax funded government grants.

If a paradigm shift in public policy was taking place as a result of the financial crash, then a significant move to raise or reduce the overall size of the public sector would be strong evidence of it. At present that does not seem to be happening despite the political rhetoric on all sides claiming that it is. The status quo appears too strong, on both the tax and the spend side. There are claims that these are the deepest cuts for a generation aimed at a substantial rolling back of the state, while supporters of the coalition claim that the cuts, if implemented, will only return public spending to the share of GDP it had in 2007. Both positions have some element of truth. The cuts are severe, but there is no intention, at least in this Parliament, to reduce public spending below 41 per cent of GDP. The reason why the cuts are severe is because GDP has dropped 5–6 per cent, a permanent reduction in British wealth which is unlikely to be made up. Cutting public services restores the status quo by permanently reducing some of the things the state has done in the past, with the brunt of the cuts being borne by local government. Some of the activity will grow back, but some will disappear forever. The real test, however, will be if the coalition government or its successor continue to cut public spending at the same rate through the next Parliament. If it were to do that, then there would be a substantial change in the size of the British state, and a potential shift to a new policy paradigm. Such a shift would require a return to normal or above-average growth to make it politically palatable.

Growth models

The debate on economic growth is a third component of the debate on the future of the economy. The financial growth model adopted in the 1980s, whose main drivers were financial services, retail, property and construction in the private sector, and education, health and universities in the public sector achieved remarkable success for the UK economy in the 1990s and up to 2007. A critical question is whether this growth model can be repaired and relaunched after some minor modifications, whether it needs a radical redesign, or whether a quite different growth model is required. Critics have suggested that this model was heavily reliant on ever-increasing levels of private and public debt, and that the extent of debt deleveraging that is now required of firms and households, and the extent of deficit reduction by government means that none of these sectors can be major drivers of growth in the immediate future. There has been much talk of the need to rebalance the economy, a phrase which has been used in at least three senses: firstly, to suggest a rebalancing between public and private consumption and investment; secondly, between the service sector, particularly financial services, and manufacturing; and, thirdly, between regions. The coalition government has embraced all three in its plans for growth (BIS, 2010, 2011) but has paid most attention to the first two. It seeks to promote recovery firstly by re-establishing fiscal discipline and sharply reducing the size of the public sector, and secondly by encouraging a major increase in private sector investment and in exports.

Whether the economy can be rebalanced and growth relaunched as the government hopes will depend on which of two contrasting scenarios about the consequences of the crash turns out to be more accurate. The more optimistic scenario, which at least until the sovereign debt crisis erupted in July 2011 reflected mainstream thinking, is that the economy will bounce back in the normal way from the unusually deep recession in 2008–9. By 2014–15 the government expected the global economy to be growing at 4–5 per cent and the UK economy by 2.9 per cent per annum. If such rates of growth could be achieved then the deficit would fall rapidly, both because of a fall in the numbers of unemployed claiming benefit, and because of the increase in tax receipts. A large part of the government's deficit reduction plan (£84 billion) depended on its growth forecast being accurate (Morgan 2011). It turned out not to be.

The second scenario is much gloomier about the prospects of growth, at least for the developed western economies. A number of analysts increasingly argue that this is no ordinary recession, and that there is unlikely to be a quick recovery from the 2008 crash as seemed possible in 2010 and the early part of 2011. As a result, the economies of the USA, the UK and the eurozone will not be able to generate the rates of growth they need to pay off their debts quickly. Their economies will struggle to cope with an increasing debt burden, and the longer this persists the more likely it becomes that they resort either to defaults or to inflation in order to manage the pressures on them (Rogoff 2011; Hutton 2011). In either case this may mean a long period of stagnation in prospect, and relative decline in relation to other parts of the international economy. Many analysts and commentators had come to believe, even before the political deadlocks in the USA and the eurozone in the summer of 2011, that the UK economy would not recover quickly and that incomes will be stagnant or falling over the next few years as the UK economy seeks to come to terms with the effects of the crash and the wiping out of so much value that was artificially created in the boom (Goodhart 2011; Warner 2011). The political implications of a long period of stagnation are naturally unwelcome to the government which during the crisis in 2011 stuck to its claim that the British economy had turned the corner and was 'showing the way to recovery' to the rest of the world (Osborne 2011). The downgrading of growth forecasts for the British economy during 2011 pointed in a different direction, and underlined the narrowing of the government's options.

There is no certainty as to which scenario is more likely. Up until 2011 the optimistic scenario had been gaining ground, but the sovereign debt crisis in 2011 drew attention to the weakness of growth in many economies, including the UK. All sides of the debate in the UK acknowledge that without growth it will be much harder to manage UK debt, and there is an increasing focus on policies which might secure faster growth, making the economy more competitive and more flexible. Such policies, however, are not new, and their effects are not necessarily long term in nature. Politicians operate on much shorter timescales and need results in the next two or three years. Recovery depends on the health of the economies of Britain's major trading partners, and if most economies are contracting demand simultaneously and seeking to lower their exchange rates, British performance is bound to suffer.

In the short term, the UK's options are determined by past decisions, and there are severe institutional constraints on what the government can do. Bold plans to rebalance the economy, for example, and shift from finance to manufacturing run up against the obstacle that financial services comprise 10 per cent of UK GDP—a higher portion than in most other major economies. The sector employs more than one million people, generated a trade surplus of £40 billion in 2009, and contributed £53 billion to the Exchequer, 11 per cent of UK tax receipts (TheCityUK 2011). Placing major restrictions on the operations of the City would further damage UK short-term economic growth prospects. Any significant rebalancing of the economy is therefore likely to be slow and take place over many years. Any sudden contraction of the role of financial services is likely to depress growth, and in the short term there are not obvious alternatives to fill the gap.

The high growth scenario for the international economy assumes that global economic growth will continue to be a positive-sum game for the OECD (Organisation for Economic Co-operation and Development) economies. The underlying factors are deemed to be positive. This is based on three assumptions: that demand will go on growing rapidly in the emerging economies; that the rate at which new technologies are deployed will increase; and that the international economy can successfully adapt to climate change. The last two are the least certain and most often questioned (Cowen 2011; Gough 2011 and chapter 4 in this volume). The scenario implies that the present check to incomes and wealth will prove temporary, that growth will revive strongly in the next few years, and that as world economic growth continues, all states, including those which already possess advanced and mature economies, will be flexible enough to find ways to continue to increase their wealth. Not all of the gains from global growth will be appropriated by rising powers. As part of the international economy the UK will benefit from global growth as it has in the past, so long as it takes steps to maintain its competitiveness. The

mainstream consensus on economic growth is articulated by the World
Economic Forum (WEF). It defines competitiveness as 'the set of institutions, policies and factors that determine the level of productivity of a
country' (WEF 2011: 4). It identifies 12 pillars of competitiveness—institutions, infrastructure, macroeconomic environment, heath and primary
education, higher education and training, goods market efficiency, labour
market efficiency, financial market development, technological readiness,
market size, business sophistication, and innovation. The UK is currently
12th on this index, firmly within the top group and has been as high as
fourth, scoring particularly highly on labour market efficiency, business
sophistication, innovation and market size, and least well currently on
macroeconomic environment (due to the build-up of private and public
debt in the last ten years). In its published growth strategy the coalition
government has stated four main aims: to create the most competitive tax
system in the G20; to make the UK one of the best places in Europe to
start, finance and grow a business; to encourage investment and exports
as a route to a more balanced economy; and to create a more educated
workforce that is the most flexible in Europe (BIS, 2010). It has begun to
develop policies to realise these goals by improving various incentives to
shape economic behaviour. These include phased cuts in corporation tax
from 2011 to 2014, reductions in the regulatory burden, relaxation of planning laws, creation of new apprenticeship schemes, and specific tax re-
liefs to encourage investment and innovations such as the creation of local
enterprise partnerships and the new Enterprise Zones (BIS 2011).

The mainstream consensus on growth policy combines market-led
and state-led elements. Market-led policy is laissez-faire in approach.
Laissez-faire is wrongly caricatured as a 'do-nothing' policy, but in fact
it is an activist policy focused on removing obstacles to competition, innovation and enterprise by reducing state activity as much as possible. It
assumes that free markets are the main engine of growth and that policy
must be designed to maximise that freedom at every level, both national
and international. Supply-side policies of reducing taxes to encourage enterprise, and competition to encourage innovation, are regarded as the
surest way to generate new jobs and new economic activities, which cannot be guessed or planned in advance. This approach has been dominant
in British policy-making since the 1980s when Nigel Lawson dismissed
the case for strategic investment in manufacturing that was made by a

concerned House of Lords Committee (Lawson 1992), in favour of allowing the market to decide which sectors should contract and which expand.
But it has always been supplemented, and in particular during the Blair
government, by strategic investment in human capital, infrastructure and
the science base to help improve long-term competitiveness.

The coalition government broadly follows this approach. Although it
talks of rebalancing the economy in favour of manufacturing and building
a strong export-led recovery, it lacks specific tools to make either happen,
and is relying instead on spontaneous private sector growth emerging
once the deficit has been brought under control. To assist this main driver
of growth the government proposes continuing strategic investment in
certain areas to create the most favourable possible climate. The growth
strategy published at the same time as the 2011 budget exemplified this
approach. Developing the themes set out in 2010, it promised to facilitate
a shift to exports and investment by making the tax system more competitive and the regulatory framework less burdensome, by removing barriers
to global trade, by targeting new emerging economies such as India and
China, by investing £40–50 billion a year in key infrastructure projects, by
improving the skills of the workforce, by improving access to finance and
by encouraging entrepreneurship (BIS 2011).

This approach continues the main lines of policy established in the
last 15 years. Critics of this approach argue that the structural weaknesses and imbalances in the British economy revealed by the financial
crash cannot be remedied by spontaneous rebalancing but require major
institutional reforms (Hay 2010; Hutton 2010) to alter the structure of economic incentives. The main institutional changes canvassed include radical reform of the financial services and corporate governance, separating
retail from investment banking and creating new financial institutions to
provide lending for innovative businesses and new technologies. Institutions like the coalition government's Green Investment Bank, which has
funds of £3 billion to dispense, would be expanded greatly. Such plans
involve a return to a much more interventionist, state-led economic policy,
in which government bodies direct investment by identifying priority sectors. Such strategies have been followed successfully in several countries
which have made export success in advanced manufacturing their key
objective. The difficulty for Britain is that it lacks many of the institutions
for such an approach, and previous attempts to create them were not very

successful (Grant 1995). The institutions it does have are part of a very different market-led model. It has been a long-running debate in British economic policy, as to whether relying on a market-led policy can enable the UK economy to continue to develop new sectors which produce internationally tradable output, as its older industries decline. This was a major theme in the tariff reform campaign at the beginning of the twentieth century (Semmel 1960) and also in the deindustrialisation debate of the 1970s and 1980s (Blackaby 1978). However, in comparison with England, the other constituent nations of the UK, Scotland, Wales and Northern Ireland, have always been subject to greater state economic control. In the future, as more powers are devolved to the other three nations and to Scotland in particular, very different priorities and models of economic development may emerge within the United Kingdom.

State-led strategic investment in skills, infrastructure, science and innovation, as well as initiatives to promote a diverse culture and a resilient civil society, in order to help economies to remain globally competitive, is less controversial. The disagreement between the laissez-faire and the strategic investment approaches is not over the need for state policies to create the environment for economic success, but over the degree of intervention in investment decisions.

A second issue is the scale of strategic investment that is required to remain competitive. Over the last ten years there has been substantial strategic investment in the science base in universities and manufacturing. This policy has been continued by the coalition, but there is a sharp contrast with Germany, which during the recession has provided a 20 per cent uplift in its spending in this area. Advocates of strategic investment argue that market-led assumptions make British strategic investment often too little and too late, and seek major institutional change to give priority across Whitehall to the requirements of manufacturing and enterprise, downplaying the role of financial services and the City of London, and the hold that it has on the thinking and policies of the British government (Ingham 1984). This would imply a significant contraction in the size of the financial sector in the UK, because the sector would no longer be treated as having the regulatory freedom which it has enjoyed over the last three decades and which made it the leading sector of the UK economy. The Independent Commission on Banking which reported in September 2011 did not propose a regulatory regime which would have seriously undermined the current role of the City, but it did call for more regulatory oversight of the City, and the ring-fencing of the retail and investment arms of the same bank, which may lead over time to a reduced role for the City. It is not, however, the radical change of direction which the critics want.

For the advocates of strategic investment, the German model of high investment, high productivity, high wages and high exports is once more ascendant and preferable to the Anglo-Saxon model. All parties once again dream of Britain becoming more like Germany. But it would be a long and painful process of restructuring for Britain to move from a predominantly liberal market economy model to a coordinated market economy (Hall and Soskice 2001). It would require sustained investment in skills and science over a long period, a major change in the organisation of the financial system and of the Civil Service, and permanent increases in spending and taxation. Some sectors of the British economy already work like this, and always have, notably defence (Edgerton 2005), but these are relatively few in number. The cultural and institutional shift required is considerable (Grant 2012), and is unlikely to occur unless the crisis became much more severe.

One of the difficulties in moving from the present model is its deep institutional roots. The British growth model as it developed in the 1990s was characterised by the increasing prominence of finance and financial services in everyday life (Langley 2008) and by a permissive attitude to the build-up of private debt, a form of 'privatised Keynesianism' as Colin Crouch has called it (Crouch 2009). The increasing prominence of finance in everyday life involves the treatment of citizens as financial subjects, obliged to make financial calculations of the assets they need or want over their lifetime, including education, health, housing and pensions, and how to fund them. It gives a major role to financial services and has wider implications for the way in which societies and economies are organised, how individuals relate to the state, and the balance between public and private sectors. It links naturally to the Big Society vision of energising communities and voluntary activity, decentralising economic activity (Blond 2010), and developing new private sector companies to deliver public services as a means of containing the cost pressures of the public sector in an increasingly competitive international economy. This increasing prominence of finance helps lock the political economy into a particular path of development.

The low growth scenario is much gloomier about the prospects of western growth, including UK growth. Tyler Cowen, for example, has argued that the western economies are facing a long period of stagnation, because all the easy sources of growth over the last two hundred years have been used up, and these economies are failing to innovate fast enough to increase their wealth (Cowen 2011). As a result living standards for the majority have been stagnating even during the boom years, and the economy was kept afloat through public and private debt, funded by the surplus economies. Realigning entitlements and incomes to what the economy can afford will be a long and painful process, because cuts will have to be much larger and last longer than currently envisaged. Other parts of the world will be able to continue to grow because they are catching up technologically and organisationally with the advanced economies, but everywhere else will stagnate at best.

This scenario removes the assumption that growth in the international economy will lift the UK economy as well. Either the UK economy may lose comparative advantage and many of its sectors cease to be competitive, or the international economy may stall, and with growing conflict over trade, resources, and currencies between the leading economies, international co-operation may weaken and countries may turn in on themselves.

In the low-growth scenario, the greatest risk is that the assumption of expanding markets and the liberalisation of trade, investment, and population flows will all stall or go into reverse. Trade protection, immigration caps and competitive devaluations might all multiply. The complex network of global and regional governance could at best become deadlocked and at worst might start to unravel. In all countries, including the UK, economic nationalists from different parts of the political spectrum have begun to emphasise the necessity of protecting national interests and disengaging from international bodies, starting with the European Union. They tend to favour much stricter control of immigration and a commercial policy which protects local jobs and makes the economy less open. The case for maintaining an open international economy and full membership of the European Union even in a time of low growth will continue to be advocated strongly by those who perceive the need for more effective coordination and cooperation at all levels of the international economy. Forums such as the WTO, the G20, and the UN Climate Conference are all regarded as essential vehicles for achieving international agreements on trade, financial regulation and carbon emissions, just as the EU is for many regional issues. From this perspective the UK's national interest, even in economically dark times, would be to seek co-operative solutions to provide a new set of rules for the international economy, in the hope of providing a secure foundation for future growth and stability. This debate raises the question of the relative openness of the British economy, how far this can be a matter of policy, and how far it is dictated by the way in which Britain is integrated into the international economy. The mainstream con-sensus since 1945 has been that Britain's interests lie in a stable international liberal order. But the arguments for a different kind of economic future for Britain—mercantilist, protectionist, nationalist, and isolationist—are already embedded in British politics, although still for the moment on the margins. They have been influential before, particularly in the 1930s, and under certain conditions could become so again (Jones 2011).

Conclusion

Returning to the Queen's question, if the problem was so large, why did no-one foresee it? The problem was large, and many had given warnings, but in retrospect no-one fully understood it and no one person or government or agency had overall responsibility for it. The cause is political rather than economic, and this is why social science, in the form of political economy as outlined here, does have something to offer policy-makers for the future. It cannot offer precise predictions of particular future events, but thinking in terms of paradigms and scenarios can alert policy-makers to a range of potential outcomes, and encourage a deeper debate on the alternatives that are feasible in particular contexts, rather than simply confining discussion within the assumptions of the ruling orthodoxy. The different approaches in political economy provide rival understandings of how the economy works, they analyse the patterns of action which constitute it, and they map out the different pathways and landscapes associated with them. At their best, political economy approaches can draw on some of the extraordinary rich-ness in social science and humanities research, only a small amount of which is presently captured in discussion of economic futures in public policy.

One of the tasks for public policy in thinking about economic futures is to build the kind of resilience and institutional flexibility that can safeguard the economy against a range of possible shocks and developments. It is the scale of the challenges ahead (Rees 2003), most obviously, but by no means exclusively, in the uncertain effects of climate change, that suggests the need for an enhanced rather than a diminished role for government. It does not imply that a larger share of national income has to pass through its hands, or that government has to become more centralised, but it does suggest that the role of government in enabling rules and frameworks which can change attitudes and behaviour and gain popular consent will become more pressing rather than less. The collective action problems which governments are called upon to solve are greater than ever, and this is particularly true in the economic sphere at both national and international levels. The range of strategies governments need to deploy are not likely to require just one approach. This again is where political economy can help, by making policy-makers reflect on the range of policies that are available and the different kinds of knowledge that are relevant in different contexts. Nothing of course guarantees that the knowledge will be used wisely, or that good political judgements will be made, but it helps prepare the ground.

References

Alesina, A. and Ardagna, S. (2010) 'Large Changes in Fiscal Policy: Taxes Versus Spending', in J. Brown (ed.) *Tax Policy and the Economy*, 24 (Chicago: University of Chicago Press).

Arestis, P. and Sobreira, R. (2010) *The Financial Crisis: Origins and Implications* (London: Palgrave Macmillan).

Bernstein, P. (1996) *Against the Gods: The Remarkable History of Risk* (New York: John Wiley and Sons).

Blackaby, F. (ed.) (1978) *De-industrialisation* (London: Heinemann).

Blanchflower, D. (2009) 'Where Next for the UK Economy?', *Scottish Journal of Political Economy*, 56(1): 1–23.

Blond, P. (2010) *Red Tory* (London: Faber and Faber).

Brown, G. (2004) 'The Budget 2004', *Guardian* 17 March 2004 [online], http://www.guardian.co.uk/money/2004/mar/17/budget.budget20044 (accessed 16 August 2011).

Cowen, T. (2011) *The Great Stagnation: How America Ate All the Low-hanging Fruit of Modern History, Got Sick, and Will (Eventually) Get Better* (New York: John Wiley & Sons).

Crouch, C. (2009) 'Privatised Keynesianism: An Unacknowledged Policy Regime', *The British Journal of Politics and International Relations*, 11: 382–399.

Davidson, P. (2009) *The Keynes Solution: The Path to Global Economic Prosperity* (London: Palgrave Macmillan).

Davies, H. (2010) *The Financial Crisis—Who is to Blame?* (Cambridge: Polity).

Department for Business, Innovation and Skills (2010) *A Strategy for Sustainable Growth* (London: BIS).

Department for Business, Innovation and Skills (2011) *A Plan for Growth* (London: BIS).

Eatwell, J. and Milgate, M. (2011) *The Fall and Rise of Keynesian Economics* (Oxford: Oxford University Press).

Edgerton, D. (2005) *Warfare State: Britain, 1920–1970* (Cambridge: Cambridge University Press).

Esping-Andersen, G. (1990) *The Three Worlds of Welfare Capitalism* (Cambridge: Polity).

Frieden, J. (2006) *The Fall and Rise of Global Ccapitalism* (New York: W.W. Norton).

Glyn, A. (2006) *Capitalism Unleashed: Finance, Globalisation, and Welfare* (Oxford: Oxford University Press).

Goodhart, C. (2010a) 'Money, Credit and Bank Behaviour: Need for a New Approach', *National Institute Economic Review* 214(1): 73–82.

Goodhart, C. (2010b) *The Regulatory Response to the Financial Crisis* (London: Edward Elgar).

Goodhart, C. (2011) 'US Economic Weakness Makes Austerity Tougher', *Bloomberg* 2 August.

Gough, I. (1979) *The Political Economy of the Welfare State* (London: Macmillan).

Gough, I. (2011) *Climate Change and Public Policy Futures*, A report for the British Academy project *New Paradigms in Public Policy* (London: British Academy Policy Centre).

Grant, W. (ed.) (1995) *Industrial Policy* (Cheltenham: Edward Elgar).

Grant, W. (2012) 'Was There Ever an Anglo-Saxon Model of Capitalism?' in T. Casey (ed.) *The Legacy of the Crash* (London: Palgrave Macmillan).

Greenspan, A. (2008) *Testimony to the House Committee of Government Oversight and Reform*, 23 October [online], http://clipsandcomment.com/wp-content/uploads/2008/10/greenspan-testimony-20081023.pdf.

Hall, P. (1993) 'Policy Paradigms, Social Learning and the State', *Comparative Politics*, 25: 275–296.

Hall, P. and Soskice, D. (eds) (2001) *Varieties of Capitalism: The Institutional Foundations of Comparative Advantage* (Oxford: Oxford University Press).

Harvey, D. (2011) *The Enigma of Capital: and the Crises of Capitalism* (London: Profile Books).

Hay, C. (2010) 'Pathology Without Crisis? The Strange Demise of the Anglo-liberal Growth Model', *Government & Opposition*, 46: 1–31.

Hayek, F. A. (1949) *Individualism and Economic Order* (London: Routledge & Kegan Paul).

HM Government (2009) *Supporting Global Growth: A Preliminary Report on the Responsiveness and Adaptability of the International Financial Institutions by the Chair of the London Summit* (London: Cabinet Office).

Hutton, W. (2010) *Them and Us: Changing Britain—Why We Need a Fair Society* (London: Little, Brown and Company).

Hutton, W. (2011) 'Our Financial System Has Become a Madhouse: We Need Radical Change', *Guardian*, 6 August.

Ingham, G. (1984) *Capitalism Divided? The City and Industry in British Social Development* (London: Macmillan).

Jones, O. (2011) *Chavs: The Demonization of the Working Class* (London: Verso).

Kaletsky, A. (2010) *Capitalism 4.0: The Birth of a New Economy* (London: Bloomsbury).

Kindleberger, C. P. (1978) *Manias, Panics and Crashes: A History of Financial Crises* (New York: Basic Books).

Knight, F. H. (1921) *Risk, Uncertainty and Profit* (Boston: Houghton Mifflin Co.).

Krugman, P. (2008) *The Return of Depression Economics and the Crisis of 2008* (London: Allen Lane).

Langley, P. (2008) *The Everyday Life of Global Finance: Saving and Borrowing in Anglo-America* (Oxford: Oxford University Press).

Lawson, N. (1992) *The View from No. 11: Memoirs of a Tory Radical* (London: Bantam).

Lawson, T. (1997) *Economics and Reality* (London and New York: Routledge).

Lindblom, C. (1977) *Politics and Markets* (New York: Basic Books).

Ludlam, S. (1992) 'The Gnomes of Zurich: Four Myths of the 1976 IMF Crisis', *Political Studies*, 40: 713–727.

Mason, P. (2009) *Meltdown: The End of the Age of Greed* (London: Verso).

McDonald, L.G. and Robinson, P. (2009) *A Colossal Failure of Commonsense: The Inside Story of the Collapse of Lehman Brothers* (New York: Crown Business).

Minksy, H.P. (1982) *Can 'it' Happen Again? Essays on Instability and Finance* (New York: M.E. Sharpe).

Morgan, T. (2011) *Thinking the Unthinkable: Might There Be No Way Out for Britain?* (London: Tullett Prebon Group).

Mullard, M. (1993) *The Politics of Public Expenditure* (London: Routledge).

NIESR (2011) 'The UK Economy', *National Institute Economic Review: Journal of the National Institute of Economic and Social Research*, April 2011: 216 [online] http://ner.sagepub.com/content/216/1.toc (accessed 16 August 2011).

Osborne, G. (2011) 'Britain is Leading the Way Out of This Crisis', *Daily Telegraph* 8 August.

Owen, G. (1999) *From Empire to Europe: The Decline and Revival of British Industry Since the Second World War* (London: Harper Collins).

Peacock, A.T. and Wiseman J. (1961) *The Growth of Public Expenditure in the United Kingdom* (Oxford: Oxford University Press).

Pennington, M. (2011) *Robust Political Economy: Classical Liberalism and the Future of Public Policy* (Cheltenham: Edward Elgar).

Pierce, A (2008) 'The Queen Asks Why No One Saw the Credit Crunch Coming', *Daily Telegraph* 5 November 2011 [online]
http://www.telegraph.co.uk/news/uknews/theroyalfamily/3386353/The-Queen-asks-why-no-one-saw-the-credit-crunch-coming.html (accessed 16 August 2011).

Pierson, P. (1994) *Dismantling the Welfare State? Reagan, Thatcher and the Politics of Retrenchment* (Cambridge: Cambridge University Press).

Redwood, J. (1993) *The Global Marketplace: Capitalism and its Future* (London: Harper-Collins).

Rees, M. (2003) *Our Final Century: A Scientist's Warning* (London: Heinemann).

Reinhart, C. and Rogoff, K. (2008) *This Time is Different* (Princeton: Princeton University Press).

Rogers, C. (2010) *The Politics of Economic Policy-making under Harold Wilson and James Callaghan and the 1976 IMF Crisis*, PhD thesis, University of Warwick.

Rogoff, K. (2011) 'The Bullets Yet to be Fired to Stop the Crisis', *Financial Times* 9 August.

Rothstein, B. (1998) *Just Institutions Matter: The Moral and Political Logic of the Universal Welfare State* (Cambridge: Cambridge University Press).

Roubini, N. (2010) *Crisis Economics: A Crash Course in the Future of Finance* (London: Allen Lane).

Ruggie, J. (1982) 'International Regimes, Transactions and Change: Embedded Liberalism in the Postwar Economic Order', *International Organisation* 36: 379–415.

Schwartz, H.M. (2009) *Subprime Nation: American Power, Global Capital, and the Housing Bubble* (Cornell: Cornell University Press).

Semmel, B. (1960) *Imperialism and Social Reform* (London: Allen & Unwin).

Shiller, R.J. (2008) *The Subprime Solution: How Today's Global Financial Crisis Happened, and What to Do About It* (Princeton: Princeton University Press).

Skidelsky, R. (2009) *Keynes: The Return of the Master* (London: Allen Lane).

Skidelsky, R. (2010) 'Britain's austerity apostles duck the debate', *Financial Times* 13 October 2010 [online], http://www.ft.com/cms/s/0/f960f190-d6fc-11df-aaab-00144feabdc0.html#axzz1Sxlh1QQQ (accessed 16 August 2011).

Sorkin, A.R. (2010) *Too Big to Fail: Inside the Battle to Save Wall Street* (London: Penguin).

Stiglitz, J. (2010) *Freefall: Free Markets and the Sinking of the Global Economy* (London: Penguin).

Sunstein, C. R. (2002) *Risk and Reason: Safety, Law and the Environment* (Cambridge: Cambridge University Press).

Tett, G. (2009) *Fool's Gold* (London: Little, Brown and Company).

TheCityUK (2011) *Economic Contribution of London's Financial Services 2010* (London: TheCityUK).

Thompson, H. (2008) *Might, Right and Consent: Representative Democracy and the International Economy, 1919–2001* (Manchester: Manchester University Press).

Thompson, H. (2009) 'The Political Origins of the Financial Crisis: the Domestic and International Politics of Fannie Mae and Freddie Mac', *Political Quarterly* 80(1): 17–24.

Thompson, H. (2010) 'The Character of the State', in C. Hay (ed.) *New Directions in Political Science* (London: Palgrave Macmillan), 130–147.

Toynbee, P. and Walker, D. (2010) *The Verdict: Did Labour Change Britain?* (London: Granta).

Turner, G. (2008) *The Credit Crunch: Housing Bubbles, Globalisation and the Worldwide Economic Crisis* (London: Pluto Press).

Wade, R. (2008) 'Financial Regime Change', *New Left Review* 53: 5–21.

Warner, J. (2011) 'Whatever George Osborne Believes, Britain Will Spend Years in the Doldrums', *Daily Telegraph* 4 August.

Wilkinson, R. and Pickett, K. (2009) *The Spirit Level: Why More Equal Societies Almost Always Do Better* (London: Allen Lane).

Williams, M. (2010) *Uncontrolled Risk: The Lessons of Lehman Brothers and How Systemic Risk Can Still Bring Down the World Financial System* (New York: McGraw Hill).

Wilson, G. (2012) 'The Crisis of Capitalism and the Downfall of the Left', in T. Casey (ed.) *The Legacy of the Crash* (London: Palgrave Macmillan).

Wolf, M. (2009) *Fixing Global Finance: How to Curb Financial Crises in the Twentieth Century* (New Haven: Yale University Press).

Wolf, M. (2011) 'Why British Fiscal Policy is a Huge Gamble', *Financial Times* 28 April 2011 [online], http://www.ft.com/cms/s/0/5f2b4b60-71c6-11e0-9adf-00144feabdc0.html#axzz1Sxlh1QQQ (accessed 16 August 2011).

World Economic Forum (WEF) (2011) *The Global Competitiveness Report 2010–11* (Geneva: WEF).

3

Squaring the public policy circle

Managing a mismatch between demands and resources

PETER TAYLOR-GOOBY

Key messages

The continuing problem of balancing the conflicting pressures on public spending presents real challenges for our democracy. It is a commonplace in discussion of public spending that the UK government must manage the conflict between insistent pressures to spend more and equally insistent pressures to curb spending. Population ageing and rising public expectations fuel the appetite for increases; the exigencies of international competitiveness and now the economic crisis demand cutbacks.

A whole range of strategies have been developed in an effort to handle these pressures. These include shifting responsibility from government to individual, the private or the voluntary sector for various areas of provision, innovative and stricter management of state provision and attempts to change people's behaviour to reduce demands. Despite some successes, there are drawbacks to all these approaches, to do with their capacity to resolve the problem and limitations on their acceptability to the public.

Current and continuing economic problems bring home the dilemma of managing contrary demands to spend more and to constrain pressures on the public purse. One outcome of a continuing failure to meet expectations is that trust in politicians will decline further. It is hard to recapture public trust without a move towards a more informed and genuinely democratic public debate.

The conflicting pressures on public spending

The conflict between pressures to constrain and to increase state spending has grown harder to manage in recent years. The 2009 recession and the sluggishness of the recovery make the problem even more difficult (see Gamble 2011 and chapter 2 of this book). This chapter examines some of the methods pursued by the UK government to square the circle of insistent demands for more spending and equally insistent pressures for cutbacks. We consider moves to encourage citizens to take greater individual responsibility, expand the private sector, promote user choice, focus provision through targets and incentives, shift the behaviour of citizens to help meet public policy goals, and extend the role of the voluntary sector. First we discuss the arguments about the contradictory pressures on government.

Commentators list a substantial number of factors that enhance demand for more spending on social and public services (for a review see Pierson 2000: 80–106). Two important factors are the changes to population age structure, which will lead to higher spending on pensions, and health and social care (HM Treasury 2009; Hills 2009: 338), and rising public expectations for better services (Glennerster 2009: 206). Developments in the first area are exacerbated by associated shifts in household structure and in women's employment that seem likely to reduce the supply of informal carers for frail older people and increase the need for child care (see Thane 2011 for a discussion). In the second area, people have become more confident in articulating and pressing home their needs. Their expectations of government services are influenced by rising standards in consumption goods (Giddens 1994: 163–164).

Figure 3.1 charts the official projections of public spending for the next half-century. These projections rely on a large number of assumptions, covering population growth, ageing and structure, work patterns and trends in employment, education and retirement, growth rates and productivity changes in the state and private sectors and demand for government services. They are based on the best available knowledge but necessarily carry a good deal of uncertainty. The projections forecast that, once the current austerity programme comes to an end, public services will consume a steadily rising proportion of GDP.

More details are given in Figure 3.2. This shows how the main areas of rising spending are health care, state pensions and long-term care, all

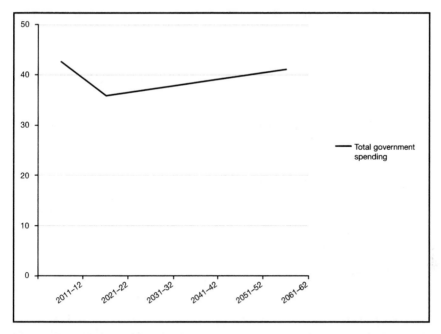

Figure 3.1 Projected government spending 2011–12 to 2061–62 (% of GDP, net of interest payments)
Source: Office for Budget Responsibility (2012: 62).

driven mainly by demography, but also by demands for better standards of provision. Spending on education, social benefits for those of working age and across all other areas is projected to remain roughly constant or fall.

The discussion of constraints on public spending emphasises the importance of globalisation. Western economies face greater competition in international markets from those with smaller public sectors (Pfaller, Gough and Therborn 1991; Bardhan, Bowles and Wallerstein 2006). Social spending becomes vulnerable to the charge that it is a 'burden' financed by more productive sectors of the economy (Scharpf and Schmidt 2000, 51–68; Alesina and Perotti 1995). It is easier to manage the dilemma when governments are confident of growth and of controlling the essential features of their own economies. The impact of international speculation on national economies brings home the point that governments face constraints if their policies are not seen to be financially prudent (Swank 2002: 2–4; McNamara 1998).

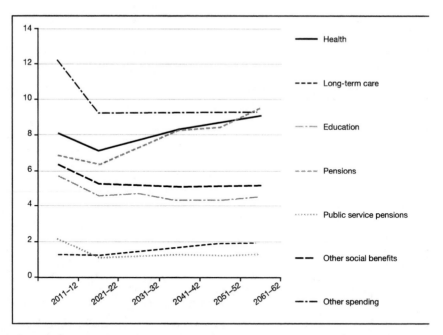

Figure 3.2   Main components in projected government spending 2011–12 to 2061–62 (% of GDP, net of interest payments)
Source: Office for Budget Responsibility (2012: 62).

These pressures are particularly intransigent at the present time. Economic recovery proceeds at a snail's pace in western countries. Policies which address demands by seeking to redistribute the proceeds of growth, as in the post-war heyday of the welfare state, face difficulties. There are also problems with policies which seek to reduce overall spending. It is enormously difficult to achieve major cuts in democracies (Pierson 2000; Weaver 1986). The expensive areas of public spending remain highly popular: health care, education and pensions have been consistently identified as top priorities for extra spending since the British Social Attitudes survey (BSA) started work in 1983 (Barnes and Tomaszewski 2011: 196).[1] Cutbacks, when pursued with sufficient vigour, have succeeded in the short term. However, long-term studies of state spending during the past century reveal an overall pattern of stability: substantial shifts in spending

[1] British Social Attitudes data are available through The British Social Attitudes information system [online], at http://www.britsocat.com (accessed on 22 August 2012).

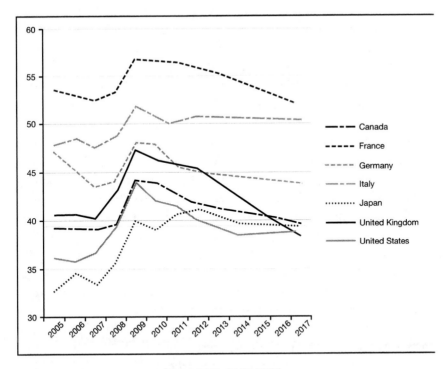

Figure 3.3 Government expenditure 2005–17 (% GDP)
Source: International Monetary Fund 2012.[2]

levels only follow from major shocks and have tended upward. The First World War lifted UK spending from a trend level of 12–15 per cent to 25–30 per cent of gross domestic product (GDP) and the Second World War raised it to 35–40 per cent (Dunsire and Hood 1989; Peacock and Wiseman 1967). Even after major cutbacks such as the Geddes Axe in 1921, the 1931 national coalition government cuts or the 1975 Labour cuts following the International Monetary Fund (IMF) loan, spending levels tend to return to trend.

The official IMF projections of public spending in the seven major capitalist economies are given in Figure 3.3. In all cases spending as a proportion of GDP rises sharply as the 2007–9 recession brings about increased spending on bank bailouts, rescue packages and social benefits, and causes GDP to fall. Public spending is then expected to decline towards the

[2] Expenditure after 2011 is based on government projections.

previous trend level, except in the cases of the USA and Japan, where it remains higher. The UK's pattern is striking in the scale of the 2007–9 increase and in the abruptness of the subsequent decline set out in the government's spending plans. These will take public spending back to the level of the 1990s. The UK starts the period is its traditional position about the middle of the G7 and ends it as the lowest spender. Whether cuts at this pace can be implemented successfully is at present unclear.

One solution might be to improve cost-efficiency in the public sector, to do more for less. Despite a large number of measures pursued by different governments during recent years, progress in this area is disappointing (OBR 2012: 54). Productivity in the public sector is difficult to measure. While the resources expended by central and local government can be measured, it is arguable that outputs should include qualitative as well as quantitative items (Atkinson 2005; Simpson 2007). For example, the public want the health service to provide treatment that allows patients dignity and a sense that nurses and doctors are committed to meeting their individual needs. The education system is expected to broaden opportunities for more deprived groups and improve standards. This complicates the measurement of output in crude terms of the volume or activity i.e. numbers of patients treated or children in school.

Recent assessments of productivity in health care and education seek to take account of qualitative issues by including service users' assessment of quality from attitude surveys and measures of the success in meeting government targets for quality of service (Judd 2011). They show that productivity in the National Health Service (NHS) has fluctuated between 1996 and 2009, with a very slight net fall, mainly due to increases in the drugs bill and staff pay (Hardie *et al.* 2011). For education, productivity also fluctuated, mainly due to changes in the school population, but it has shown little change over the whole period (Ayoubkhani *et al.* 2010). Resources were squeezed up to 1999 as the cuts of the Major government continued to feed through. From the beginning of the twenty-first century, spending, and with it the aspirations of policy-makers, rose substantially. Despite a wide range of interventions, it has proved difficult for governments to make progress in getting more for less. Under current plans spending on health care faces, at best, a steady state, while other areas of social provision will be cut back substantially (HM Treasury 2010a: Institute for Fiscal Studies 2011; Taylor-Gooby and Stoker 2011).

The UK government, like those in other western countries, has the task of managing conflicting pressures to provide better (and more expensive) public services while containing state spending. The problem has become increasingly difficult as demographic and other pressures intensify and as national economies face the need to ensure international competitiveness. The current financial crisis tightens the screw.

This chapter reviews some of the ways in which diverse but rising demands and constrained resources influence policy-making, and considers the implications for the broad shape of the public policy debate in the medium-term future. This is a vast field and we focus particularly on new policy directions which seek to shift the balance between the state, the private sector, the individual citizen and the community in provision. The longer-term history of public policy discusses responses to the pressures people experienced in the rapidly urbanising and industrialising society of the eighteenth and nineteenth centuries. Ordinary citizens developed collective institutions to meet their needs as best they could: friendly societies, benefit clubs, unions and building societies which pooled savings to provide the members with housing (Thane 1996; Thompson 1992). Charitable relief played a role in hospitals and poor relief. Market provision also developed in step with opportunities. The subsequent growth of the welfare state has largely been a story of the incorporation and expansion of much of the working-class and civil society provision into a more comprehensive and better funded framework (Lowe 1999; Alldritt *et al.* 2009). The boundaries between state, market and voluntary, community, individual and family provision for social needs shifted as governments expanded provision for social needs (Power 2012; see chapter 7 of this book).

Current tensions are leading to the development of policies which draw on the private sector, the market, the community and individual citizens in new ways. These developments can conveniently be grouped under six main headings: strengthening individual incentives; expanding the private sector; using market systems to extend user choice; introducing targets and associated incentives to improve the quality and cost-efficiency of state provision; operating 'with the grain' of everyday life heuristics and choice strategies; and extending the role of the voluntary sector and enhancing democratic engagement.

Greater individual responsibility: Work incentives

National governments have promoted the transfer of responsibility from state to individual in the move from more passive to more active bene-fits for those of working age (European Commission 2008). The UK's approach to activation has incorporated two elements: stringent restric-tions on entitlement that limit the number of people who can claim out of work benefits and the level of benefits they can claim, and wage top-ups or tax credits so lower-paid people can meet their needs (Millar 2009). Current policies limit entitlement further, most importantly by further tests of eligibility for the rather higher Incapacity Benefit and the restruc-turing of the Disabled Living Allowance. These measures are expected to move more than half the current 2.5 million disabled claimers to cheaper benefits, to Jobseekers' Allowance or into work and save in excess of £2 bil-lion (HM Treasury 2010a: 2.123; Grant and Wood 2011: 28–29). They also cut the levels of some benefits, including some top-up benefits. Claimers face strong financial incentives to pursue paid work. .

New policies will bring all benefits, apart from pensions, together into the new Universal Credit. The objective is to simplify the system so that the circumstances under which people are entitled to support, and the incentives they face to move off benefit and into work, are more trans-parent (Department for Work and Pensions (DWP) 2010: 1). The logic of withdrawing state support from those assumed to be able to pay for themselves also emerges in discussion of means-testing for the currently universal over-60s winter fuel payment and bus passes (Cooke 2011: 18). Debates about the future of child benefit, previously universal but removed from higher rate taxpayers in the 2010 spending review (HM Treasury 2010a: 8), also raise the issue of shifting responsibility through the exten-sion of means-testing. A strong element in public opinion endorses the work ethic and supports policies which strengthen incentives for those of working-age who are deemed able to work (Butt and Curtice 2010: 23–25; Taylor-Gooby 2013). Whether a greater role for individual responsibility in relation to benefits for other groups is accepted is less clear.

Shifting provision to the private sector

Privatisation policies have developed since the 1980s with the goals of improving cost-efficiency, allowing greater public choice and reducing state expenditure. The policies include: the Right to Buy for council tenants, the expansion of private pensions and the outsourcing of services across a wide range of central and local government provision. Less substantial programmes have been pursued in education and health care. These policies have been implemented with varying enthusiasm and varying degrees of success by different governments (Letwin 1988).

Right to Buy, introduced under the 1979–80 Conservative government, tapped a strong desire for home ownership. Over two million dwellings had been bought under the scheme by 2010 (Office for National Statistics (ONS) 2010a: 142; ONS 2001: 174). Despite new building programmes, the social housing sector, including council and housing association dwellings, has shrunk from about a third to about a fifth of all housing (ONS 2010a: Figure 10.4). Home ownership is highly popular and the associated changes to public housing finance, effectively shifting housing support from rent subsidy for social housing to means-tested support for low-income tenants, reduced government transfers to local housing providers massively. However, by 2010 spending on rent benefits at £22 billion effectively outstripped previous levels of local housing subsidy, increasing at more than three times the rate of retail prices between 2004–05 and 2009–10 (HM Treasury 2010b: Table 5.2). This illustrates a problem: even when privatisations are popular and appear to offer immediate savings by reducing state commitment to direct provision, costs may still rise if the relevant need remains pressing.

Policies in the 1980s to encourage people to transfer from state supplementary to private pensions were also effective in achieving large numbers of transfers. However, many pensions were mis-sold, leading to a scandal and compensation (Goode 1993). Subsequent governments have retained the objective of expanding the role of the private sector, but have failed to find a system of regulation that encourages private provision at a level where it is attractive to both providers and purchasers (Béland and Gran 2008; Pensions Commission 2004: Chapter 3 annex). Current policies move cautiously to promote more pension saving by employees and employers but at a relatively low level (DWP 2011). Governments of both parties have retained a commitment to a strong basic state pension.

Privatisation has been vigorously pursued in the outsourcing of a wide range of services, from street cleaning and rubbish collection to architecture and planning, the management of government offices and, more recently, the contracting out of programmes such as the 2010 government's Work Programme (Lindsay 2011: 36). A Department for Business review of the UK public services industry showed that it was the second-largest such industry in the world, after the USA, accounted for some £80 billion by 2008 (roughly one-fifth of total government spending on services), and had more than doubled in size during the last decade (Julius 2008: ii). It reported from a review of academic literature that savings from transfers to the private sector amounted to between 10 and 30 per cent.

The fact that a step change in the proportion of outsourcing is predicted as the most likely response to the sharp local spending cuts from 2011 to 2015 suggests that the approach is widely seen as cost-efficient (Moore 2010). A survey of members by the Local Government Association (LGA) shows that two-thirds of respondents, particularly larger authorities, are pursuing outsourcing in order to manage cuts (LGA 2011: 4). The public sector workforce is to be cut further, by more than 5 per cent by 2014 (Office for Budget Responsibility (OBR) 2012, Table A). The 2011 Localism Bill encourages the use of a wide range of providers to substitute for state services (Institute of Local Government Studies 2011). It is unclear how far radical moves in this direction will be popular. The councils leading the move (Suffolk and Bury St Edmunds) put their plans on hold in 2011 following unfavourable local election results (Johnstone 2011).

In the highly popular areas of education and health care, moves to privatise services have been cautious. The Assisted Places Scheme from 1980 to 1997 provided a relatively small number of places at private schools for students from low-income families selected by the schools. The places cost more than state provision and tended to be allocated to middle-class children whose parents had suffered a loss of income (most commonly through divorce). They were popular with users but not cost-effective and the scheme was ended by the following government (Edwards, Fitz and Whitty 1989). The current academies and faith schools programmes allow state-financed schools in England to contract out parts of their spending.

A number of Independent Sector Treatment Centres dealing with specific time-limited and predictable health conditions (varicose vein and cataract surgery for example) were established in the 2000s. The objective was to expand competition in NHS front-line services. It proved necessary to pay a premium of 11 per cent over the in-house cost yardstick to encourage new players to enter the market. It was difficult to identify benign competitive impacts on NHS practice (House of Commons Health Committee 2006). Political controversy over proposals to open up competition in the health service to any qualified provider in the 2011 NHS bill (Department of Health 2011) and the government's decision to put the plans on hold indicates the strength of public concern in this area.

The government limits the range of treatments available on the NHS according to an assessment of cost-effectiveness provided by the National Institute for Health and Clinical Excellence (NICE). Since 2009, patients have been permitted to top-up NHS care with private payments for drugs or treatment that are not included on the list (Department of Health 2009). This is only allowed where the NHS and private elements can be clearly separated, for example when they are delivered by different staff or in different clinics. One possibility would be for the health service to fund basic treatment or contribute to private treatment with the payment topped up by the patient. This raises the question of whether private provision might expand into areas previously covered by the NHS as the pressures on state provision grow stronger.

This brief review shows that governments have sought to make greater use of private provision. Privatisation appears to be more successful in generating savings and more acceptable to the public in the transfer of assets such as council housing, and in the provision of back-office and general services. It is much less popular and effective in relation to core public services such as the NHS and state schooling and may generate problems in local government. There are real difficulties in developing private provision so that it is both attractive to all parties and achieves savings, particularly within the heartland of the public sector. This point is illustrated most forcefully by the pensions and NHS examples, but is also relevant to other areas of provision.

State and market: user choice

Since the late 1980s an established strand in policy-making has emphasised the decentralisation of bureaucratic state providers and the reconstitution of individual front-line agencies (hospitals, clinics, schools, community social care or health services) as separate budget holders (Pollitt and Talbot 2004). Resources follow service users within the state sector so that choice and competition become powerful forces, compelling agencies to respond to people's demands and meet them cost-effectively (Le Grand 2007; Enthoven 2002). Further developments allow private providers, commercial or not-for-profit, to enter the market (for a summary of recent developments see Organisation for Economic Co-operation and Development (OECD) 2011).

The expansion of markets and of choice through public services is both a direct response to public demands and a mechanism to intensify the pressures on managers to deliver a more responsive service. Choice is in principle highly popular, and, where it gives real control over budgets, appears to have had some success. Survey evidence indicates that while choice is enthusiastically endorsed (when offered as a costless good), consultation is also popular, but the introduction of private providers into competitive markets is not (Curtice and Heath 2009). In addition, choice is valued much less than other outcomes such as quality or speed of provision, so that it is of most interest as a means to achieving these ends. However, choice may offer a way of addressing the issue of diverse and competing demands. There are persistent concerns that prioritising individual choice erodes the public service ethos (Plant 2003) and damages public trust (Halpern 2010; Taylor-Gooby 2009). In the first case, consumerism limits the scope for the exercise of professional discretion by providers. In the second, the perception that providers' decisions are dominated by market considerations erodes confidence in their commitment to meeting individual needs.

Choice within state-financed services has been introduced in education, through open enrolment under the Education Reform Act of 1988; in health care through patient choice between different (state and non-state) providers for non-urgent treatment and proposals to allow a free choice of GP; and in social care through the recently implemented personal budgeting system.

Problems emerge in providing effective consumer choice where there is limited spare capacity. This has led to dilemmas in education, where over-subscribed schools choose between students, and where the growing diversity of academies, faith schools and other specialised schools in the state sector allows opportunities for providers to impose conditions on entry. In practice there is a tendency for schools to choose the most attractive pupils, who tend to come from the more privileged social groups, widening social class divisions, unless this is prevented. When parents are able to choose between competing providers, middle-class parents appear in practice to exercise choice more advantageously and over a wider range (Gewirth, Ball and Bowe 1995; Burgess, Proper and Wilson 2005; Ball 2008; Machin and Wilson 2009). However, it is also established that neighbourhood schooling does not prevent social sorting; and housing in the catchment area of a popular school commands a substantial premium, 20 per cent in one study (Leech and Campos 2003; see also Burgess *et al.* 2009). Studies of the impact of greater choice on outcomes indicate little change in class inequalities in the UK (Gibbons, Machin and Silva 2008) or in Nordic countries where social inequalities and inequalities in school resources are typically less marked (Böhlmark and Lindahl 2008; Holmlund and McNally 2009; Allen 2010).

Social class inequalities in education appear to persist whether legislation provides more or less choice of school. A converse issue arises for less successful institutions and those who are unable, for whatever reason, to escape them. Issues of provider selection in health and social care are less well documented in the UK (see Propper *et al.* (2008) for a study of US experience and earlier discussion of school entry) but indicate corresponding problems (Le Grand 2007: 127–140; Dixon and Thompson 2006).

The move to personal budgets in social care takes the idea of user choice one step further. Under this system, the share of the total budget for each individual deemed to need the service is allocated under their control, either as a direct payment, which they then spend on approved services, or to finance the particular package of services they would prefer (and can afford) from the available range (Social Care Institute for Excellence (SCIE) 2011a). This approach has gained strength since its introduction in the 1996 Community Care Act. It has achieved 'impressive early results', with high levels of user satisfaction, and offers the potential for administrative savings (Glasby, Le Grand and Duffy 2009: 495). It also enables the service user to access resources across the full range of possible providers, from state agencies through voluntary sector to local arrangements with neighbours and in the community. It is being extended across all adult social care. Experiments are currently being conducted by DWP into using a similar system of direct control in relation to payments for disabled people.

This approach locates respect for the autonomy of service users to make decisions about how to spend social resources in ways that best meet their needs within the general theme of user choice. Direct payments and personalised budgeting provoke different reactions among different groups of users. The more knowledgeable and self-confident individuals are and the more predictable their needs, the more able they feel to play a large part in decisions on the package of services they need; less confident groups, particularly older people and those with conditions that are difficult to manage, are more equivocal (SCIE 2011b; Glendinning *et al.* 2009).

Experience across most areas of state provision is that choice is popular and that choice procedures tend to make services more responsive, leading to greater satisfaction by service users (Le Grand 2007: 38–62). Flexibility in supply and rigorous controls are necessary to avoid 'cherry-picking' by providers and to prevent more privileged users getting preferential access to the best services. Where direct payments enable service users to purchase effectively from a broad range of providers, the more vulnerable groups often wish to have the support of professionals as advisers.

Targets and incentives

The imposition of targets refines and strengthens the range of incentives facing service providers and their managers. The 1997 government promoted the use of targets and incentives in the public sector to achieve efficiency savings and direct resources and activities in desired directions (Hood *et al.* 2009). At the same time, efforts were made to improve the professionalism of service providers through new training programmes, in-service training and incentives for qualified staff. Coupled with the mechanisms to allow greater choice to service users discussed above, these developments are sometimes considered as part of a 'New Public Management' (Flynn 2007; Bartlett *et al.* 1998). Recent governments have used targets linked to a range of incentives for key actors, including the dismissal of unsuccessful managers (Bevan and Hood 2006), rewards, penalties, reputational advantage and extra resources for those who meet targets. Over 360 targets were established in the first comprehensive spending reviews from 1998 onwards, these were cut back to 60 in 2007 and have now been further reduced as current policies stress local responsibility for outcomes and focus on spending reductions (Baldock, Gray and Jenkins 2007: 278–283; Taylor-Gooby 2009: 119–123; HM Treasury 2010a).

A substantial literature indicates some successes, some weaknesses, misleading assumptions and strict limitations on the scope for effective use of this approach (see Wilson 2010 for a summary). It is difficult to disentangle the independent effect of the target regime since the use of targets from 1999 to 2010 was been coupled with substantial increases in funding in health, education and social care. In any case, some targets follow pre-established trends, so that the goals might arguably have been achieved without the targets.

High-profile targets in relation to waiting times, waiting lists, mortality from cancer and cardiovascular disease and in relation to GP activity in the health service have been achieved. Comparisons with Scotland, Wales and Northern Ireland, where rather different regimes are in place (Propper *et al.* 2008; Le Grand 2007), indicate an independent effect from the target regimes. However, the Quality and Outcomes Framework (QOF) targets for GPs, intended to encourage good practice through incentive payments, appear to have been set at or below the level of current performance (NAO 2008). The mortality targets largely followed existing trends. There is indicative evidence that waiting time targets were subject to gaming (Bevan and Hood 2006). In education, test score targets achieved some improvement, at least initially (Wilson and Piebaga 2008; Hood, Dixon and Wilson 2009), but there is also evidence of cream-skimming in schools entry policies (Whitty, Power and Halpin 1998; West, Barham and Hind 2011) and perverse effects on examination entry policies (Wilson, Croxson and Atkinson 2006). Targets are unpopular among the managers and professionals whose behaviour they seek to direct (Hoggett *et al.* 2006), and also among the general public (Taylor-Gooby and Wallace 2009: 418).

Recent overviews of evidence on inequalities in relation to health (Sassi 2009), education (Lupton *et al.* 2009) and early years provision (Stewart 2009) show real but modest achievements. Two main factors underlie the difficulty in making greater gains: the complexity of the tasks that public services undertake and the multiplicity of stakeholders including service users, taxpayers, providers, managers, professional bodies, government and citizen interests (Wilson 2010). The target-plus-incentive approach is most likely to succeed when the objective and the associated incentive structure are simple and transparent, and when there is a clear consensus on the priority of various activities. The approach can achieve some success in containing costs, but has faced difficulties in practice in addressing the dilemma of meeting insistent and diverse demands. It is not popular.

Behaviour change

If people made rather different choices in a number of areas, the pressures on public provision would be mitigated. A higher rate of personal savings would reduce the demand for means-tested pension supplements (Pensions Commission 2004), different dietary and exercise choices would improve public health (Cabinet Office 2011), better separation of rubbish would cut the cost of local authority refuse collections (Rediscovering the Civic 2010), and greater involvement of local people might improve management of open spaces (John and Richardson 2012) and so on. Since behavioural change policies work with the reality of people's assumptions and aspirations they are likely to be popular, but are not, so far, well-developed in practice.

An influential stream of work has identified a number of heuristics that people use in everyday life to simplify practical choices (Tversky and Kahneman 1974). The most important are anchoring, loss aversion and the discounting of future gains at a high rate (Hargreaves-Heap *et al.* 1992: 365; Breakwell 2007: 28). Anchoring involves overweighting an arbitrary starting point in estimates of loss or gain, leading to an irrational attachment to the status quo. Loss aversion refers to an excessive concern about losses so that they are overvalued compared to monetarily equivalent gains. Excessive discounting minimises the value of more distant future benefits or penalties. Other work on real-world behaviour highlights the importance of cognitive dissonance (Festinger 1957) and tendencies to conformity (Martin and Hewstone 2003). These refer to the observed tendency for people to shift their beliefs to suit their behaviour, rather than vice versa, and the way in which people often seek to change their behaviour to fit in with a group with which they identify.

Behavioural change policymaking seeks to exploit these tendencies (New Economics Foundation 2005; Prime Minister's Strategy Unit (PMSU) 2004; Halpern 2010). Examples based on loss aversion typically incorporate attachment to the status quo. In the new voluntary third-tier pension scheme, starting in October 2012, employees are automatically blanketed in, and must choose to leave rather than choose to join. Leaving is a rejection of the default and experienced as a loss. The Child Trust Fund (now closed) effectively presented saving as a fait accompli with an initial endowment and then further incentivised it with matching grants for savers.[3] Top-up pension contributions involve extra spending. However, schemes which take larger contributions in good years may address loss aversion by taking some of the surplus from an unexpectedly higher income. Providers may exploit future discounting by offering contribution rates which start low but increase in the future (Thaler and Sunstein 2008: 112–115). Loss aversion is also exploited in behavioural schemes to stop smoking, such as that being pioneered by the government in collaboration with Boots. Individuals' deposit money is only returned, with a bonus, if they succeed in their goal (Cabinet Office 2011: 9; Thaler and Sunstein 2008: 232).

Future discounting may also be addressed by creating a current contract which then commits behaviour to achieve a distant goal, for example, school–parent homework contracts, or commitments to exercise or diet. This approach may also overcome the problem of cognitive dissonance by strengthening the motivation to align future behaviour with current intentions, rather than allowing the weight of behaviour to shift intentions when dissonance between the two occurs.

One issue is the obvious limits to the extent to which government can modify choices (Stoker and Moseley 2010). Other agencies may offer alternative framings with different implications for action. For example, the framing of measles, mumps and rubella (MMR) vaccination as potentially damaging may undermine public health programmes (Fitzpatrick 2005). Other examples of conflicts about how issues are to be understood concern the impact of immigration on job opportunities (Mulley 2010: 1) and whether care by one's mother is more important for young children than the higher living standard resulting from the mother's employment (Duncan 2007).

An authoritative overview by Marteau *et al.* (2011) concludes that changes to choice environments can certainly improve people's health behaviour. However, most of the intentional modifications to choice architecture in contemporary society are pursued by commercial interests rather

---

[3] See HM Revenue and Customs, The Child Trust Fund [online], http://www.hmrc.gov. uk/ctf/ (Accessed on 27 August 2011).

than government, and lead to choices that damage health, such as fast food rather than healthy food; car-driving rather than cycling; the normalisation of alcohol consumption and so on. The implication is that behavioural approaches may be useful, but that government has other resources available to it in improving outcomes in areas such as health, for example: the regulation of food quality and of alcohol consumption; subsidy of sports facilities; and redesign of transport systems. Why retreat to nudge, where other influences may shape choices?

These points imply that, while useful, the potential for developing these approaches may be limited unless government is in a position to confront the social traditions and commercial interests framing many choices. They are acceptable to the public in the areas indicated.

Shared values: the third sector

Policy-makers have displayed increasing interest in the capacity of not-for-profit, voluntary and informal groupings of citizens to meet social needs. Responsibility is transferred away from government, as in the individualisation or privatisation policies discussed earlier. Here the frame of reference is one of collective values rather than individual deliberative choices. Third sector policies would reduce pressure on the state, enable people to play a role in meeting the demands on government services and also, perhaps, promote greater cohesion and inclusiveness across society. These themes lay behind the New Deal for Communities programme and the National Strategy for Neighbourhood Renewal (Social Exclusion Unit 2001). A number of proposals seek to tap the energies of the sector further and involve neighbourhood and community groups (Mumford and Power 2003; Young Foundation 2010) and the more established charities (National Council for Voluntary Organisations (NCVO) 2010) in helping to resolve the pressures on government. The 2010 government has placed considerable emphasis on a loosely-defined notion of the Big Society: 'a broad culture of responsibility, mutuality and obligation' (Cameron 2009).

Civil society groupings have a strong tradition of providing for a range of social needs. NCVO estimates that some 171,000 large voluntary organisations can be identified in the UK (NCVO 2010: 25), with some 600,000 smaller unregistered groups (Phillimore and McCabe 2010).

These groups pursue a huge variety of objectives, from university education, to animal welfare, to environmental activities, to culture and recreation, to the promotion of religion, to youth work, to trade union activity, to international aid, to human rights work. They range from a relatively small number of large, well-structured organisations employing a substantial number of staff and providing a range of services, often under contract to local government and other bodies, to small agencies concerned with fundraising for particular local needs.

For our purposes, three considerations are relevant: voluntary sector activities and resources tend to be focused on particular needs and areas (Breeze 2010; Kendall 2003), they are unevenly spread across the country (Mohan 2011; Lyon and Sepulveda 2009), and the voluntary sector typically works hand-in-hand with government (NCVO 2011: 5). The sector may find it hard to take on the role of alternative provider, making a substantial contribution to the problem of resource constraint, because its scope is narrower than that of government and the organisations that are closest to public services rely on state support.

About 70,000 organisations operate in the fields of social services, housing, health and social care, education and community development (NCVO 2010: 29). They tend to be concentrated in the better-off parts of the country (Lyon and Sepulveda 2009). Mohan shows a clear inverse relationship between the density of neighbourhood organisations within an area and the level of deprivation of the area (Mohan 2011: 7). As a result, more public funds go to organisations in less deprived areas, although a greater proportion of the voluntary organisations working in large urban centres in the north of the country than in the south receive public support (ibid.: 12). Studies of the capacity of voluntary and charitable organisations to substitute for services like the NHS on a substantial scale indicate that they are not in a position to make a major contribution (Heims *et al.* 2010).

Support from the general public is again directed chiefly at particular needs. The largest numbers of volunteers support education, religious groups and sporting activities (NCVO 2010: vi, 10; Scott 2007: 322). Donations also favour specific groups. The leading areas by numbers giving are medical research (20 per cent), hospitals and hospices (25 per cent), and children and young people (14 per cent). By amount, religious causes receive 15 per cent of all donations, followed by medical research, hospitals and hospices, overseas aid and children and young people (NCVO 2009: 8–9).

Many charities and voluntary organisations, and also community interest companies and similar bodies established by social entrepreneurs, operate to fulfil public policy or statutory goals, mainly with state finance and under contract to state agencies. Nearly a quarter (24 per cent) of charities receives funding from local government (Office of the Third Sector (OTS) 2008). This accounts for 36 per cent of total voluntary sector income (£12.8 billion). Five sectors (employment and training, law and advocacy, education, housing, and social services) receive more than half their income from government. By 2007–08 45 per cent of local government funding and 30 per cent of central government funding was in the form of contracts for the provision of services (ONS 2010b: 23–24). The vast majority of these resources go to the larger charities: 79 per cent is received by 3,742 of the largest organisations with over 5,000 employees, with only 3.3 per cent going to organisations with fewer than 50 employees (NCVO 2010: 27). For these charities it is difficult to disentangle the impact of their activities from that of the public services with which they work. The significance of government engagement and its role in relation to the growth of a 'Big Society' is indicated by a recent Community Development Foundation (CDF) survey of community development workers. This shows that lack of access to funding (62 per cent), working to specific policy agendas (48 per cent) and working on short-term project funding (41 per cent) are the three most significant problems mentioned by workers in this sector (CDF 2009).

Voluntary activity is popular. It offers ways of providing services relatively cheaply and draws on resources of goodwill and commitment that can supplement, but not replace, public provision (Frey 1997: 123). However, the close links between the parts of the voluntary sector most engaged in social provision and the state, make it difficult to separate the impact of community-run from state-run provision. This is particularly relevant in those sectors mainly funded by government, where most of that finance is directed through contracts: employment and training, law and advocacy, education, housing and social services. The fact that voluntary activity appears to have its strongest base in the better-off parts of the country points to further limitations in directing resources where they are most needed. The voluntary sector makes a major contribution but there are limits to how far it can substitute for government.

Discussion

Public policy is trapped between pressures to contain spending and demands for improvements and expansion. This tension is increasingly difficult to balance. In this chapter we have reviewed six public policy responses. All can contribute to some aspect of the problem but none seems likely to offer an independent resolution, suggesting that governments will pursue them in combination.

Cutbacks, particularly those affecting the highly valued areas of public policy which absorb the greater share of resources (health care, education, pensions), are unpopular and come at a high political cost. The various pressures on spending lead to a continual search for methods to improve productivity in public services. So far as we can see, these efforts achieve no more than the maintenance of the status quo, itself a difficult task given the level of demand. It is unclear whether the exceptional circumstances of the 2009 recession and its aftermath will lead to a step change in public expectations, and whether the cuts currently being implemented will be made to stick.

Policies structured around work incentives and individual responsibility follow a strong theme in public attitudes, but one that applies most clearly to specific areas of provision. Privatisation has been pursued in the outsourcing of state provision, and has achieved some savings. It is unpopular in relation to core services such as health care and education, and is unlikely to generate savings here without damaging public support.

Greater choice in public services is popular, whether through the patient choice system in the NHS, open enrolment in schools, or personalised budgets in social care. Choice programmes, when introduced as part of a new public management strategy, have not been directly concerned to contain spending pressures, but have been one element in market competition designed to confront providers with incentives that require them to be both responsive to demand and cost-efficient. These approaches may improve the way resources are deployed but the evidence discussed earlier indicates no step change in productivity in the period during which they expanded most rapidly.

Policies which establish and enforce targets reassert central control. Target policies were most widely deployed during a period of relative spending growth from 1999 to 2007 and appear to have had some effect in directing the extra resources towards policy goals. They are unpopular with the managers who had to implement them and, perhaps more importantly, with the general public.

A less obtrusive approach to central direction involves modifying the contexts in which people make choices, to encourage behaviour conducive to the objectives of policy-makers. Experience with the approach is limited. It is at present unclear how far the behavioural change strategy can go in taking some of the pressure away from public spending, or in what areas it is most effective. In principle, it offers opportunities to do this in ways that work with the demands that people make of the public sector. However, the extent to which government is in a position to reframe the choices that people make is restricted, so that such a strategy can only make a partial contribution to the dilemma.

Finally, the voluntary sector writ large scores highly in relation to people's demands, since voluntary activity is concentrated in fields where people believe there are needs and feel able to contribute to meeting them. This component of civil society is rich and diverse in the UK. Harnessing its contribution to public policy issues is politically attractive. There is considerable uncertainty about the potential for expansion of these activities, particularly where needs are most pressing. Voluntary activity is strongest in better-off areas. Most resources are directed to health care and education, not to poverty, poor housing and joblessness in disadvantaged parts of the country. In any case, state finance and support appear essential to much of the work. This applies particularly to those areas which are closest to state provision and are most likely to be seen as potentially capable of substituting for it. The expansion of what is sometimes termed a 'third sector' is popular and valuable but unlikely to make major inroads on spending issues.

Future directions in policy

The variety and incompleteness of the various solutions opens the way to different scenarios for the future development of public policy. The immediate future is overshadowed by the financial crisis, spending cuts and sluggish recovery. Previous experience indicates real problems in sustaining the level of cutbacks required to move spending substantially away from the post-war trend line of about 40 per cent of GDP. There may be room for some modest expansion once the GDP lost in recessions is made up. Governments may seek to combine spending constraint, choice, markets and privatisation, targets, behavioural change, and a greater role for the non-state sector in different ways.

Possible approaches could be ranged along two dimensions, one running from an emphasis on state centralisation to the transfer of responsibility to the private or voluntary sector or to individuals, and one from greater to lesser generosity in the level of benefits and services. Centralised approaches might favour target-setting and imposed cuts, while more decentralised approaches pursue a greater role for choice, markets and the private sector and for voluntary provision. The degree of generosity would be reflected in spending levels, the extent to which redistributive measures were pursued, and enthusiasm for, or avoidance of, direct cuts. One reason for the current interest in behavioural change and in the voluntary sector may be that they appear equivocal in relation to spending and uncertain but probably positive in gaining public acceptance. If real transfers of responsibility could be achieved by influencing behaviour or by substituting voluntary for state effort this might contribute to spending constraint.

The dilemma between growing public demands for services that meet a diverse range of needs and the pressures to contain spending seems likely to play a continuing role in shaping the context of policy-making. Pierson's argument that the future of western welfare states is one of 'permanent austerity' appears prescient (Pierson 2000: 456). Governments, wherever they locate their policies on the above dimensions, will continue to combine the various strategies with different emphases and the search for new ways of delivering policies to meet the pressures will grow, if anything, more persistent.

This leads to a further point. Many commentators point out that citizens are becoming increasingly mistrustful of politicians and unwilling to engage in political debates (see Stoker 2011 and chapter 8 of this book). One reason for the growth of 'anti-politics' is the evident mismatch between the promises contained in policy platforms and the outcomes experienced in ordinary people's lives (Crouch 2004). Permanent austerity means that there are real limits to what government can do in relation to the demands placed upon it. If the conflict between expanding demand and constrained resources cannot be resolved, the question becomes one of finding the best way to live with it. Our political traditions are not well adapted to considered discussion of unattractive policy choices.

Politicians are reluctant to take the lead in opening a debate on these issues that would seek to identify the standards of provision and the priorities between them that can credibly be provided. The need for such a debate is now stronger than it has ever been and will become even more clamorous in the future. A final scenario is one in which, in a direct attempt to recapture public trust, our political leadership opens up the dilemma of containing spending and meeting demands directly to the public. Such an approach would require a sufficiently high level of general political awareness to enable realistic discussion of these issues, so that solutions can be made to stick. It is hard to see how a political debate which seeks to reconcile rising demands with severely constrained spending can recapture public trust if it does not move in such a direction.

References

Alesina, A. and Perotti, R. (1995) 'The Political Economy of Budget Deficits', *Staff Papers – International Monetary Fund*, 42: 1–31.

Alldritt, C., Masters, J., Gerritsen, S. and Kippin, H. (2009) *A Brief History of Public Sector Reform*, The 2020 Public Services Trust at the RSA [online], http://clients.squareeye.net/uploads/2020/documents/STC%20A%20Brief%20History%20of%20Public%20Service%20Reform.pdf (accessed on 26 August 2010).

Allen, R. (2010) 'Replicating Swedish Free School Reforms in England', *Research in Public Policy (CMPO Bulletin)* 10: 4–7.

Atkinson, A. (2005) *Atkinson Review: Final Report. Measurement of Government Output and Productivity for the National Accounts* (Basingstoke: Palgrave Macmillan).

Ayoubkhani, D., Baird, A., Munro, F. and Wild, R. (2010) 'Education Productivity', *Economic and Labour Market Review* 4: 55–60.

Baldock, J., Gray, A. and Jenkins, B. (2007) 'Public Expenditure Decision-making', in J. Baldock, N. Manning and S. A. Vickerstaff (eds) *Social Policy*, third edition (Oxford, Oxford University Press), 275–306.

Ball, S.J. (2008) *The Education Debate* (Bristol: The Policy Press).

Bardhan, P., Bowles, S. and Wallerstein, M. (2006) *Globalization and Egalitarian Redistribution* (Princeton, NJ: Princeton University Press).

Barnes, M. and Tomaszewski, W. (2010), 'Lone Parents and Benefits', in A. Park, J. Curtice, K. Thomson, M. Phillips, E. Clery and S. Butts (eds) *British Social Attitudes 26th Report* (London: Sage), 193–216.

Bartlett, W., Roberts, J and Le Grand, J. (1998) *A Revolution in Social Policy* (Bristol: Policy Press).

Béland, D. and Gran, B. (eds) (2008) *Public and Private Social Policy: Health and Pension Policies in a New Era* (Basingstoke: Palgrave Macmillan).

Bevan, G. and Hood, C. (2006) 'Have Targets Improved Performance in the English NHS?', *British Medical Journal* 332: 419–422.

Böhlmark, A. and Lindahl, M. (2008) 'Does School Privatisation Improve Educational Achievement? Evidence from Sweden's Voucher Reform', Institute for the Study of Labour (IZA), DP No. 3691 [online], http://ftp.iza.org/dp3691.pdf (accessed on 26 August 2011).

Breakwell, G. (2007) *The Psychology of Risk* (Cambridge: Cambridge University Press).

Breeze, B. (2010) *Coutts Million Pound Donors Report,* The Centre for the Study of Philanthropy, Humanitarianism and Social Justice, University of Kent [online], http://www.kent.ac.uk/sspssr/cphsj/documents/mpdr2010.pdf (accessed on 26 August 2011).

Burgess, S., Propper, C. and Wilson D. (2005), *Will More Choice Improve Outcomes in Education and Health Care?,* The Centre for Market and Public Organisation, University of Bristol [online], http://www.bris.ac.uk/Depts/CMPO/choice.pdf (accessed on 26 August 2011).

Burgess, S., Greaves, E., Vignoles, A. and Wilson, D. (2009) *What Parents Want,* wp 09/222, CMPO, Bristol [online], http://www.bristol.ac.uk/cmpo/publications/papers/2009/wp222.pdf (accessed on 28 September 2011).

Butt, S. and Curtice, J. (2010), 'The Public as Weather-vane', in A. Park, J. Curtice, K. Thomson, M. Phillips, E. Clery and S. Butts (eds) *British Social Attitudes 26th Report* (London: Sage), 1–18.

Cabinet Office (2011), *Applying Behavioural Insight to Health* [online], http://www.cabinetoffice.gov.uk/sites/default/files/resources/403936_BehaviouralInsight_acc.pdf (accessed on 26 August 2011).

Cameron, D. (2009) 'The Big Society', Hugo Young Lecture [online], http://www.conservatives.com/News/Speeches/2009/11/David_Cameron_The_Big_Society.aspx (accessed 28 September 2011).

Chamberlain, E. (2010), *Briefing on the Big Society,* National Council for Voluntary Organisations [online], http://www.ncvo-vol.org.uk/sites/default/files/Big_Society_Programme_briefing_final_0.pdf (accessed on 26 August 2011).

Community Development Foundation (CDF) (2009) *Survey of Community Development Workers and Managers* [online], http://www.cdf.org.uk//c/document_libary/get-file?uuid=de048626-344c-4a9c-8e90-8249c97df0cb&groupId=10128 (accessed on 27 August 2011).

Cooke, G. (2011) *National Salary Insurance,* Institute for Public Policy Research [online], http://www.ippr.org/images/media/files/publication/2011/07/national-savings-insurance_110726_7775.pdf (accessed on 26 August 2011).

Crouch, C. (2004) *Post-democracy* (Cambridge: Polity).

Curtice, J. K. and Heath, O. (2009) 'Do People Want Choice and Diversity of Provision in Public Services?', in A. Park, J. Curtice, K. Thomson, M. Phillips and E. Clery (eds) *British Social Attitudes 25th Report* (London: Sage), 55–78.

Department of Health (2009) *Guidance on NHS Patients Who Wish to Pay for Additional Private Care* [online], http://www.dh.gov.uk/prod_consum_dh/groups/dh_digitalasset/dh_096576.pdf (accessed on 22 August 2012).

Department of Health (2011), *Modernisation of Health and Care* [online], http://healthandcare.dh.gov.uk/any-qualified-provider-2/ (accessed on 11 January 2013).

Dixon, A. and Thompson, S. (2006) 'Choices in Health Care: The European Experience', *Journal of Health Services Research and Policy* 11: 167–171.

Duncan, S. (2007) 'What's the Problem With Teenage Parents? And What's the Problem With Policy?', *Critical Social Policy* 27: 307–334.

Dunsire, A. and Hood, C. with Huby, M. (1989) *Cutback Management in Public Bureaucracies* (Cambridge: Cambridge University Press).

Department of Health (2011) *NHS and Social Care Bill* [online], http://www.dh.gov.uk/en/ Publicationsandstatistics/Legislation/Actsandbills/HealthandSocialCareBill2011/index. htm (accessed on 28 September 2011).

Department for Work and Pensions (DWP) (2010) *Universal Credit: Welfare That Works,* Cm 7957 (London: TSO).

Department for Work and Pensions (DWP) (2011) *A State Pension for the 21st Century,* Cm 8053 (London: TSO).

Edwards, T., Fitz, J. and Whitty, G. (1989) *The State and Private Education: An Evaluation of the Assisted Places Scheme* (Lewis: Falmer Press).

Enthoven, A. (2002) *Introducing Market Forces into Health Care: A Tale of Two Countries,* The Nuffield Trust [online], http://www.nuffieldtrust.org.uk/sites/files/nuffield/publication/ introducing-market-forces-into-healthcare-jun02.pdf (accessed on 26 August 2011).

European Commission (2008) *Renewed Social Agenda* [online], http://ec.europa.eu/social/ main.jsp?catId=547 (accessed on 22 August 2012).

Festinger, J. (1957) *A Theory of Cognitive Dissonance* (Stanford, CA: Stanford University Press).

Fitzpatrick, M. (2005), 'Why Can't the Daily Mail Eat Humble Pie over MMR?', *British Medical Journal,* 331: 1148.

Flynn, N. (2007) *Public Sector Management,* fifth edition (London: Sage).

Frey, B. (1997) *Not Just for the Money: An Economic Theory of Personal Motivation* (Cheltenham: Edward Elgar).

Gamble, A. (2011) *Economic Futures.* A report for the British Academy project *New Paradigms in Public Policy* (London: British Academy Policy Centre).

Gewirth, S., Ball, S. J., and Bowe, R. (1995) *Markets, Choice and Equity* (Milton Keynes: Open University Press).

Gibbons, S., Machin, S. and Silva, O. (2008) 'Choice, Competition and Pupil Achievement', *Journal of the European Economic Association,* 6: 912–947.

Giddens, A (1994), *Beyond Left and Right: The Future of Radical Politics* (Cambridge: Polity Press).

Glasby, J., Le Grand, J. and Duffy, S. (2009) 'A Healthy Choice? Direct Payments and Healthcare in the English NHS', *Policy and Politics* 37(4): 481–497.

Glasby, J. and Littlechild R. (2009) *Direct Payments and Personal Budgets: Putting Personalisation into Practice* (Bristol: The Policy Press).

Glendinning, C., Arksey, H., Jones, K., Moran, N., Netten, A. and Rabiee, P. (2009) *Individual Budgets Pilot Projects: Impact and Outcomes for Carers,* Social Policy Research Unit, University of York [online], http://www.york.ac.uk/inst/spru/research/pdf/ IBSENCarersRep.pdf (accessed on 22 August 2012).

Glennerster, H. (2009), *Understanding the Finance of Welfare: What it Costs and How to Pay for It* (Bristol: The Policy Press).

Goode, R. (1993) *The Pension Law Reform: Report v. 1: The Report of the Pension Law Review Committee,* Cm 2432 (London: TSO).

Grant, E. and Wood, C. (2011), 'Disability Benefits', in N. Yeates, T. Haux, R. Jawad and M. Kilkey (eds) *In Defence of Welfare: The Impacts of the Spending Review,* Social Policy

Association [online], http://www.social-policy.org.uk/downloads/idow.pdf (accessed on 22 August 2012).

Halpern, D. (2010) *The Hidden Wealth of Nations* (Cambridge: Polity).

Hardie, M., Cheers, J., Pinder, C. and Qaeser, U. (2011) *Public Sector Outputs, Inputs and Productivity: Healthcare no 5* (London: ONS).

Hargreaves-Heap, S., Hollis, M., Lyons, B., Sugden, R. and Weale, A. (1992) *The Theory of Choice* (Oxford: Blackwell).

Heims, E., Price, D., Pollock, A. M., Miller, E., Mohan, J. and Shaoul, J. (2010) 'A Review of the Evidence of Third Sector Performance and its Relevance for a Universal, Comprehensive Health System', *Social Policy and Society 9*: 515–526.

Hills, J. (2009) 'Future Pressures', in J. Hills, T. Sefton and K. Stewart (eds) *Towards a More Equal Society* (Bristol: The Policy Press).

HM Treasury *(2009) Long-term Public Finance Report: An Analysis of Fiscal Sustainability [online]*, http://www.hm-treasury.gov.uk/d/pbr09_publicfinances.pdf (accessed on 2 August 2012).

HM Treasury (2010a) *Spending Review 2010*, Cm 7942 (London: TSO), http://www.hm-treasury.gov.uk/spend_index.htm (accessed on 2 August 2012).

HM Treasury (2010b) *Public Expenditure Statistical Analyses*, Cm 7890 (London: TSO).

Hoggett, P., Beedell, P., Jiminez, J., Mayo, M. and Miller, C. (2006) 'Identity, Life History and Commitment to Welfare', *Journal of Social Policy* 35(4): 689–704.

Holmlund and McNally, S. (2009) 'A Swedish Model for UK Schools?', *Centrepiece* 10, 23–24, (London: Centre for Economic Performance), http://cep.lse.ac.uk/pubs/download/cp306.pdf (accessed on 29 September 2011).

Hood, C., Dixon, R. and Wilson, D. (2009) *'Managing by Numbers': The Way to Make Public Services Better*, ESRC Public Services Programme, [online], http://www.christopherhood.net/pdfs/Managing_by_numbers.pdf (accessed on 27 August 2011).

Horne, M. and Shirley, T. (2009) *Co-production in Public Services: A New Partnership with Citizens* (London: Cabinet Office).

House of Commons Health Committee (2006), *Independent Sector Treatment Centres: Fourth Report of Session 2005–06*, HC 934-1 (London: TSO).

Institute for Fiscal Studies (2011) *The IFS Green Budget* [online], http://www.ifs.org.uk/budgets/gb2011/gb2011.pdf (accessed on 22 August 2012).

Institute of Local Government Studies (2011) *The World Will Be Your Oyster?*, University of Birmingham [online], http://www.tsrc.ac.uk/LinkClick.aspx?fileticket=pUV9gMRqse0%3D&tabid=508 (accessed on 22 August 2012).

International Monetary Fund (2012), *World Economic Outlook Data,* September edition [online], http://www.imf.org/external/pubs/ft/weo/2012/01/weodata/index.aspx (accessed on 22 August 2012).

John, P. and Richardson, E. (2012) *Nudging Citizens Towards Localism?*, British Academy Policy Unit, London, http://www.britac.ac.uk/policy/Nudging-citizens-towards-localism.cfm (accessed on 22 August 2012).

Johnstone, R. (2011), 'Council Outsourcing Plans Could Take Decade', *Public Finance,* 11 May 2011 [online], http://www.publicfinance.co.uk/news/2011/05/council-outsourcing-plans-could-take-decade/ (accessed on 22 August 2012).

Judd, A. (2011) *Public Service Labour Productivity* (London: ONS).

Julius, D. (2008), *Public Services Industry Review – Understanding the Public Services Industry: How Big, How Good, Where Next?* (London: Department for Business, Enterprise and Regulatory Reform).

Kendall, J. (2003) *The Voluntary Sector: Comparative Perspectives in the UK* (London: Routledge).

Le Grand, J. (2007) *The Other Invisible Hand* (Princeton, NJ: Princeton University Press).

Leech, D. and Campos, E. (2003) 'Is Comprehensive Education Really Free? A Case-Study of the Effects of Secondary School Admissions Policies on House Prices in One Local Area', *Journal of the Royal Statistical Society* 166: 135–154.

Letwin, O. (1988) *Privatizing the World: A Study of International Privatization in Theory and Practice* (New York: Thomson).

Local Government Association (LGA) (2011) *Report of the Council Budgets, Spending and Saving Survey 2011* [online], http://new.lga.gov.uk/lga/core/page.do?pageId=17710284 (accessed on 22 August 2012).

Lindsay, C. (2011) 'Welfare That Works?', in N. Yeates, T. Haux, R. Jawad and M. Kilkey (eds) *In Defence of Welfare: The Impacts of the Spending Review*, Social Policy Association [online], http://www.social-policy.org.uk/downloads/idow.pdf (accessed on 22 August 2012).

Lowe, R. (1999) *The Welfare State in Britain Since 1945*, second edition (Basingstoke: Macmillan).

Lupton, D., Heath, N. and Salter, E. (2009) 'Education', in J. Hills, T. Sefton and K. Stewart (eds) *Towards a More Equal Society* (Bristol: Policy Press), 71–90.

Lyon, F. and Sepulveda, L. (2009) 'Mapping Social Enterprises: Past Approaches, Challenges and Future Directions', *Social Enterprise Journal* 5: 83–94.

Lyon, F., Teasdale, S. and Baldock, R. (2010) *Approaches to Measuring the Scale of the Social Enterprise Sector in the UK*, working paper 43, Third Sector Research Centre [online], http://www.tsrc.ac.uk/ (accessed on 22 August 2012).

Machin, S. and Wilson, J. (2009) 'Academy Schools and Pupil Performance', *CentrePiece Spring 2009* [online], http://cep.lse.ac.uk/pubs/download/cp280.pdf (accessed on 22 August 2012).

Macmillan, R. (2010) *The Third Sector Delivering Public Services: An Evidence Review*, working paper 20, Third Sector Research Centre [online], http://www.tsrc.ac.uk/LinkClick.aspx?fileticket=l9qruXn%2fBN8%3d&tabid=712 (accessed on 22 August 2012).

Marteau, T., Ogilvie, D., Roland, M., Suhrcke, M. and Kelly, M. (2011) 'Judging Nudging: Can Nudging Improve Population Health?', *British Medical Journal* 342: d228.

Martin, R. and Hewstone, M. (2003) 'Majority Versus Minority Influence: When, Not Whether, Source Status Instigates Heuristic or Systematic Processing', *European Journal of Social Psychology* 33: 313–330.

McNamara, K. (1998) *The Currency of Ideas: Monetary Politics in the European Union* (Ithaca, NY: Cornell University Press).

Millar, J. (ed.) (2009) *Understanding Social Security: Issues for Policy and Practice*, second edition (Bristol: The Policy Press).

Mohan, J. (2011) *Mapping the Third Sector*, working paper 62, Third Sector Research Centre [online], http://tsrc.ac.uk/LinkClick.aspx?fileticket=izLuarcAwMs%3D&tabid=500 (accessed on 27 August 2011).

Moore A. (2010) 'Outside In: Outsourcing in Government', *Public Finance*, 29 July 2011 [online], http://www.publicfinance.co.uk/features/2010/07/outside-in/ (accessed on 27 August 2011).

Mulley, S. (2010) *Immigration and Employment: Anatomy of a Media Story*, Institute for Public Policy Research [online], http://www.ippr.org/images/media/files/publication/2011/05/ImmigrationandemploymentAug10_1791.pdf (accessed on 27 August 2011).

Mumford, K. and Power, A. (2003) *Eastenders: Family and Community in East London* (Bristol: The Policy Press).

National Audit Office (2007), *The Academies Programme* [online], http://www.nao.org.uk/news/0607/0607254.aspx (accessed on 27 August 2011).

National Audit Office (NAO) (2008) *NHS Pay Modernisation*, HC307, 2007–8, 28 February, http://www.nao.org.uk/publications/0708/new_contracts_for_general_prac.aspx (accessed on 28 September 2011).

National Council for Voluntary Organisations (NCVO) (2009) *UK Giving 2009: An Overview of Charitable Giving in the UK, 2008/09* [online], http://www.ncvo-vol.org.uk/sites/default/files/UploadedFiles/NCVO/Publications/Publications_Catalogue/Sector_Research/FINAL_UK_Giving_2009_FINAL.pdf (accessed 27 August 2011).

National Council for Voluntary Organisations (NCVO) (2010) *The UK Civil Society Almanac 2010* (London: NCVO).

National Council for Voluntary Organisations (NCVO) (2011) *Counting the Cuts: The Impact of Spending Cuts on the UK Voluntary and Community Sector* [online], http://www.ncvo-vol.org.uk/sites/default/files/counting_the_cuts.pdf (accessed on 27 August 2011).

New Economics Foundation (2005) *Behavioural Economics: Seven Principles for Policymakers* (London: New Economics Foundation).

Office for Budget Responsibility (OBR) (2012) *Fiscal Sustainability Report* [online], http://budgetresponsibility.independent.gov.uk/fiscal-sustainability-report-july-2011/ (accessed on 22 August 2012).

Organisation for Economic Co-operation and Development (OECD) (2011) *Privatisation in the 21st Century: Summary of Recent Experiences* [online], http://www.oecd.org/dataoecd/44/58/43449100.pdf (accessed on 27 August 2011).

Office for National Statistics (ONS) (2001) *Social Trends, 30* (London: Stationery Office).

Office for National Statistics (ONS) (2010a) *Social Trends, 40* (Basingstoke: Palgrave Macmillan).

Office for National Statistics (ONS) (2010b) *Measuring Outcomes for Public Service Users: Final Report* [online], http://www.ons.gov.uk/ons/guide-method/method-quality/measuring-outcomes-for-public-service-users/mopsu-reports-and-updates/index.html (accessed on 29 September 2011).

Office of the Third Sector (OTS) (2008) *National Survey of Third Sector Organisations* (London: Cabinet Office).

Peacock, A. and Wiseman, J. (1967) *The Growth of Public Expenditure in the United Kingdom 1890–1955* (London: George Allen & Unwin).

Pensions Commission (2004) *Pensions: Challenges and Choices. The First Report of the Pensions Commission* (London: TSO).

Pfaller, A., Gough, I. and Therborn, G. (1991) *Can the Welfare State Compete? A Comparative Study of Five Advanced Capitalist Countries* (Basingstoke: Palgrave Macmillan).

Phillimore, J. and McCabe, A. (2010) *Understanding the Distinctiveness of Small-scale Third Sector Activity*, working paper 33, Third Sector Research Centre [online], http://www.tsrc.ac.uk/LinkClick.aspx?fileticket=iBB6cFBtNYU%3D&tabid=500 (accessed on 27 August 2011).

Pierson, P. (ed.) (2000) *The New Politics of the Welfare State* (Oxford: Oxford University Press).

Plant, R. (2003) 'The Public Service Ethic and Political Accountability', *Parliamentary Affairs* 56: 560–579.

Pollitt, C. and Talbot, C. (eds) (2004) *Unbundled Government* (London: Taylor & Francis).

Power, A. (2012) *The Big Society and Concentrated Neighbourhood Problems*, a report for the British Academy project *New Paradigms in Public Policy* (London: British Academy Policy Centre).

Prime Minister's Strategy Unit (PMSU) (2004) *Personal Responsibility and Changing Behaviour: The State of Knowledge and Its Implications for Public Policy* [online], http://cdi.mecon.gov.ar/biblio/docelec/dp4105.pdf (accessed on 27 August 2011).

Propper, C., Sutton, M., Whitnall, C. and Windmeijer, F. (2008) *Incentives and Targets in Hospital Care: Evidence from a Natural Experiment*, Working Paper 08/205, Centre for Market and Public Organisation, University of Bristol [online], http://www.bristol.ac.uk/cmpo/publications/papers/2008/wp205.pdf (accessed on 27 August 2011).

Rediscovering the Civic (2010) *How to Get the Recycling Boxes Out: A Randomised Controlled Trial of a Door to Door Recycling Service*, policy briefing no. 1, Universities of Manchester and Southampton [online], http://www.civicbehaviour.org.uk/documents/EmergePolicyBrief1June2010.pdf (accessed on 27 August 2011).

Sassi, F. (2009) 'Health Inequalities', in J. Hills, T. Sefton and K. Stewart (eds) *Towards a More Equal Society* (Bristol: Policy Press), 135–156.

Scharpf, F.A. and Schmidt, V.A. (2000), 'Conclusion', in F.A. Scharpf and V.A. Schmidt (eds) *Welfare and Work in the Open Economy Volume 1: From Vulnerability to Competitiveness* (Oxford: Oxford University Press), 310–336.

Social Care Institute for Excellence (SCIE) (2009) *The Implementation of Individual Budgets in Adult Social Care*, research briefing 20 [online], http://www.scie.org.uk/publications/briefings/files/briefing20.pdf (accessed on 27 August 2011).

Social Care Institute for Excellence (SCIE) (2011a) *SCIE Guide 10: Direct Payments. Answering Frequently Asked Questions* [online], http://www.scie.org.uk/publications/guides/guide10/files/guide10.pdf (accessed on 27 August 2011).

Social Care Institute for Excellence (SCIE) (2011b), *SCIE Report 40: Keeping Personal Budgets Personal: Learning from the Experiences of Older People, People With Mental Health Problems and Their Carers* [online], http://www.scie.org.uk/publications/reports/report40/keyissues/index.asp (accessed on 27 August 2011).

Scott, D. (2007) 'The Role of the Voluntary and Community Sectors', in J. Baldock, N. Manning and S.A. Vickerstaff (eds) *Social Policy*, third edition (Oxford: Oxford University Press), 307–46.

Simpson, H. (2007) *Productivity in the Public Services*, working paper 07/164, Centre for Market and Public Organisation University of Bristol [online], http://www.bristol.ac.uk/cmpo/publications/papers/2007/wp164/pdf (accessed on 27 August 2011).

Social Exclusion Unit (2001) A New Commitment to Neighbourhood Renewal: National Strategy Action Plan (SEU, Cabinet Office) [online], http://www.neighbourhood.statistics.gov.uk/HTMLDocs/images/NationalStrategyReport_tcm97-51090.pdf (accessed 28 September 2011).

Stewart, K. (2009) '"A Scar on the Soul": Child Poverty and Disadvantage under New Labour', in J. Hills, T. Sefton and K. Stewart (eds) Towards a More Equal Society (Bristol: Policy Press), 47–70.

Stoker, G. (2011) Building a New Politics? A report for the British Academy project New Paradigms in Public Policy (London: British Academy Policy Centre).

Stoker, G. and Moseley, A. (2010) Motivation, Behaviour and the Micro-Foundations of Public Services (London: The 2020 Public Services Trust) [online], http://clients. squareeye.net/uploads/2020/documents/2020_ESRC_stoker_27.07_v3.pdf (accessed 28 September 2011).

Swank, D. (2002) Global Capital, Political Institutions and Policy Change in Developed Welfare States (Cambridge: Cambridge University Press).

Talbot, C. (2006) 'Public Domain – There's No Debate', Public Finance, 23 June 2006 [online], http://www.publicfinance.co.uk/features/2006/public-domain-theres-no-debate-by-colin-talbot/ (accessed on 27 August 2011).

Taylor-Gooby, P. (2009) Reframing Social Citizenship (Oxford: Oxford University Press).

Taylor-Gooby, P. and Wallace, A. (2009) 'Public Values and Public Trust', Journal of Social Policy 38: 401–420.

Taylor-Gooby, P. (2013) 'Why Do People Stigmatise the Poor at a Time of Rapidly Increasing Inequality, and What Can Be Done About It?', Political Quarterly 84(1).

Taylor-Gooby, P. and Stoker, G. (2011) 'The Coalition Programme: A New Vision for Britain or Politics as Usual?', Political Quarterly 82(1): 4–27.

Thaler, R.H. and Sunstein, C.R. (2008) Nudge: Improving Decisions About Health, Wealth, and Happiness (New Haven, CT: Yale University Press).

Thane, P. (1996) Foundations of the Welfare State, second edition (London: Longman).

Thane, P. (2011) Demographic Futures: Addressing Inequality and Diversity Among Older People. A report for the British Academy project New Paradigms in Public Policy (London: British Academy Policy Centre).

Thompson, F.M.L. (1992), The Cambridge Social History of Britain, 1750–1950: Volume 2. People and Their Environment (Cambridge: Cambridge University Press).

Tversky A. and Kahneman, D. (1974), 'Judgement Under Uncertainty: Heuristics and Biases', Science New Series 185: 1124–31.

Weaver, R. (1986) 'The Politics of Blame Avoidance', Journal of Public Policy 6: 371–398.

West, A., Barham, E. and Hind, A. (2011) 'Secondary School Admissions in England 2001 to 2008: Changing Legislation, Policy and Practice', Oxford Review of Education 37(1): 1–20.

Whitty, G., Power, S. and Halpin, D. (1998) Devolution and Choice in Education: The School, the State, and the Market (Milton Keynes: Open University Press).

Wilson, D., Croxson, B., and Atkinson, A. (2006) 'What Gets Measured Gets Done', Policy Studies 27: 153–171.

Wilson, D. and Piebaga, A. (2008) 'Performance Measures, Ranking and Parental Choice: An Analysis of the English School League Tables', International Public Management Journal 11: 344–366.

Wilson, D. (2010) Targets, Choice and Voice, 2020 Public Services Trust, http://clients.squareeye.nt/uploads/2020/documents/esrc_targets.pdf (accessed on 28 September 2011).

Young Foundation (2010) Investing in Social Growth: Can the Big Society be More Than a Slogan? [online], http://www.youngfoundation.org/files/images/YF_Bigsociety_Screen__2_.pdf (accessed on 27 August 2011).

4

Climate change and public policy futures

IAN GOUGH

Introduction

Climate change poses the most intractable questions about our future and the role of public policy. It has been described as 'a truly complex and diabolical policy problem' (Steffen 2011; cf. Garnaut 2008). In the words of the *Stern Review* (2007: 25) climate change is a new risk that is 'big, global, long-term, persistent and uncertain'. Together these five descriptors make it a unique threat. It thus poses an utterly novel challenge for public policy-making. According to Giddens *et al.* (2009: 14), current presentations of the climate change 'threat' come across as 'both overwhelming and existential, yet at the same time unspecific and distant'—a baffling combination to address.

This chapter addresses just a few of the issues posed by climate change for thinking about public policy futures. Many big issues are left to one side. Most ethical and normative perspectives and arguments are not addressed directly, including intergenerational justice and its links with other conceptions of social justice, and the relationship between sustainability, development and well-being (though these do crop up). Moreover, all other aspects of environmental policy are ignored, including air and water pollution, waste management, biodiversity protection, and the protection of natural resources, wildlife and endangered species. This chapter concentrates solely on climate change or global warming, given general agreement that it poses the most egregious challenge to the sustainability of the planet's natural resources and of contemporary economic and social systems—though some argue the loss of biodiversity and the breakdown of the nitrogen cycle are equally urgent and menacing (Rockström *et al.* 2009).

Most models predict substantially greater direct negative impacts on habitats and livelihoods in tropical and subtropical regions, which are also in general poorer than the temperate zones and bear little responsibility for the historic accumulation of greenhouse gases (GHGs) in the atmosphere—a double injustice. Emissions in a third zone, the fast-rising capitalist economies of Asia, are escalating from a low-moderate level. These patterns give rise to profound issues in global governance, which this chapter also ignores. The international governance of climate change comprises a plethora of relatively uncoordinated institutions, including the UN Framework Convention on Climate Change (UNFCCC) and the Global Environmental Facility (Held and Hervey 2011). Suffice it to say that the former hit a brick wall in Copenhagen in December 2009 and that the way forward is as yet unclear.[1] But this chapter only considers the impact of climate change on public policy-making in the UK and the rich countries of the West.

To anticipate, climate change is already setting severe constraints on policy-making. The UK government is said to have adopted the world's most demanding and legally binding targets to reduce CO_2 and other GHGs. The Climate Change Act 2008 commits the UK to reduce GHG emissions by at least 80% by 2050 and by at least 34% by 2020, compared with the base year of 1990. Furthermore, it has set three intermediate carbon budgets of an average of 604 million tonnes of carbon dioxide equivalent ($MtCO_2e$) in 2008–12, 556 $MtCO_2e$ in 2013–17 and 509 $MtCO_2e$ in 2018–22, and in May 2011 the coalition government committed the UK to the radical reduction targets for the fourth Budget period 2023–27. Figure 4.1 sets out the remarkable transformation in our economic and social structure to which this commits us. These commitments have radical implications for public policy futures.

The remainder of this chapter is organised in six sections. First, I summarise the scientific consensus and the case of climate change sceptics; I also consider public opinion and the interests behind the 'denial industry'. The second section develops a framework for thinking about the policy

[1] One achievement was agreement on the Fast Start finance programme, promising $30 billion up to 2012 to help developing countries adapt to climate change and protect forests. The UK government would appear to be at least achieving its share: the Overseas Development Assistance budget is one of the few areas of public spending planned to grow in real terms up to 2014 and £1.5 billion is planned to be spent on Fast Start.

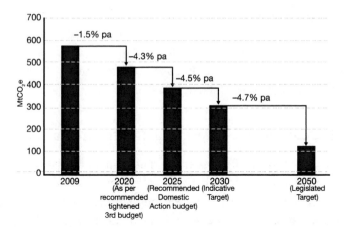

Figure 4.1 Rate of reduction of greenhouse gas emissions, excluding international aviation and shipping 2009–50
Source: UK Committee on Climate Change (2010: 25).

impacts of climate change risks and briefly summarises direct and indirect impacts. The rest of the chapter concentrates on the impact of climate change *mitigation* policies (CCMPs) on public policy futures, because I regard these as the most significant. We begin in the next section with a note on the economics and political economy of CCMPs. This is followed by a survey and appraisal of current carbon mitigation policies in the UK. I then present three contrasting future scenarios and some of their policy implications, before concluding.

This chapter develops an interdisciplinary political economy approach. Drawing on Caporaso and Levine (1992) and Gamble (1995), modern political economy is characterised by two assumptions. The first is that political and economic processes, though analytically distinct under capitalism, are interlinked and should be studied as a complex and interrelated whole. The second is that the economy, the sphere of 'material provisioning', carries a special weight in explaining and properly understanding the polity and politics. The approach adopted here also rests on a 'punctuated equilibrium' view of history with two further corollaries. First, national institutions, including economic, welfare and environmental structures, demonstrate complementarities and follow distinct adjustment paths to common challenges such as globalisation. Examples are national varieties of capitalism and welfare regimes, which exhibit strong path dependency over time (Crouch and Streeck 1997; Hall and Soskice

2001; Esping-Andersen 1990). Once a particular course of development is established, they tend to stick to it. Second, interactions between different causal sequences can sometimes lead to periods of systemic change ('switching points') when institutions and regimes may get shunted on to new tracks (Pierson 2004; cf. Gough 2010).

Scientific consensus, scepticism and the denial industry

There is a strong scientific consensus that climate change is happening, that it is largely man-made, that it is global, cumulative and potentially destructive, and that it will have to be brought under control sooner or later if disaster is to be avoided. The science of climate change, and the extent of agreement versus debate on its various aspects, is presented in numerous places (see, for example, the Intergovernmental Panel on Climate Change (2007), Stern (2007) and the Royal Society (2010)).[2] To quote summaries from a report of the UK Committee on Climate Change (CCC), 'It is close to certain that increasing atmospheric concentrations of GHGs since the industrial revolution are due to human activity ... It is close to certain that the planet has warmed since the late 19th century ... There is a high degree of confidence that human emissions have caused most of the observed warming since the mid-20th century' (CCC 2010: 54–59). Looking to the future it concludes 'precise scientific projections are uncertain, but they are the best evidence on which to base policy. Current evidence points to major potential impacts on human welfare and ecological systems if efforts are not made to curb emissions' (CCC 2010: 62).

A critical issue in shaping global carbon targets is the relationship between future stabilisation levels of CO_2 and other warming gases (expressed as parts per million of CO_2 equivalent) and likely global temperature increases. Table 4.1, taken from the *Stern Review*, summarises a number of these estimates. The Hadley estimate shows that if CO_2e (carbon dioxide equivalent) reaches 550 parts per million (ppm), then global temperatures are likely to rise by between 2.4°C and 5.3°C above pre-industrial levels. The current global level of CO_2e is 430ppm and it is rising by about 25ppm a decade. Yet the *Stern Review* used a stabilisation target of 550ppm which

---

[2] Some amendments have been made to correct errors in these reports since their initial publication.

Table 4.1   Temperature projections at stabilisation levels of CO_2

Stabilisation level (ppm CO_2 equivalent)	Temperature increase at equilibrium relative to pre-industrial (°C)		
	IPCC TAR 2001 (Wigley and Raper)	Hadley Centre Ensemble	Eleven studies
400	0.8–2.4	1.3–2.8	0.6–4.9
450	1.0–3.1	1.7–3.7	0.8–6.4
500	1.3–3.8	2.0–4.5	1.0–7.9
550	1.5–4.4	2.4–5.3	1.2–9.1
650	1.8–5.5	2.9–6.6	1.5–11.4
750	2.2–6.4	3.4–7.7	1.7–13.3
1,000	2.8–8.3	4.4–9.9	2.2–17.1

Source: Stern (2007: 16).

entailed a mean global temperature rise of around 4°C, now recognised as dangerously high.

The consensus view on desirable global emissions has hardened in the last few years. Lenton *et al.* (2008) argue that the Greenland ice sheet could melt if regional temperatures rise by around 3°C. And Stern (in Kaul *et al.* 2009: 136) writes:

> Five degrees is absolutely enormous. It would redraw the physical geography of the world. Large parts of the world would become desert, including most of southern Europe and the southern part of France. Other areas would be inundated. You'd see massive movements of population. If we've learnt anything from the last 200 or 300 years, it is that big movements of population have a high probability of conflict. This isn't a black swan, a small probability of a big problem; this is a big probability of a huge problem.

Stern himself now uses a 500ppm target. This, he estimates, would require annual global emissions by 2050 of some 20 billion tonnes CO_2e (compared with 40 billion tonnes in 1990). When dividing this by the then global population—some nine billion people—this equals just over two tonnes per capita (pc). The US currently emits over 20 tonnes pc and most of Europe around 10–12 tonnes pc. The European Union (EU) commitment to cut emissions by 80% by 2050 would thus roughly achieve this global target, but it would need to be matched by all other countries to attain the 500ppm goal.

However, arguments are now mounting that this is still too risky a goal. Meinshausen *et al.* (2009) stress that the total stock of emissions matters more than the final stabilisation target. To stand a 75 per cent chance of keeping temperatures below 2°C, cumulative emissions of all GHGs must be limited to 1.5 trillion tonnes between 2000 and 2050—a drastic scenario. Weitzman (2007) argues for deep emission cuts, building on the fact that the probability functions of distant-future temperature changes are 'fat-tailed' and thus presents a higher probability of a rare event, including catastrophic temperature rises. Thus agreement has been coalescing (up to now) around a still lower target rise in maximum temperature of $2^{\circ}C$ and the lower emissions target of 450ppm CO_2e by 2050. Jackson (2009) models a 450ppm target and concludes that this would require enormous reductions in global emissions to reach just four billion tonnes in 2050—under *one-half* of a tonne per person on the planet. These differences in targets have scale effects on mitigation costs, as discussed below.

The range of probabilities illustrates that climate modelling is an inherently uncertain exercise due mainly to natural climate variability, uncertainty about the evolution of emissions, and model uncertainties, including how to model feedbacks and other complex interactions. Yet, there is broad scientific agreement on the basic picture.

The above consensus is vigorously challenged by climate change deniers. These are represented in the UK by those such as Nigel Lawson and the Global Warming Policy Foundation, but are notably active in three of the highest emitting developed countries—the USA, Canada and Australia (Christoff and Eckersley 2011). Behind these deniers is often well-financed lobbying by interest groups representing energy-intensive sectors of the economy, as revealed by Oreskes and Conway (2010). Business interests also regularly express concern about the short-term implications of climate change policies for profitability and competitiveness. The Institute of Directors continually warns that UK competitiveness will suffer if we act alone (see, for example, Muspratt and Seawright 2006), a message amplified in the current crisis.

Most surveys show public opinion in western countries to be ambivalent—wishing to protect the earth's environment but unwilling to pay a significant price to achieve this. There has been some increase in climate change scepticism in the UK between 2005 and 2010, but it began from a low base. A substantial majority (78 per cent) of respondents believe that climate change is happening, though this is a fall from 91 per cent in 2005. Overall levels of concern about the issue have also fallen, as have risk perceptions (Spence *et al.* 2010). There is also, however, a surprising level of concern about energy security. Most people say they would be willing to pay more for renewable energy and would vote in favour of spending taxpayers' money on projects designed to tackle climate change. Yet a large majority do not accept that the main responsibility for taking action against climate change lies with individuals and families. Possible explanations for growing scepticism include issue fatigue, recession, a desire to diminish 'cognitive dissonance' or the uncomfortable feeling caused by holding conflicting ideas simultaneously, the failure of the 2009 UN Climate Change Conference in Copenhagen (COP15) and the 'climategate' email revelations.[3] However, outside of the USA, scepticism about man-made climate change and lack of interest in mitigation policies does not approach a majority position.

Climate change is contested terrain and, given the uncertainties and the very long time scales, will perhaps always be so. The CCC (2010: 17) summarises these conflicting trends: 'While developments in science since our 2008 report have marginally increased the strength of the case for forceful global action to reduce emissions, the likelihood of getting early global agreement has decreased'.

It can be argued that modern liberal democracies are unsuited to tackling collective action problems and particularly climate change due to short-termism, the influence of well-organised interest groups (notably business), and the absence of political constituencies voicing the concerns of future generations and of peoples outside the borders of the nation state (Held and Hervey 2011). The favourable record of democracies in tackling specific environmental problems may not apply to such a diffuse problem as future climate change (for instance, see Haas 1990). Bättig and Bernauer (2009) suggest that political democracies generate positive policy commitments to tackling climate change but their effect on outputs and outcomes is ambiguous. Radical long-term commitments to carbon reduction, such as those of the UK, *do* reflect public concerns, but implementation will likely be derailed by other political pressures (Held and Hervey 2011).

---

[3] Posted emails from the University of East Anglia Climatic Research Unit fuelled an internet storm of activity by climate change 'sceptics'. For a detailed account and evaluation, see the Muir Russell Report http://www.guardian.co.uk/environment/2010/jul/07/findings-muir-russell-review.

The interaction of public policy and climate change risks: a framework

Our concern here is the impact of climate change on the economic and social future of countries like the UK, and thus its implications for future public policies. The causal chain is long; a simple and incomplete model linking these is shown below:

Economic activity →
    Energy consumption →
        Greenhouse gas emissions →
            GHG cumulative concentrations →
                Global temperature →
                    Regional climate change →
                        Impact on human habitats →
                          Social well-being

It is common to distinguish two categories of climate change *policies*: mitigation and adaptation.[4] *Mitigation* policies act to reduce greenhouse gas emissions or to increase greenhouse gas sinks. *Adaptation* policies reduce the damaging effects of climate change that does occur, but do nothing directly to prevent it. Broadly speaking, mitigation policies address the first three factors in the model above and adaptation policies address the last two.

Gough *et al.* (2008) identify four impacts of climate change on the public policy environment in rich countries such as the UK:

Direct impacts of climate change itself, distinguishing
    impacts in the UK
    the results in the UK of impacts overseas
The impacts of climate change *policies*, distinguishing
    adaptation policies
    mitigation policies

This review will concentrate on mitigation policies, but I will deal briefly with the first three. The *direct* impacts of climate change on habitats and well-being will hit tropical and subtropical areas harder and earlier, but this does not mean the northern, richer world will be unaffected. Southern Europe, Australia and the southern United States will experience rising

---

[4] A third category is geo-engineering—that is, the large-scale engineering of the earth's environment to counteract trends in atmospheric chemistry, which is not considered here.

heat and water stress, and low-lying coastal regions such as the Netherlands will be vulnerable to rising sea levels. Arctic areas of Europe and Canada may experience dramatic temperature rises with direct consequences for indigenous communities. According to a Foresight report (2011a), direct impacts on the UK are likely to be mild over the next two decades. The Joseph Rowntree Foundation is currently promoting research on the direct impacts of likely climate change on social welfare and social justice in Britain, including flood risks, drought risks and heatwaves (Benzie *et al.* 2011). The Department of Health first published its heatwave plan for the UK in 2004 and it has been revised several times since. In my view these risks, and the costs of managing them, are not likely to be especially burdensome for a rich country over the next three decades. However, there will be distributive consequences as direct impacts are likely to affect lower-income groups more, as more live in higher-risk areas, such as floodplains, and fewer have adequate insurance (Walker and Burningham 2011).

Necessary *adaptation* policies will follow from these direct impacts, such as investing in flood defences to protect against storm surges, extra reservoir capacity, and making buildings more resilient to climate change. The *Stern Review* (2007: 417–429) estimates that member countries of the Organisation for Economic Cooperation and Development (OECD) would need to invest between 0.05 per cent and 0.5 per cent of GDP extra each year in adaptive measures, and more if temperature rises exceed the central forecast (Fankhauser (2010) provides more recent but still widely varying estimates.) These figures are high but not daunting. The contrasts with the poorer developing world are extreme. In the words of Desmond Tutu, 'Rich countries can use their vast financial and technological resources to protect themselves against climate change, at least in the short term... But as climate change destroys livelihoods, displaces people and undermines entire social and economic systems, no country—however rich or powerful—will be immune to the consequences. In the long-run, the problems of the poor will arrive at the doorstep of the wealthy' (quoted in United Nations Development Programme 2007: 166).

This leads on to the *indirect* effects on the UK of global climate change beyond our borders. One major potential impact for the EU and the UK is rising levels of distress migration from tropical Africa and South Asia: the subject of another Foresight report (2011b). Potential impacts discussed in the first Foresight report (2011a) cover a vast range of issues including:

resource scarcity, epidemics, degraded coastal infrastructure impeding shipping, disruption of vital oil and gas supplies, insecurity of food supplies and rising and more volatile prices, disruption of international economic networks and chains, growing restrictions on free trading which may harm the City of London, slowing global economic growth, collapse of weak states, and growing international tensions weakening global governance. The report recognises that these threats can be accompanied by opportunities, such as the potential role of London in global insurance and carbon trading markets. This list reveals the problems of envisaging future scenarios in a global context. In the light of these, I will not say anything more here about indirect impacts from overseas.

The remainder of this chapter will concentrate on the impacts of CCMPs on public policy futures for two reasons: first, that mitigation is the prime global responsibility of the rich industrialised world as recognised (inadequately) in the Kyoto framework; secondly, that CCMPs will have the greatest impact in the medium-term on domestic living standards and on UK public policy.

The economics of mitigation policies: a short note

CCMPs raise difficult issues given the uncertainties over: (a) desirable mitigation goals and their respective risks and consequences; (b) the rate at which future costs and benefits should be discounted; and (c) the likely costs of implementing effective programmes—all of these over a global scale and over long time periods. The benchmark here is the *Stern Review*, whose central conclusion was that the costs of taking action now to reduce emissions will be far lower than the costs of business as usual, 'If we don't act the overall costs and risks of climate change will be equivalent to losing at least 5% of global GDP each year, now and forever' (Stern 2007: vi) and could reach more than 20 per cent of GDP. The costs of action were estimates at 1 per cent of global GDP each year up to 2050. I have already stated that this rather benign view was based on too high a global emissions target that Stern has now revised downwards raising future cost estimates. This section briefly considers the other two issues: the discount rate and the costs of mitigation.

A discount rate is used to calculate the present values of future costs and benefits. The case for a positive discount rate arises for two major reasons:

first, that future generations will have higher incomes than us and therefore the utility of an extra unit of consumption then will be less; secondly, the 'pure time preference' argument that consumption now is preferred to consumption in the future. The *Stern Review* (2007) allows for the first and embodies assumptions of continuing high global growth rates of 1.3 per cent per annum (in the North as well as the South). However, it argues on ethical grounds against making any allowance for the second. This has been criticised by orthodox economists who, assuming that consumers are the best judges of their preferences, contend that this contradicts the low savings rates of the current generation (Nordhaus 2007; Dasgupta 2006). However, Stern firmly endorses the prescriptive, normative approach to evaluating discount rates over such long time spans, as do others (for example Broome 1992).

Neumayer (2007) welcomes this, but contends that Stern still misses the real question of whether climate change inflicts irreversible and non-substitutable damage to 'natural capital'—that is, the multiple and various services of nature that benefit human beings. If damage to natural capital is non-substitutable, then it cannot be compensated by any amount of growth in future consumption. This implies larger benefits to mitigation. It also supports a more radical rights-based approach to thinking about the future where future generations have a fundamental and inalienable right to the non-substitutable services of nature and the current generation has a duty of intergenerational stewardship.

Turning to the costs of mitigating climate change, the '1 per cent of GDP' estimate of the *Stern Review* has come under criticism. Using the tougher target of 500ppm, Stern now estimates costs at around 2 per cent of world GDP. His back-of-the-envelope justification is as follows: achieving 500ppm CO_2e by 2050 would require taking out 50 billion tonnes of CO_2 a year compared to 'business as usual'; assuming a cost of \$40 a tonne this would cost \$2,000 billion (or \$2 trillion); assuming world GDP has doubled in the meantime to about \$100 trillion, this amounts to about 2 per cent of 2050 world GDP (Stern in Kaul 2009: 155). It is important to stress that this figure is expressed as a share of future GDP and seems to imply that the mitigation costs will rise over time with GDP rather than being front-loaded.

These cost estimates have been heavily criticised by Helm (2009) among others on several grounds. Firstly, the *Stern Review* assumes an 'optimal' supply function of technologies, and 'optimal policies' to support this. In practice the activities of energy suppliers and others are partly driven by rent-seeking, and policies are affected by special interest groups and their lobbying (some of which come into being as a result of the CCMPs, such as those around the EU Emissions Trading Scheme (ETS)—see below). These factors may also reduce the future rate of growth and thus raise the cost of mitigation as a share of future GDP. The list of potential indirect impacts of climate change on the UK, noted above, will also likely affect the efficiency of policy responses.

Secondly, some argue that the 'rebound effect', first noticed by Jevons (1865), undermines the effectiveness of many energy-saving policies and that this is likely to be large (Sorrell 2009). Rebound can occur in many ways, as when consumers use the cost savings from improvements in domestic energy efficiency to turn up the thermostat, or purchase other goods and services which may be even more energy intensive, or when producers use cost savings to raise output and emissions. (The average internal temperature of British houses rose by $6^{0}C$ from 1970 to 2001 (Shorrock and Utley 2003).)

Such critics also doubt that the models take full account of increasing returns to scale from present non-renewable energy patterns. Much capital stock in the developed world is locked into high-carbon patterns that include long asset lives in the electricity distribution systems, existing road networks which result in very low marginal costs of driving, and dispersed urban settlement patterns. As Helm (2009: 14) comments, 'A carbon economy embeds fossil fuels into the fabric of its infrastructure'. Thus changes cannot be limited to the marginal changes analysed by orthodox economic models. Stern recognises that 'mitigating climate change does not constitute a small perturbation around business-as-usual, but a shift from one economic growth path to another' (in Hepburn and Stern 2009: 40), but this sits uneasily alongside the marginal cost approach in the *Stern Review*.

The conclusion is that 'economic growth may not be so easily compatible with the effects of, and mitigation costs of, climate change' (Helm 2009: 31). Sorrell concludes that the *Stern Review* 'assumes that rebound effects are small, mitigation is relatively cheap, and decoupling is achievable. In contrast, the perspective presented above suggests that rebound effects are large, mitigation is relatively expensive, and decoupling is difficult' (2009: 361). In this light it would be wise to assume that CO_2 abatement will be, in Martin Weitzman's words, 'very expensive' (in Kaul *et al.* 2009: 149).

UK climate change mitigation policies

In terms of policy aspirations the UK is a leading figure in the fight against climate change. The UK Climate Change Act 2009 was hailed as the world's most demanding and legally binding commitment to reduce CO_2 and other GHGs. As well as statutory targets the act established the CCC as an independent body to advise the government on setting and meeting carbon budgets. At the same time the new Department of Energy and Climate Change, headed then by Ed Miliband, published the UK *Low Carbon Transition Plan* which set out detailed targets and programmes to achieve these goals.[5] This, and the subsequent very detailed reports of the CCC, analyse plans and achievements in reducing emissions under five main headings: power and heavy industry (which accounts for about one-half of all emissions), transport, homes and communities, workplaces and jobs, and farming, land and waste.

According to a range of indicators for large developed economies, the UK was the leading country alongside Germany in achieving reductions in emissions in the period 1990–2005, mainly due to the 'dash for gas' replacing coal in electricity generation (Christoff and Eckersley 2011—though note their survey excludes small European countries with good records). The recent CCC report illustrates just how tough it will be to build on this success to reach the 2050 target: the UK needs to reduce total GHG emissions to 80 per cent below 1990 levels; excluding international aviation and shipping they need to fall by 85 per cent; and excluding other GHGs carbon emissions need to fall by around 90 per cent; finally, these emissions must be achieved entirely domestically without resort to buying carbon credits from abroad (CCC 2010: 18).

There is, however, a fundamental concern about all such figures, namely that these are production-based emissions, and do not include the carbon emitted in producing goods elsewhere in the world which are then consumed in Britain. The two diverge widely: in 2006 UK CO_2 emissions were 33 per cent higher when offshore production of goods we consume was taken into account, and emissions of all greenhouse gases were astonishingly 51 per cent higher. This is a difference between 10.7 tonnes per head and 16.2 tonnes per head—one of the biggest gaps in the world, due

---

[5] I understand that the coalition government is no longer formally following the plan as a policy document.

to deindustrialisation in Britain and the high import ratio (Gough *et al.* 2011). According to Helm *et al.* (2007), taking this into account reverses the success of the UK record: the greenhouse gas emissions produced in the UK have fallen by 15 per cent since 1990, but those consumed here have risen by 19 per cent over the same period (Helm *et al.* 2007: 23).

Nevertheless, we will start from the UK government Kyoto-based targets. What CCMPs have been implemented to date? The picture is one of 'a proliferation of climate change policies, targets, direct subsidies, market-based support, levies, pricing schemes, and various trading schemes' (Hepburn 2009: 365).

In theory there are at least three methods of influencing GHG emissions: market incentives; information, education and behaviour change; and direct regulation. Each can take many forms. I will consider each of these three in turn.

Economic incentives

There is a division within economic incentive policies between those influencing the price of carbon, such as a carbon tax, to which the quantity of emissions adjusts, and those capping or otherwise influencing the quantity of carbon emitted, to which its price adjusts. The main driver of carbon reduction over the three budget periods to 2022 is planned to be the EU ETS which applies to large industrial concerns including power generation across Europe. It sets an overall cap and requires companies to submit allowances to cover their verified emissions. Companies can trade their allowances and also use credits from economies achieved in developing countries. We are now approaching phase three of the ETS which will run for the period 2013–20. So far all of the UK allowances have been loaded on to the power generation sector. It has encountered numerous problems in the first two phases (National Audit Office 2009): early allowances were given free which generated windfall profits, and implementation resulted in a 'highly complex economic and regulatory landscape' with substantial monitoring and verification costs. The impact of phase two on UK emissions is likely to have been small, though the National Audit Office (NAO) regards the system as too complex to properly evaluate. Nevertheless, it has put in place the world's most ambitious cap-and-trade system, and it is expected that the ETS will deliver two-thirds of the first three UK carbon budgets (Department of Energy and Climate Change 2011).

The broad alternative to cap-and-trade is carbon taxation, which has several theoretical and practical arguments in its favour (Weitzman 1974). Yet the popularity of carbon taxes waxed in the 1980s and early 1990s and has waned ever since (Environmental Tax Policy Institute 2008). The UK Climate Change Levy, an indirect tax on notional units of energy supplied to non-domestic consumers which exempts electricity generated from renewables, was introduced in 2001 but raises trivial sums. Helm (2009) and Hepburn (2009) both ask why cap-and-trade has triumphed over carbon taxation despite its manifold weaknesses. They conclude that it initially reflected the hegemony of market mechanisms. Once established, the ETS created opportunities for gaming and vested interests which then lobbied heavily for its continuation and for less restrictive implementation. Futures trading in carbon also generated a powerful financial industry interest. Industrial lobbying and 'lock-in' raise the costs of change. The only realistic option now, they argue, is to build in a price floor to the ETS carbon price, which the coalition government is committed to.

Present UK fiscal commitments to climate change mitigation are very small (Gough and Marden 2011). Total spending on CCMPs is tiny— 0.3 per cent of GDP—and one-half of this is mandated spending by energy companies. Environmental taxes, notably fuel duties, are more important, raising about 2.5 per cent of GDP, but their share is falling. The burden of CCMPs including the ETS falls ultimately on households—and this is intended. Thus CCMPs immediately raise issues of distributive justice and collide with other goals of public policy. Household energy use rises with income but falls rapidly as a share of income. However, household size and type and employment status also influences emissions, as well as lifestyle and 'lock-in' (the shaping of consumption patterns by spatial, economic and social factors not amenable to short-term modification). These findings undermine simplistic arguments for raising carbon prices and using revenues to compensate low-income households as the 'losing' households are too heterogenous. Yet more is spent on poorly targeted winter fuel payments to compensate for fuel poverty than on all programmes to improve insulation for households (such as Decent Homes, which provides funds to improve standards in social housing, and Warm Front, which has now ended). The current policy mix is both inefficient and inequitable.

Alternative policies are essential if both climate change and social justice goals are to be served (Gough *et al.* 2011).

Information, education and behaviour change

This heading embraces at least three very different policies based on distinct theoretical foundations (Seyfang and Paavola 2008). First, there is orthodox economic consumer behaviour theory, which condones providing information to improve the decisions of rational individuals. There is much evidence that this has failed in effectively reducing high carbon consumption. Numerous studies show that many energy reduction programmes in the home would pay for themselves, yet householders are loath to take up the schemes on offer. This can be explained by the second, social model of consumer behaviour, which recognises multiple drivers, such as identity, belonging, social norms and self-esteem. This model can endorse targeted measures, such as DEFRA's *Framework for pro-environmental behaviours* (2008). This distinguishes between seven segments of the population according to their understanding of environmental issues, their willingness to act and their ability to act, as applied to different types of behaviour (using a car less for short journeys, wasting less food, and so on). However, it still ignores broader determinants of consumption, for example, pitting 'individuals against global corporations in the struggle to shift consumption patterns' (Seyfang and Paavola 2008: 672).

The third approach recognises material constraints on consumer behaviour—the way that 'systems of provision' lock households into patterns of consumption, as when rural and suburban residents have no viable alternatives to driving the car. This moves attention from individual motivations to institutions and everyday practices and supports very different climate change mitigation policies. For Dobson (2006) it requires the cultivation of 'green citizenship' to overcome several problems with economic incentives, such as the existence of very low price elasticities (found, for example, in taxes on 'gas-guzzler' vehicles), the way such policies may encourage more self-interested behaviour, and the existence of rebound effects. The strong sustainability necessary to forestall future climate change, he claims, will require a more ethical sense of mutuality, collective interest and the common good. This in turn entails public action and collective engagement, such as carbon reduction action groups and transition towns, and numerous discrete movements such as farmers' markets (Whitmarsh 2011). It supports Ostrom's (2009) 'polycentric' approach of building a strong commitment to action in small to medium governance units linked through information networks and monitoring. Yet, Whitmarsh (2011) contends that growing distrust and apathy among voters and citizens is today undermining beliefs in the need for, and the efficacy of, grassroots activism in the environmental field (cf. Stoker 2011).

There is a wide gap between these appeals—to rational consumers at one extreme and to engaged citizens at the other. Moreover, the policies may conflict; incentives that appeal solely to self-interest may degrade intrinsic motivations such as altruism and solidarity—and thus fail to deliver their intended outcomes (Taylor-Gooby 2011 and chapter 3 in this volume). Public policies will need to be aware when economic incentives and intrinsic motivations cannot run side by side and choices must be made.

Regulation

Traditional 'command-and-control' regulation prescribes a level of pollution abatement and uses institutional measures aimed at directly influencing the environmental performance of polluters by regulating processes or products (OECD 1994). This leaves the polluter with no alternative other than to comply with the regulation or face penalties for non-compliance. Because of the equal burden put on all polluters, irrespective of their specific abatement costs, environmental regulation is usually considered by economists to be cost-inefficient. Yet, when compliance and implementation costs and the scope for evasive action by firms are taken into account, regulation can be effective (Hepburn 2009). Indeed, many effective regulations exist, notably at the EU level, covering the energy performance of buildings and limits for car emissions, and filament light bulbs will soon be banned. However, it will take a serious engagement with critics of the nanny state for a significant shift to rationing, regulation and controls to make progress.

To summarise the record, the UK Climate Change Act and the *Low Carbon Transition Plan* are radical initiatives but can be criticised on several grounds. There is a major disjuncture between the vaulting ambitions of the targets and the policies and programmes thus far announced. The CCC has called for a 'step change' to address this gap. Current programmes target 'low-hanging fruit' and there is insufficient upfront investment and, in my view, quite inadequate public subsidies. The legal backing to the commitments is hazy and difficult to reconcile with the British political system. The main emphasis in UK mitigation policy has been on economic incentives, and, within this, on cap-and-trade or indirect market systems. Lifestyle changes and direct regulations have had little attention.

This profile reflects the continuing domination of neoclassical economics and models of consumer behaviour, which study characteristics internal to the individual, such as attitudes, values and habits. Policy to alter behaviour then focuses on improving information or altering prices to internalise environmental externalities. Yet, at the same time, the plans call for some major reversals in neo-liberal ideology, for example in energy policy. Some of this has been forthcoming, such as the cancellation of the third runway at Heathrow, but the coalition government's radical reduction of the scope of the public sector appears to conflict with further progress here. There are many areas where policy integration is ill thought out, such as recognising the regressive consequences of loading the costs of insulation and renewals on households' energy bills. Above all, the issue of the UK's (and other developed countries') wide 'emissions gap' in foreign trade lies outside all current thinking.

Future scenarios

I distinguish three scenarios according to views about the future potential for economic growth in the developed world: (a) that more growth is the solution; (b) that growth can be decoupled from emissions—'green growth'; and (c) that growth is the dominant problem. In practice in Europe all countries subscribe to variants of the second position, and we have also noted the extensive commitments by UK governments to decarbonise the economy whilst maintaining growth. However, it is useful to frame this scenario within the two more controversial positions.

'Irrational optimism': More growth is the solution
A neo-liberal alternative is emerging, growing out of climate change denial but going beyond it, which can be summarised as more growth, freer markets and technological optimism. Ridley (2010: 347) is optimistic about future warming and its effects: 'The probability of rapid and severe climate

change is small; the probability of net harm from the most likely climate change is small; the probability that no adaptation will occur is small; and the probability of no new low-carbon energy technologies emerging in the long run is zero.' The source of the latter two optimisms is a lasting belief in Adam Smith's theory of exchange and in the ability of modern-day markets to prompt never-ending technological improvements. Faster global growth will equip future populations to cope with climate change, mainly through adaptation, though this should be guided by policy initiatives to spur a wide range of techno-fixes, including various forms of geo-engineering (Lomborg 2010).

Another variant is the recent *Hartwell Paper* (Prins *et al.* 2010) which is premised on a Hayekian view of cognitive fallibility and support for incremental, 'clumsy' solutions (cf. Verweij and Thompson (2006)). This is coupled with a realist questioning of whether scientific consensus can ever engender political consensus. Copenhagen was a necessary failure based on a top-down, utopian perspective which ignored social and political realities; the appropriate alternative is a precautionary, disaggregated, indirect, bottom-up approach. In particular, climate change policies must build on other policy goals, notably a desire for more secure energy supplies, where there are more supportive political constituencies. Notwithstanding the overriding argument, the report nevertheless concludes with a decidedly top-down call for sustained public investment in alternative energy sources financed by a hypothecated carbon tax.

This first scenario is close to the Republican (and currently the dominant) mainstream in the US federal government, though not to many state, city and community initiatives across the USA. Energy security is a major policy driver amid scepticism and/or denial about climate change. Favoured solutions are first and foremost deregulated drilling for oil and exploitation of Canadian tar sands, plus some federal subsidies and loan guarantees for alternative energy sources notably nuclear, carbon capture and storage, and biofuels, with energy conservation bringing up the rear (Graham 2011). A supporting role for public policy is accepted but this would necessarily lead to further reductions in most other areas of state intervention. These positions hardly amount to a coherent response to mid-range temperature projections, let alone more extreme scenarios. But buoyed with optimism in self-regulating systems they do not need to be.

Green growth—ecological modernisation—low-carbon industrial revolution

The ecological modernisation thesis was developed in Germany in the 1980s and has been much discussed since (Christoff 1996; Mol *et al.* 2009). This reform-oriented school of environmental social science essentially argues that environmental interests, including climate change mitigation, can be incorporated within a successful capitalist economy. This is to be achieved via 'policy integration' across environmental, economic and social decision-making (Nilsson and Eckerberg 2007). In this way the interests of business and national competitiveness can be harnessed to support a radical restructuring of the economy, which will gradually decouple carbon emissions from economic activity. Allied notions are sustainable development, first advocated by the Brundtland Commission, which distanced itself from 'limits to growth' arguments, 'green growth' (Brundtland Commission Report 1987; OECD 2010), the 'low-carbon industrial revolution' (Stern 2011) and 'a green new deal' (NEF 2008).

Weaker and stronger forms of ecological modernisation have been identified, and the UK is usually placed at the 'weak' end of the continuum (Christoff 1996; Revell 2005). However, two features are common to most forms. First, a recognition that low-carbon technology is likely to drive the next technological revolution and that early innovation and investment in this field will enhance national competitiveness. This is now a policy focus across the world including the EU, USA, Korea and China. Second, there is a need for integration across environmental, economic and social policy domains. This will require a much more active state than the dominant model under neo-liberalism. Giddens (2009) contends that this implies a return to planning in order, inter alia, to set goals and targets, manage risks, promote industrial policy, realign prices, and counter negative business interests.

Since 2007, two more 'contingent' events have strengthened this strategic approach. The first was fears over the future of oil and gas—of declining production, rising prices and insecurity of supplies. 'Peak oil' is the point in time when the maximum rate of global production is reached, after which the rate of production enters terminal decline. There is still considerable dispute about when this will be, but oil prices peaked in July 2008 at over $147 per barrel and, despite the recession, have remained persistently high. There is also growing concern in Europe over excessive reliance on oil and gas from the unstable Middle East and authoritarian Russia. The link between climate change mitigation and energy security is not a direct one, but in Europe the two now reinforce each other and are driving a reversal of previous energy policy. In 1982 the Secretary of State for Energy Nigel Lawson announced the privatisation and liberalisation of energy markets, stating: 'I do *not* see the government's task as being to try to plan the future shape of energy production and consumption' (quoted in Giddens 2009: 43). The result was under-investment and growing dependence on imports once North Sea oil began to decline. This has now fostered a new policy in the Energy Act 2008 which recognises shortfalls in generation, plans for replacement investment and requires a directive role for the state. There are growing synergies between these concerns and climate mitigation programmes.

The second event was the financial crisis of 2008 and subsequent recession of 2009 onwards which engendered various proposals for a 'Green New Deal' (UNEP 2009; NEF 2008). These call for a sustained public programme to invest in renewable energy and to deploy radical conservation measures. This would at the same time boost demand in slow-growing post-crisis economies like the UK and create new employment opportunities, via, for example, creating and training a 'carbon army' of workers to achieve the reconstruction programme. It is a radical exercise in policy integration for a post-crisis economy. Given the inherent contradictions of savage deficit reduction programmes, it is likely that green new deal proposals will see a revival.

It is difficult to summarise in any detail proposals for a green growth strategy. The sheer scope of the exercise often leads to long lists of disparate policy initiatives. The policy integration required extends to many existing domains. Take social policy as an example (Gough and Marden 2011); a higher carbon price, however achieved, will impact much more severely on low-income households, so there is a regressive distributional impact which will worsen already high levels of 'fuel poverty'. Yet it is difficult to compensate low- and middle-income losers via the social security system, because they are so heterogenous—rural households dependent on car transport, elderly 'empty-nesters', people in poorly insulated housing (even by the very low standards current in Britain).

Thus, alternatives to compensation must enter the policy toolbox. One is 'reverse block pricing' by utility companies—that is, lowering the marginal costs of initial units of electricity or gas consumed, and raising the marginal costs of successive units. This would recognise the 'basic need' component of the first block of household energy and the progressive choice element in successive units, and thus would be intrinsically progressive and would tackle fuel poverty directly (CCC 2008: 409). Though this solution has been raised by the CCC it would require a radical shift in the pricing policies and regulation of private utility companies—a reversal of the liberalisation and deregulation agenda of the past three decades. Another alternative is a serious commitment to 'eco-social investment' as part of a green new deal—for example street-by-street retrofitting of the existing housing stock, investment in public transport and the encouragement of cycling and non-car alternatives. To achieve this, the raft of government programmes needs to link up with the wealth of initiatives in civil society and alternative policies to encourage pro-environmental behaviours. This gives some indication of the revolution in policy integration that a realistic programme of climate change mitigation would entail.

Theory and history suggest that path dependency will be strong and that different types of economic, political and welfare regime will vary in their abilities to transform into 'eco-states' and achieve green growth (Meadowcroft 2005). According to Dryzek, 'social democratic welfare states and what Hall and Soskice call coordinated market economies ... are better placed to handle the intersection of social policy and climate change than the more liberal market economies with more rudimentary welfare states' (in Gough *et al.* 2008: 336). In a recent cross-national analysis of environmental governance regimes Duit (2008) identifies six 'thick eco-states' combining high levels of government involvement with high scores for civic involvement: Denmark, Norway, Sweden, Finland, Germany and Austria. The first four are social democratic welfare states and the latter two are paradigm coordinated market economies.

Yet, in a cross-national study of climate change policies by Christoff and Eckersley (2011), the UK emerges as a leading country both in past and present performance and in aspirations, despite the absence of several predisposing structures such as corporatist political institutions and proportional representation. Perhaps more important, they suggest, is a 'European' framing of issues which does not regard climate science as an 'ideological marker' underpinning adversarial politics in the way it has become in the USA and Australia, for example (Christoff and Eckersley 2011). There is also a gap between the institutionalisation of 'carboniferous capitalism' in the USA, Canada and Australia, and the dominant discourse of ecological modernisation in the EU. Thus the UK is in an ambivalent position. The CCC (2009) has welcomed recent signals from British governments of a turn towards an active industrial policy, which may be taken as some recognition of this pattern. Yet to fundamentally switch the UK's political economy and path of development is a daunting challenge and current indicators of this are zero or negative.

'Degrowth' and radical transformation

The fundamental premise underlying the third scenario is that endless economic growth is impossible within a bounded system—including a planet. This was the thesis of *The limits to growth* (Meadows *et al.* 1972): exponential growth in population and material output is unsustainable. If ecological equilibrium is not restored the limits to growth will be over-shot and an uncontrolled decline will occur. The Ehrlich–Holdren (1971) equation I=PAT represents environmental impact—'I' as the product of population 'P', affluence 'A', and a technology transformation factor 'T'. Neither the *Limits to growth* argument or the Ehrlich–Holdren equation necessarily imply that economic growth must be curtailed ('T' could adjust sufficiently to ensure green growth), but they lend support for a more radical questioning of the imperatives of industrial, capitalist and consumerist societies. The UK Sustainable Development Commission published a report in 2009 by Tim Jackson titled *Prosperity without Growth?* (with the question mark added after pressure from the Treasury). This developed a sophisticated 'degrowth' argument marrying together arithmetic, ethics, recent research into the sources of well-being, and a political economy of modern capitalism (see also Jackson 2009).

First, Jackson joins others in attacking the 'myth of decoupling'. Inbuilt drivers in the world economy are pushing up emissions at a *growing* rate: coal-fired electricity generation in China and India, a predicted 2.3 billion more cars by 2050, 97 new airports in China by 2020, and so on. There is as yet *no* global decoupling of economic activity and emissions (Garnaut *et al.* 2009). Indeed, the global financial crisis and recession of 2008–09 has alone delayed the growth of global emissions by three years according to one estimate—the emissions level projected for 2015 will not now be reached until 2018.

To stabilise climate change on relatively optimistic assumptions may require global carbon emissions of below four billion tonnes per annum by 2050, one-fifth of the target in the *Stern Review*. To achieve this with continued global population growth (0.7 per cent a year) and past rates of income growth (1.4 per cent a year) would require a 7 per cent a year—in sum a *twentyfold*—improvement in the current global average carbon intensity (grams of carbon dioxide per dollar of GDP). The world economy would need an improvement in decoupling of 11.2 per cent per year in order to achieve a world where the entire population enjoyed an income comparable with EU citizens in 2050 (assuming their incomes keep growing). Jackson concludes, 'There is as yet no credible, socially just, ecologically sustainable scenario of continually growing incomes for a world of nine billion people' (Jackson 2009: 86).

This case is backed by two supporting arguments. First, prosperity (Latin *pro-speres*) is about living well and hopefully, and is by no means equivalent to growing GDP or throughput of economic activity. This draws on much recent material on happiness, well-being and alternative measures (Layard 2005; NEF 2009; Stiglitz *et al.* 2009). Second, deep structures within capitalist society reproduce a system within which an absence of growth is simply inconceivable: 'Someone once said that it is easier to imagine the end of the world than to imagine the end of capitalism' (Jameson 2003: 76). This argument rests on the role of efficiency in developed market societies which by continually raising labour productivity thus requires continuing growth to employ displaced labour. It also generates an 'iron cage of consumerism' which requires more and more private consumption, rather than more public goods and investment in ecological maintenance (Jackson 2009: 87–102, 143–56).

A low-growth or no-growth scenario would require a radical transformation in a range of public policies, and more policy integration. There are very few signposts (though see the work of Herman Daly 1996 and 2008). A new macroeconomics of 'degrowth' would be necessary, including a sustained reduction in working hours, according to Victor (2008). The logic of commodification would need to be challenged—perhaps via rationing and personal carbon allowances and trading (PCAT) (Environmental Audit Committee 2008; Gough and Meadowcroft 2011). The suggestion is that in a steady-state economy, a radically different environmental/welfare policy regime would need to integrate the redistribution of carbon, work/

time, and income/wealth (NEF 2010). At present these are mainly studied, and policies developed, within separate silos, but that would need to change. These are just a few of the implications of a zero growth economy for future public policy integration.

Conclusions

There is a strong scientific consensus that the world is warming due to human-induced economic activity and GHG emissions. This is recognised by majorities of public opinion in all western countries, though least in the USA, and with some decline in the last few years. The direct impacts of this climate change are likely to be mild in the UK in the next two to three decades, but the indirect effects of climate change outside our borders are uncertain and potentially large.

The countries of the EU are now committed to a radical reduction in GHG emissions of 80 per cent by the year 2050, and UK governments are committed to five-year planned reductions up to 2027. Yet there is no 'silver bullet' in climate change mitigation and the costs are likely to be very large. Growth in developed countries like the UK could be slower, which would help emissions, but would raise the relative costs of mitigation policies. Moreover, these targets for emissions produced within the UK are much lower than the emissions generated by UK consumers, due to the deindustrialisation of the UK economy and the outsourcing of production to countries like China. There is at present no mechanism within the Kyoto or UNFCCC frameworks to account for and rectify these global emission flows.

Notwithstanding the radical nature of the UK's *Low Carbon Transition Plan*, present climate mitigation policies fall far short of what is needed to reach the targets. They are based on upstream cap-and-trade, notably the EU ETS, and mandated market solutions. Planned upfront investment and public carbon taxation and subsidies are inadequate. There is as yet insufficient recognition of the scale of policy integration—across economic, environmental and social policies—that will be required. The legal basis of the carbon commitments is also hazy.

This mismatch between goals and implementation may reflect public opinion within a democratic political system faced with a 'diabolical' policy problem stretching across time and space. It also reflects, I have argued, the continuing dominance of economic models with a marginal, equilibrium-based methodology and a simplistic view of motivations and behaviour change. A political economy approach provides a more realistic, but far more challenging, framework for climate mitigation policies.

The implicit political-economic scenario in Europe and the UK is 'green growth'—that economic activity can be decoupled from carbon emissions via big investment in new technology, coupled with reframed carbon pricing and integrated policies to shift consumer behaviour. This strategy can access support from other political constituencies by improving energy security in the transition period and by boosting business competitiveness in low-carbon technologies. Yet this again requires substantial policy integration. It also challenges the still-dominant neo-liberal economic model. It would appear to be a more realistic way forward for social democratic and coordinated market economies. It is far more challenging for the UK's finance-based market economy. It will require new forms of public mobilisation and building of political constituencies.

In any case, it is impossible for the large Asian economies to follow the western growth model. It may well be easier for newly emerging economies to fashion a new path of development and there will be lessons the older economies can learn from them. But if the economics of a finite planet point to the end of economic growth in the West, still more radical thinking and action will be required. Either way, climate change will transform public policy futures.

Acknowledgements

Thanks to Anna Coote, Monica Guillen Royo, John Hills and two anonymous referees for comments on an earlier version. They are in no way responsible for the final result.

References

Bättig, M. and Bernauer, T. (2009) 'National Institutions and Global Public Goods: Are Democracies More Cooperative in Climate Change Policy?', *International Organisation* 63: 281–308.

Benzie, M., Harvey, A., Burningham, K., Hodgson, N. and Siddiqi, A. (2011) *Vulnerability to Heatwaves and Drought: Case Studies of Adaptation to Climate Change in South-west England*, Joseph Rowntree Foundation [online], http://www.jrf.org.uk/sites/files/jrf/climate-change-adaptation-full.pdf (accessed 11 June 2011).

Broome, J. (1992) *Counting the Cost of Global Warming* (Cambridge: White Horse Press).

Brundtland Commission Report (1987) *Our Common Future* (Oxford: Oxford University Press).

Caporaso, J. and Levine, D. (1992) *Theories of Political Economy* (Cambridge: Cambridge University Press).

Christoff, P. (1996) 'Ecological Modernisation, Ecological Modernities', *Environmental Politics* 5: 476–500.

Christoff, P. and Eckersley, R. (2011) 'Comparing State Responses', in J.S. Dryzek, R.B. Norgaard and D. Schlosberg (eds) *Oxford Handbook of Climate Change and Society* (Oxford: Oxford University Press).

Committee on Climate Change (CCC) (2008) *Building a Low-carbon Economy—the UK's Contribution to Tackling Climate Change* (London: HMSO).

Committee on Climate Change (CCC) (2009) *Meeting Carbon Budgets—the Need for a Step Change* (London: HMSO).

Committee on Climate Change (CCC) (2010) *The Fourth Carbon Budget—Reducing Emissions Through the 2020s* (London: HMSO).

Crouch, C. and Streeck,W. (1997) *Political Economy of Modern Capitalism: Mapping Convergence and Diversity* (London: Sage).

Daly, H. (1996) *Beyond Growth* (Washington, DC: Beacon Press).

Daly, H. (2008) *A Steady State Economy* (London: Sustainable Development Commission).

Dasgupta, P. (2006) *Comments on the Stern Review's Economics of Climate Change* [online], http://www.econ.cam.ac.uk/faculty/dasgupta/STERN.pdfs (accessed 11 June 2011).

Department of Energy and Climate Change (2009) *The Low Carbon Transition Plan* (London: Her Majesty's Government).

Department of Energy and Climate Change (2011) *EU ETS Phase III (2013–2020)* [online], http://www.decc.gov.uk/en/content/cms/emissions/eu_ets/phase_iii/phase_iii.aspx (accessed 24 June 2011).

Department for Environment, Food and Rural Affairs (DEFRA) (2008) *A Framework for Pro-environmental Behaviours* [online], http://archive.defra.gov.uk/evidence/social/behaviour/documents/behaviours-jan08-report.pdf (accessed 11 June 2011).

Dietz S., Michie, J. and Oughton, C. (eds) (2011) *The Political Economy of the Environment: An Interdisciplinary Approach* (Abingdon: Routledge).

Dobson, A. (2006) *Environmental Citizenship* (Cambridge, MA: MIT Press).

Duit, A. (2008) *The Ecological State: Cross-national Patterns of Environmental Governance Regimes*, EPIGOV Paper 39 (Berlin, Ecologic: Institute for International and European Environmental Policy).

Ehrlich, P.R. and Holdren, J.P. (1971) 'Impact of Population Growth', *Science* 171: 1212–1217.

Environmental Audit Committee (2008) *Personal Carbon Trading: Fifth Report of 2007–08*, House of Commons HC 565.

Environmental Tax Policy Institute and the Vermont Journal of Environmental Law (2008) *The Reality of Carbon Taxes in the 21st Century* [online] http://www.vermontlaw.edu/Documents/020309-carbonTaxPaper(0).pdf (accessed 11 June 2011).

Fankhauser, S. (2010) 'The Costs of Adaptation', *Interdisciplinary Reviews of Climate Change* 1: 1757–1780.

Foresight (2011a) *International Dimensions of Climate Change: Final Project Report* (London: The Government Office for Science).

Foresight (2011b) *Migration and Global Environmental Change. Final Project Report* (London: The Government Office for Science).

Gamble, A. (1995) 'The New Political Economy', *Political Studies* 43: 516–530.

Garnaut, R. (2008) *The Garnaut Climate Change Review: Final Report* (Cambridge: Cambridge University Press).

Garnaut, R., Howes, S., Jotzo, F. and Sheehan, P. (2009) 'The Implications of Rapid Development for Emissions and Climate-change Mitigation', in D. Helm and C. Hepburn (eds) *The Economics and Politics of Climate Change* (Oxford: Oxford University Press), 81–106.

Giddens, A. (2009) *The Politics of Climate Change* (Cambridge: Polity).

Giddens, A., Latham, S. and Liddle, R. (eds) (2009) *Building a Low-carbon Future* (London, Policy Network).

Gough, I. (2010) 'Economic Crisis, Climate Change and the Future of Welfare States', *21st Century Society: Journal of the Academy of Social Sciences* 5: 51–64.

Gough, I., Meadowcroft, J., Dryzek, J., Gerhards, J., Lengfeld, H., Markandya, A. and Ortiz, R. (2008) 'Climate Change and Social Policy: A Symposium', *Journal of European Social Policy* 18: 325–344.

Gough, I. and Meadowcroft, J. (2011) 'Decarbonising the Welfare State', in J.S. Dryzek, R.B. Norgaard and D. Schlosberg (eds) *Oxford Handbook of Climate Change and Society* (Oxford: Oxford University Press).

Gough, I. and Marden, S. (2011) *Fiscal Costs of Climate Mitigation Programmes in the UK: A Challenge for Social Policy?*, CASE papers CASE/145 (London: CASE).

Gough, I., Abdallah, S., Johnson, V., Ryan-Collins, J. and Smith, C. (2011) *The Distribution of Total Embodied Greenhouse Gas Emissions by Households in the UK, and Some Implications for Social Policy*. CASE papers (in press) (London: CASE).

Graham, L.O.G. (2011) 'US Energy and Climate Change Policy', Grantham Research Institute on Climate Change and the Environment public lecture, LSE, 24 March.

Haas, P.M. (1990) 'Obtaining International Environmental Protection through Epistemic Consensus', *Journal of International Studies* 19(3): 347–363.

Hall, P.A. and Soskice, D. (2001) *Varieties of Capitalism: The Institutional Foundations of Comparative Advantage* (Oxford: Oxford University Press).

Held, D. and Hervey, A. (2011) 'Democracy, Climate Change and Global Governance', in D. Held, A. Hervey and M. Theros (eds) *The Governance of Climate Change* (Cambridge: Polity), 89–110.

Helm, D. (2009) 'Climate-change Policy: Why Has So Little Been Achieved?', in D. Helm and C. Hepburn (eds) *The Economics and Politics of Climate Change* (Oxford: Oxford University Press), 9–35.

Helm, D., Smale, R. and Phillips, J. (2007) 'Too Good to be True? The UK's Climate Change Record' [online] http://www.dieterhelm.co.uk/sites/default/files/Carbon_record_2007.pdf (accessed 11 June 2011).

Hepburn, C. (2009) 'Carbon Taxes, Emissions Trading and Hybrid Schemes', in D. Helm and C. Hepburn (eds) *The Economics and Politics of Climate Change* (Oxford: Oxford University Press), 365–384.

Hepburn, C. and Stern, N. (2009) 'The Global Deal on Climate Change', in D. Helm and C. Hepburn (eds) *The Economics and Politics of Climate Change* (Oxford: Oxford University Press), 36–57.

Intergovernmental Panel on Climate Change (IPCC) (2007) *Climate Change 2007: Mitigation of Climate Change. Fourth Assessment Report* (Cambridge: Cambridge University Press).

Jackson, T. (2009) *Prosperity Without Growth? Economics for a Finite Planet* (London: Earthscan).

Jackson, T. (2011) 'Confronting Consumption: Challenges for Economics and for Policy', in S. Dietz, J. Michie and C. Oughton (eds) *The Political Economy of the Environment: An Interdisciplinary Approach* (Abingdon: Routledge), 189–212.

Jameson, F. (2003) 'Future City', *New Left Review*, 21 (May–June): 65–79.

Jevons, W.S. (1865) *The Coal Question; An Inquiry Concerning the Progress of the Nation, and the Probable Exhaustion of Our Coal Mines* (London: Macmillan and Co.).

Kaul, I., Schelling, T., Solow, R.M., Stern, N., Sterner, T. and Weitzman, M.L. (2009) 'Round Table Discussion: Economics and Climate Change. Where Do We Stand and Where Do We Go From Here?', in J.-P. Touffut (ed.) *Changing Climate, Changing Economy* (Cheltenham: Edward Elgar), 135–164.

Layard, R. (2005) *Happiness: Lessons from a New Science* (London: Allen Lane).

Lenton, T., Held, H., Kriegler, E., Hall, J.W., Lucht, W., Rahmstorf, S. and Schellnhuber, H.J., (2008) 'Tipping Elements in the Earth's Climate System', *Proceedings of the National Academy of Sciences of the USA*, 105: 1786–1793.

Lomborg, B. (2010) *Smart Solutions to Climate Change: Comparing Costs and Benefits* (Cambridge: Cambridge University Press).

Meadowcroft, J. (2005) 'From Welfare State to Ecostate?', in J. Barry and R. Eckersley (eds) *The State and the Global Ecological Crisis* (Cambridge, MA: MIT Press), 3–23.

Meadows, D.H., Meadows, D.L., Randers, J., and Behrens III, W.W. (1972) *The Limits to Growth: A Report to the Club of Rome* (New York: Universe Books).

Meinshausen, M., Meinshausen, N., Hare, W., Raper, S.C.B., Frieler, K., Knutti, R., Frame D.J. and Allen, M.R. (2009) 'Greenhouse Gas Emission Targets for Limiting Global Warming to 2°C', *Nature* 458: 1158–1162.

Mol, A., Sonnenfeld, D. and Spaargaren, G. (eds) (2009) *The Ecological Modernisation Reader: Environmental Reform in Theory and Practice* (London and New York: Routledge).

Muspratt, C. and Seawright, S. (2006) 'Amber Alert Over Green Taxes', *The Telegraph*, [online], http://www.telegraph.co.uk/finance/2949852/Amber-alert-over-green-taxes. html (accessed 11 June 2011).

Nair, C. (2011) *Consumptionomics: Asia's Role in Reshaping Capitalism and Saving the Planet* (Oxford: Infinite Ideas).

National Audit Office (NAO) (2009) *European Union Emissions Trading Scheme: A Review* [online], http://www.nao.org.uk/publications/0809/eu_emissions_trading_scheme.aspx (accessed 11 June 2011).

New Economics Foundation (NEF) (2008) *A Green New Deal* [online], http://www. neweconomics.org/sites/neweconomics.org/files/A_Green_New_Deal_1.pdf (accessed 11 June 2011).

New Economics Foundation (NEF) (2009) *The Happy Planet Index 2.0* [online], http://www. neweconomics.org/sites/neweconomics.org/files/The_Happy_Planet_Index_2.0_1.pdf (accessed 11 June 2011).

New Economics Foundation (NEF) (2010) *21 Hours: Why a Shorter Working Week Can Help Us All to Flourish in the 21st Century* [online],http://www. neweconomics.org/publications/21-hours (accessed 11 June 2011).

Neumayer, E. (2007) 'A Missed Opportunity: The Stern Review on Climate Change', *Global Environmental Change* 17: 297–310.

Nilsson, M. and Eckerberg, K. (2007) *Environmental Policy Integration in Practice: Shaping Institutions for Learning* (London: Earthscan).

Nordhaus, W. (2007) *The Stern Review on the Economics of Climate Change* [online], http://nordhaus.econ.yale.edu/stern_050307.pdf (accessed 11 June 2011).

Organisation for Economic Cooperation and Development (OECD) (1994) *Improving the Quality of Law and Regulations: Economic, Legal and Managerial Techniques* (Paris: OECD).

Organisation for Economic Cooperation and Development (OECD) (2010) *Interim Report of the Green Growth Strategy: Implementing Our Commitment for a Sustainable Future* (Paris: OECD).

Oreskes, N. and Conway, E.M. (2010) *Merchants of Doubt* (New York: Bloomsbury Press).

Ostrom, E. (2009) *A Polycentric Approach for Coping with Climate Change*, World Bank, Policy research working paper 5095.

Pierson, P. (2004) *Politics in Time: History, Institutions, and Social Analysis* (Princeton, NJ: Princeton University Press).

Prins, G., Galiana, I., Green, C., Grundmann, R., Korhola, A., Laird, F., Nordhaus, T., Pielke Jnr, R., Rayner, S., Sarewitz, D., Shellenberger, M., Stehr, N. and Tezuko, H. (2010) *The Hartwell Paper 2010: A New Direction for Climate Policy after the Crash of 2009* [online] http://eprints.lse.ac.uk/27939/1/HartwellPaper_English_version.pdf (Accessed 11 June 2011).

Revell, A. (2005) 'Ecological Modernisation in the UK: Rhetoric or Reality?', *European Environment* 15: 344–361.

Ridley, M. (2010) *The Rational Optimist: How Prosperity Evolves* (London: Fourth Estate).

Rockström, J., Steffen, W., Noone, K., Persson, Å., Chapin III, F.S., Lambin, E., Lenton, T.M., Scheffer, M., Folke, C., Schellnhuber, H., Nykvist, B., De Wit, C.A., Hughes, T., van der Leeuw, S., Rodhe, H., Sörlin, S., Snyder, P.K., Costanza, R., Svedin, U., Falkenmark, M., Karlberg, L., Corell, R.W., Fabry, V.J., Hansen, J., Walker, B., Liverman, D., Richardson, K., Crutzen, P., and Foley, J. (2009) 'Planetary boundaries: Exploring the safe operating space for humanity', *Ecology and Society* 14: 32 [online] http://www.ecologyandsociety.org/vol14/iss2/art32 (Accessed 11 June 2011).

Royal Society (2010) *Climate Change: A Summary of the Science* [online], http://royalsociety.org/climate-change-summary-of-science/ (accessed 11 June 2011).

Seyfang, G. and Paavola, J. (2008) 'Inequality and Sustainable Consumption: Bridging the Gaps', *Local Environment* 13: 669–684.

Shorrock, L. and Utley, J. (2003) *Domestic Energy Fact File* (Watford: Building Research Establishment).

Sorrell, S. (2009) 'Improving Energy Efficiency: Hidden Costs and Unintended Consequences', in D. Helm and C. Hepburn (eds) *The Economics and Politics of Climate Change* (Oxford: Oxford University Press), 340–361.

Spence, A., Venables, D., Pidgeon, N., Poortinga, W. and Demski, C. (2010) 'Public Perceptions of Climate Change and Energy Futures in Britain: Summary Findings of a Survey Conducted in January–March 2010', Technical report, Understanding Risk working paper 10-01 (Cardiff: School of Psychology).

Steffen, W. (2011) 'A Truly Complex and Diabolical Policy Problem', in J.S. Dryzek, R.B. Norgaard and D. Schlosberg (eds) *Oxford Handbook of Climate Change and Society* (Oxford: Oxford University Press), 21–37.

Stern, N. (2007) *The Economics of Climate Change: The Stern Review* (Cambridge: Cambridge University Press).

Stern, N. (2011) 'The Low-carbon Industrial Revolution' [lecture], 17 March, London School of Economics and Political Science.

Stiglitz, J., Sen, A. and Fitoussi, J. (2009) Report by *the Commission on the Measurement of Economic Performance and Social Progress* [online], http://www.stiglitz-sen-fitoussi. fr/documents/rapport_anglais.pdf (accessed 11 June 2011).

Stoker, G. (2011) *Building a New Politics?* A report for the British Academy project *New Paradigms in Public Policy* (London: British Academy Policy Centre).

Taylor-Gooby, P. (2011) *Squaring the Public Policy Circle: Managing Demands that Outstrip Resources.* A report for the British Academy project *New Paradigms in Public Policy* (London: British Academy Policy Centre).

United Nations Development Programme (2007) *Human Development Report 2007/2008: Fighting Climate Change* (Basingstoke: Palgrave Macmillan).

United Nations Environment Programme (2009) 'Global Green New Deal—a Policy Brief' [online], http://www.slideshare.net/dabydeen/global-green-new-deal-policy-brief (accessed 11 June 2011).

Verweij, M. and Thompson, M. (eds) (2006) *Clumsy Solutions for a Complex World: Governance, Politics and Plural Perceptions* (Basingstoke: Palgrave Macmillan).

Victor, P. (2008) *Managing Without Growth: Slower by Design, not Disaster* (Cheltenham: Edward Elgar).

Walker, G. and Burningham, K. (2011) 'Flood Risk, Inequality and Environmental Justice', *Critical Social Policy* 31: 216–240.

Weitzman, M. (1974) 'Prices vs. Quantities', *Review of Economic Studies* 41: 477–491.

Weitzman, M. (2007) 'A Review of the Stern Review on the Economics of Climate Change', *Journal of Economic Literature* XLV: 703–724.

Whitmarsh, L. (2011) 'Social and Psychological Drivers of Energy Consumption Behaviour and Energy Transitions', in S. Dietz, J. Michie and C. Oughton (eds) *The Political Economy of the Environment: An Interdisciplinary Approach* (Abingdon: Routledge), 213–228.

5

Citizenship in a diverse and multicultural society

TARIQ MODOOD

European urban diversity

Currently most of the largest, especially the capital, cities of north-west Europe are about 25–40 per cent non-white (that is, people of non-European descent, including Turks). The non-white groups are relatively young. Even without further large-scale immigration, they will continue to expand for at least one generation before they stabilise in size, reaching or exceeding 50 per cent in some cities in the next few decades or sooner. The trend will include some of the larger urban centres of southern Europe. A high degree of racial, ethnic and religious mix in its principal cities will be the norm in twenty-first-century Europe, and will characterise its national economic, cultural and political life, as it has done in twentieth- (and will do so in twenty-first-)century USA. Of course, there will be important differences between Western Europe and the USA. Amongst these is that the majority of non-whites in the countries of Europe are Muslims; the UK, where Muslims form about a third of non-whites or ethnic minorities, is one of the exceptions. With an estimated nearly 20 million Muslims in Western Europe today, the Muslim population in the former EU-15 is only about 1 per cent and is relatively evenly distributed across the larger states (Pew Forum 2011). However, in the larger cities the proportion which is Muslim is several times larger and growing at a faster rate than most of the population (Lutz, Skirbekk and Testa 2007; Kaufman, Goujon and Skirbekk 2011).

The riots in the banlieues of Paris and elsewhere in 2005, the Danish cartoon affair and other issues about offence and freedom of speech and the proliferating bans on various forms of female Muslim dress are just some in a series of conflicts focused on minority–majority relations. In this context, questions about integration, equality, racism and Islam have become central to European politics. In the USA race and ethnicity have been a strong factor in the granting of citizenship and the organisation of politics. The contexts of Britain and the rest of Europe differ in important ways (Brubaker 1992; Triandafyllidou *et al.* 2012). Moreover, continuing migration flows are very likely as the West European population ages. With a very low birth rate, it will be difficult for the continent to meet its labour needs (see Pat Thane's chapter in this volume). Alongside Eastern Europe and Russia, North Africa, with its burgeoning population, unemployed youth, and a source and conduit of illegal migration flows, may be a major contributor to Europe's future population, as may be Turkey. Transcontinental extended families are also likely to contribute workers. Such families usually become of less importance over time but can remain significant for several generations in some groups. For example, estimates suggest that about 50 per cent of marriages of British Pakistanis are with Pakistani nationals coming to Britain as spouses (Dale 2008).

Fear of and hostility towards immigrants, and to Muslims specifically, are exacerbated by concerns about security, both in terms of international relations and transnational Islamist terrorist causes and in terms of networks that can be attractive to some second-generation Muslims and converts, and that have actual and potential recruits in Europe. In addition, Islam is seen as culturally threatening and/or illiberal and undemocratic in its values. This is strongly reflected in opinion polls and in the rise of extreme right parties across Western Europe, leading mainstream parties to take into account, if not actually tap into, such sentiments. Fear, polarisation and conflict are likely to get worse if there is a prolonged economic recession as both ethnic minorities and those whites most likely to swing to extreme right views are most vulnerable to job losses and cuts in public services and welfare budgets (Searchlight Educational Trust 2011).

While all these considerations are relevant to thinking about current trends and future scenarios, there is a more fundamental analytical and political issue, which I will call 'minority–majority relations' or 'integration'. The political problem is that Britain and the various Western European countries have tried, or at least discussed, different approaches but no one approach has gained stable and widespread acceptance or is considered successful. This is partly due to a limited realisation of how the ethnic mix is changing in European societies. For example, between the 1950s and early 1970s Germany brought in large numbers of temporary overseas workers (*Gastarbeiter*) and allowed them to stay on renewed contracts, rather than rotating the migrants as they had originally planned. The migrants were allowed to bring their families to join them in Germany (in accordance with international conventions on rights to family life) and their children were often given a segregated Turkish-based education. Societal expectations were allowed to persist that this population was not settling in Germany, and that 'Germany was not a country of immigration'.[1] In short, collective denial meant that integration was not addressed. Some social scientists spoke of 'the myth of return' (the mistaken belief that immigrants would return to countries of origin). They urged the country to wake up to the facts and think constructively about minority–majority relations rather than allow the pattern of exclusion to grow through neglect (Schmitter Heisler 1986: 79–80). They also took the lead in Germany and elsewhere in speaking up against the rise of discourses that hold migrants and the second generation responsible for lack of integration when, for decades, the majority society and its institutions practised formal or informal discrimination and exclusion.

Yet intellectuals themselves can also be mistaken about issues and trends, and therefore about the important political questions. This has been the case with British social scientists in relation to post-immigration 'difference'.

Paradigms and biases

In Britain, until at least the 1990s, the study of and policy-making about post-immigration 'difference' suffered from two serious biases. One was a trans-Atlantic bias which perpetuated the idea that the issues were best understood in terms of race relations—meaning the black–white relations in the North Atlantic world. US cities, especially inner cities, were taken as paradigms and it was often assumed that whatever the USA does

---

[1] This was prominently stated in the coalition agreement between the Christian Democrats and Liberals in 1982 and became the conservative credo towards immigration in the following decades.

today, the UK will do tomorrow. The focus was on issues such as colour-racism, poverty, educational underachievement, drugs, crime, and children brought up by single mothers. Having now seen the development of tight, patriarchal kinship networks, educational overachievement amongst South Asians (though there is simultaneous educational underachievement amongst Pakistanis and Bangladeshis, especially males) and the upward social mobility of Indians and Chinese, not to mention a disproportionate number of millionaires and billionaires from those ethnic groups, we see how flawed the original taken-for-granted paradigm was in relation to Britain. This is related to the second bias.

The secularist bias in Britain is more European than American.[2] Until the 1990s, few social scientists or policy-makers foresaw that the issues conceptualised by 'race', 'ethnicity' and 'multiculturalism' were going to be dominated by aspects of religion. Nor did they foresee that this would be brought about by the power of British ethnic minority agency and its transnational connections. Despite those social scientists who always see power in top-down ways (through class and/or racism or 'governmentality' analyses), no British politician ever wished religion to have the political salience that it has acquired and now will have for at least some time; rather, some minorities rejected certain racial identities as self-identities in favour of religious ones and set the terms of a new agenda (Modood 1990, 2005). It is now clear that the dominant frame is neither Atlantocentric black-white nor religion-blind but perhaps some version of Europe-Islam (Caldwell 2009) and/or civic integrationism (Joppke 2010).

The issue of immigrant integration illustrates how problems and the way in which they are framed can shift in unexpected ways, from cheap labour and 'race', to public religion, secularism and international conflict. Both theorists and policy-makers are running to catch up with events and social movements, both at grassroots and at transnational levels. We find ourselves at a point where models of analysis and policy have failed, but there is uncertainty and disagreement about how they should be replaced. Each of the paradigms that has been nationally dominant—for example, the

---

[2] Foner and Alba (2008) argue that negative perceptions of Muslims in western European social science compared to its US counterpart is due to the fact that religion is more positively valued in the USA in general and as an integrative vehicle. They may, however, underestimate the growing hostility to Muslims in the USA (as evidenced in the 'Ground Zero mosque' controversy) even if it has not yet reached European proportions.

multiculturalism of the Netherlands with its separate 'pillars' for Catholic, Protestant and social-democratic groupings[3] or the more integrationist British version, the *Gastarbeiter* approach in Germany, and the republican *laïcité* in France—is thought to have failed or at least become outdated (Vertovec and Wessendorf 2010). The Netherlands probably took multiculturalism furthest in Europe but it has also experienced the most visible retreat (Joppke 2004). In Britain, the riots in the northern English towns in 2001, soon followed by the terrorist attacks of September 11 in the USA, led to a perception that multiculturalism created separate and hostile communities (Cantle 2001; McGhee 2008). France experienced riots daily for 22 days in more than 250 localities in the autumn of 2005, leading President Chirac to speak of a 'crisis of identity' (Simon and Sala Pala 2010), a theme that President Sarkozy made central to his politics. In Germany, a book that declares that Turkish immigrants are ruining the country had unprecedented sales figures of over a million copies in less than a year (Fekte 2011). While most discourses appeal to common values and/or national integration and eschew separatism, there is no clear agreement on an approach that identifies the issues in a way consistent with the basic principles of European democracies. The task is not so much speculating about the future, as urgently identifying a viable and acceptable framework for analysis and policy. In what follows I seek to offer an analytical framework by clarifying concepts and discussing existing trends and possible scenarios.

Identifying and responding to 'difference'

The need for integration arises when an established society is faced with people whom it perceives, and therefore treats, unfavourably by comparison with other members. Typically these outsiders also perceive themselves as 'different', though not necessarily in a negative way. This challenge may relate to different areas or sectors of society and policy, such as employment, education and housing. For example, someone is integrated into the labour market when s/he is able to enjoy equality of opportunity in

[3] The consociational model of separate, parallel civic institutions ('pillars') for Catholics and Protestants that emerged in the nineteenth century declined sharply in the middle of the twentieth century, but its formalised institutional structure persisted and opened opportunities for the organisation and representation of ethnic and religious minorities in the latter part of the twentieth century (Bader 2011).

accessing jobs and careers, as well as the education and training necessary to compete for such jobs; and when the labour market is not segmented into different parts with radically different monetary rewards and working conditions for those with broadly similar qualifications and experience. This is particularly relevant where the segmentation is, formally or informally, based on the categories of 'difference' such as race, ethnicity, religion and so on. What is true of labour markets can be applied more generally.

The purpose of integration is equality of opportunity in a society, where membership of any sector of society—such as employment, education, and so on—is not based on criteria such as race and ethnicity. Integration has a number of components based on opportunities to participate which are context-specific and need to be secured by law and policy initiatives. It also has a subjective and symbolic dimension, which has some context-specific features, but which also has a more general or 'macro' character: how a minority is perceived by the rest of the country and how members of a minority perceive their relationship to society as a whole. Even if members of ethnic minorities are fully integrated in terms of legal rights, access to employment or education that does not mean they have achieved full social integration. This also requires some degree of subjective identification with the society or country as a whole—what the Commission on Multi-Ethnic Britain called 'a sense of belonging' (CMEB 2000: Introduction)—and acceptance from the majority population that the minority persons are full members of society and have the right to feel that they belong.

Sectoral integration and the general sense of integration can happen at an individual level. An individual may choose to integrate or not, and may be given opportunities to participate or not. The interest here is not in individual choices and opportunities themselves, but in examining their impact at the level of groups or society as a whole. A sense of belonging is dependent on how others perceive and treat you, not just as an individual but also as a member of a racial group or ethno-religious community. Each policy area will have its own imperatives and difficulties, for example concerning qualification levels or residential segregation,[4] but there is also a

---

[4] Different groups may integrate to different degrees across sectors. For example, Jews in Britain are highly integrated in relation to employment but are the most residentially segregated religious minority (Peach 2006).

general understanding that we as members of society have about what our society is and what it is to be a member. This informs popular understanding as well as political ideas and the general terms of policy paradigms. As the Quebec Consultative Commission put it: 'the symbolic framework of integration (identity, religion, perception of the other, collective memory, and so on) is no less important than its functional or material framework' (Bouchard and Taylor 2008; see also Bouchard 2011). This is particularly relevant because the sense of 'crisis' about multiculturalism and integration operates at this general and societal level. This is evident when one considers how few are the policies directed at integration or how small the funds involved are, compared to the headline importance that the issues regularly achieve. In thinking about policy paradigms and—of a general ethos or orientation at a national level—it is therefore important to engage at this broader societal level.[5]

I consider this larger, macro-symbolic sense of integration with its implied policy paradigms or framings when I discuss four modes of integration: assimilation, individualist-integration and two versions of multiculturalism, one of which I will call cosmopolitanism.[6] Each mode offers its own distinctive interpretation of the core values of European democracy (freedom, equality and civic unity, or 'fraternity'), and is a developing model.[7] The issue or 'problem' addressed by these paradigms is post-immigration 'difference' (Modood 2007). Large-scale immigration into Europe has been by people marked by 'difference'. The 'difference' is not confined to the fact of migration, or how long the migrants and their families have been in Europe, or the fact that they come from less economically developed parts of the world. 'Difference' primarily refers to how people are identified: how they identify themselves (for example as 'white', 'black', 'Chinese', 'Muslim', etc.), how they identify others (again as

---

[5] For an alternative view that at a moment when general conceptions are confused, we can best grasp what the real issues are by focusing on 'the everyday', see Fox and Miller-Idris (2008).

[6] The concern here is not primarily in relation to socio-economic integration, for which see Loury, Modood and Teles (2005) and Heath and Cheung (2007). The bigger challenge, for another occasion, is to connect the socio-economic with the issues discussed in this chapter. The issues of 'difference', however, are as important as the socioeconomic in relation to equal citizenship and have to be understood in their own terms.

[7] In doing so I follow Charles Taylor's treatment of the concept of secularism (Taylor 2009), though without claiming that he would wish to use it as I do in relation to integration.

'white', 'black', 'Chinese', 'Muslim', etc.) and how they are identified by others ('white' etc.).

These identities fall (not necessarily unambiguously or discretely) within the fields of 'race', ethnicity, religion, culture and nationality as various forms of difference. They will no doubt be classed or gendered in specific or generalisable ways but the important point from which everything else follows is that these identities are not reducible to, or, stronger still, are not primarily socioeconomic or 'objective' in classical sociological terms. The identities involve subjectivity and agency. The relationship between migrants and the 'hosts', or, more accurately, given that the migrations in question took place mainly in the third quarter of the twentieth century, the minority–majority relations, cannot be understood without the forms of difference. The relevant interactions cannot be explained, the position of different actors cannot be predicted (or even guessed at), and political preferences cannot be expressed without the explicit or implicit use of the idea of difference. It is commonly said that we must distinguish between *multiculturalism* as social description and *Multiculturalism* as political understanding of those social facts. Interestingly, the same could be but is rarely said about class/Class, nation/Nation, or gender/Gender. In fact, social description and sociological concepts are not normally politically neutral. The concepts I analyse below, then, are normative and policy-oriented but they presuppose an understanding of what the social phenomenon is that demands a political response. The problem then, is how to integrate difference, or to put it another way, the processes whereby difference ceases to be problematic. I shall consider four modes of integration (summarised in Table 5.1).

Modes of integration

Assimilation is the term used to describe a situation when the processes affecting change and the relationship between social groups are seen as one-way. The preferred result is one where the newcomers do little to disturb the society they are settling in and become as much like their new compatriots as possible.[8] We may think of it as one-way integration. This

---

[8] When US sociologists use the term 'assimilation', they usually mean what is meant by integration in the UK, as in the 'segmented assimilation' proposed by Portes and Zhou (1993).

may simply be a laissez-faire approach with few policies but the state can play an active role in bringing about the desired outcome, as in early twentieth-century 'Americanisation' policies towards European migrants in the United States. The desired outcome for society as a whole is seen as involving least change in the ways of doing things for the majority of the country and its institutional policies. Assimilation seeks to erase difference so that the occasions for discrimination and conflict are not allowed to take root. From the 1960s onwards, beginning with anglophone countries and spreading to others, assimilation as a policy has come to be seen as impractical (especially for those who stand out in terms of physical appearance), illiberal (requiring too much state intervention) and inegalitarian (treating indigenous citizens as a norm to which others must approximate). It was as early as 1966 that Roy Jenkins, the then UK home secretary, declared that in the view of the British government integration is 'not a flattening process of assimilation but equal opportunity accompanied by cultural diversity in an atmosphere of mutual tolerance' (Jenkins 1967: 267). Accordingly, 'assimilation' as a term has come to be dropped in favour of 'integration'. Yet, even today, when some politicians use the term 'integration', they actually, consciously or not, mean what here has been defined as assimilation (Fekete 2008: 8–19). The use of these terms in public discourse cannot be taken at their face value but should be critically inspected.

In the three modes of integration that go beyond assimilation, processes of social interaction are seen as two-way, where members of the majority community as well as immigrants and ethnic minorities are required to do something; so the latter cannot alone be blamed for failing to, or not trying to, integrate. Assimilation—in policy terms, not merely as reference to personal choices—has recently come to the fore most often in relation to naturalisation, with the introduction of language requirements and tests of national knowledge. The established society is the site of institutions, including employment, civil society and the state, in which integration has to take place. The prospective citizens' rights and opportunities must be made effective through the anti-discrimination laws and policies that regulate these institutions. At this point we should distinguish between the two-way modes, *individualist-integration* and *multiculturalism*. The former sees the institutional adjustments in relation to migrants or minorities as only relevant to claimants as individuals and bearers of rights as equal citizens (Barry 2001). Minority communities may exist as private associations but are not recognised or supported in the public sphere.

Multiculturalism is where processes of integration are seen as two-way, as involving groups as well as individuals, and as working differently for different groups (CMEB 2000; Parekh 2000; Modood 2007). In this understanding, each group is distinctive, and thus integration cannot consist of a single template (hence the 'multi'). 'Culturalism' refers to the fact that the groups in question are likely not just to be marked by newness or phenotype or socioeconomic location but by certain forms of group identity. The integration of groups is in addition to, not as an alternative to, the integration of individuals, anti-discrimination measures and a robust framework of individual rights. Multiculturalism, like most concepts, takes different forms in different contexts and at different times. For example, it has been differently understood in the Netherlands and in Britain (Joppke 2004; Koopmans *et al.* 2005). It is also understood differently in Quebec compared to in anglophone Canada (Bouchard and Taylor 2008: 115–117). The meaning of any mode of integration is subject to debate and contestation. Those who originate the policy may start with one meaning, as, for example, Roy Jenkins did in relation to race and culture. Then others, including latecomers to the debate, may push it or extend it in other directions by, for example, making religion central, as Muslims in Britain have done (Modood 2005).

Equality is central to multiculturalism, as it is to other conceptions of integration. The key difference between individualist-integration and multiculturalism is that the concepts of group and of the equal status of different kinds of groups (racial, ethnic, religious and so on) are essential to the latter. Post-immigration minorities are groups differentiated from the majority society or the norm in society by two factors: on the one hand, negative 'difference', alienness, inferiorisation, stigmatisation, stereotyping, exclusion, discrimination and racism; on the other, by the senses of identity that groups so perceived have of themselves. The two together are the key data for multiculturalism. The differences at issue are those perceived both by outsiders or group members—from the outside in and from the inside out—to constitute not just some form of distinctness but a form of alienness or inferiority that diminishes or makes difficult equal membership in the wider society or polity.

Multiculturalism has recently been defined as 'where ethno-cultural-religious minorities are, or are thought of, as rather distinct communities, and where public policy encourages this distinctiveness' (Emmerson 2011). This, however, is only part of it. Multiculturalism allows those who wish to encourage such distinctiveness to do so; but it also seeks forms of social unity that are compatible with this, what Hartmann and Gerteis (2005) call 'new conceptions of solidarity', grounded in a concept of equality (Bouchard and Taylor 2008). Each mode of integration must be understood in terms of its interpretation of free choice, equality and fraternity (as displayed in Table 5.1). Characterisations of multiculturalism that omit unity as a key component are extremely common but incomplete.

Further unpacking multiculturalism and integration

Multicultural accommodation of minorities, then, is different from individualist-integration because it explicitly recognises the social reality of groups, not just of individuals and organisations. There may, however, be considerable complexity about what is meant by the social reality of groups. Ideas of groups as discrete, homogeneous, unchanging, bounded populations are not realistic when we are thinking of multicultural recognition (Modood 2007: 93–97).[9] Disagreement about the extent to which post-immigration groups exist and/or ought to exist and be given political status means that there are two kinds of multiculturalism (Modood 1998; Meer and Modood 2009a). I shall use 'multiculturalism' to refer to the view that group membership is a central feature of people's identity in our society.[10] I shall use 'cosmopolitanism' to refer to the view that 'difference' is perceived as valuable (or pragmatically accepted) but that group identity is not of importance or, if it exists, that it should not be politically recognised (Waldron 1991). The contention is that in the early stages of migration

[9] Cf. 'The ethnic group in American society became not a survival from the age of mass immigration but a new social form' (Glazer and Moynihan 1963: xvii). To emphasise the point that one needs to be using the concept of groups but not in its most simplest traditional meaning, perhaps one should use the term 'groupness'.

[10] This is how the term has been used by the leading political theorists such as Taylor (1994), Kymlicka (1995) and Parekh (2000) and, by the Canadian government; it is also consistent with CMEB (2000) and other exponents of multiculturalism—see Modood (2007: 14–20) for details.

and settlement, especially in the context of a legacy of racism, colonial-ism and European supremacism, processes of social exclusion created or reinforced certain forms of 'groupness' such as white and black. However, as a result of social mixing, cultural sharing and globalisation in which the dominant identities of modernity (such as of race and nation) are dissolv-ing, people have much more fluid and multiple identities, combine them in individual ways and use them in context-sensitive ways (Hall 1992a). For example, the ways that Caribbean-origin Britons have socially blended into a 'multiculture' and have sought conviviality and sociability rather than separate communities may perhaps not be fully captured as a form of individualistic integration (Gilroy 2000). While remaining economically marginal and over-represented in relation to the social problems associ-ated with deprived inner-city areas, they have become a feature of popular culture in terms of music, dance, youth styles and sport, in all of which they have become significantly over-represented (Hall 1998). To the extent that football teams, Olympians and television programmes such as *The X Factor* are central to popular and national identities, Caribbean-origin people are placed at the centre of British national imaginaries. Moreover, Britain and most other countries in Western Europe have recently expe-rienced and are experiencing a new wave of immigration and will con-tinue to do so, including that from within the European Union. Given the diversity of the locations from which migrants are coming, the result, it is argued, is not communities, but a churning mass of languages, ethnicities and religions, all cutting across each other and creating a 'super-diversity' (Vertovec 2007). This may be setting a pattern for the future, and it may be allied to a further argument that globalisation, migration and telecommu-nications have created populations dispersed across countries that interact more with each other, and have a greater sense of loyalty to each other, than they might to their fellow citizens.

In what ways does cosmopolitanism go beyond individualist-integration? Its distinctive ethos is that we should value diversity and create the condi-tions where it is individually chosen. We should oppose all forms of impo-sition of group identities on individuals and therefore the ideas, images and prejudices by which individuals are rendered inferior or portrayed as threatening, and so excluded from full membership of society. We should not require assimilation or conformity to dominant group norms. Inherited or ascribed identities which slot people into pigeonholes not of

Table 5.1   Four modes of integration*

	Assimilation	Individualist-integration	Cosmopolitanism	Multiculturalism
Objects of policy	Individuals and groups marked by 'difference'.	Individuals marked by 'difference', especially their treatment by discriminatory practices of state and civil society.	Individuals marked by 'difference', especially their treatment by discriminatory practices of state and civil society, and societal ideas, especially of 'us' and 'them'.	Individuals and groups marked by 'difference', especially their treatment by discriminatory practices of state and civil society, and societal ideas, especially of 'us' and 'them'.
Liberty	Minorities must be encouraged to conform to the dominant cultural pattern.	Minorities are free to assimilate or cultivate their identities in private but are discouraged from thinking of themselves as minority, but rather as individuals.	Neither minority nor majority individuals should think of themselves as belonging to a single identity but be free to mix and match.	Members of minorities should be free to assimilate, to mix and match or to cultivate group membership in proportions and combinations of their own choice.
Equality	Presence of difference provokes discrimination and so is to be avoided.	Discriminatory treatment must be actively eliminated so everyone is treated as an individual and not on the basis of difference.	Anti-discrimination must be accompanied by the dethroning of the dominant culture.	In addition to anti-discrimination the public sphere must accommodate the presence of new group identities and norms.
Fraternity	A strong, homogeneous national identity.	Absence of discrimination and nurturing of individual autonomy within a national, liberal democratic citizenship.	People should be free to unite across communal and national boundaries and should think of themselves as global citizens.	Citizenship and national identity must be remade to include group identities that are important to minorities as well as majorities; the relationship between groups should be dialogical rather than one of domination or uniformity.

*In all cases it is assumed that a backdrop of liberal democratic rights and values operate. The features highlighted here are in addition or interaction with them.

their choosing, giving them a script to live by, should be refused: they not only reduce the options of the kind of person one can be but divide society up into antagonistic groups (Appiah 1994).[11] Cosmopolitanism is a conception of multiculturalism as maximum freedom, for minority as well as majority individuals, to mix with, borrow and learn from all, whether they are of your group or not. Individual identities are personal amalgams of bits from various groups and heritages and there is no one dominant social identity to which all must conform. The result will be a society composed of a blend of cultures: a 'multiculture'.

While this is an attractive image of contemporary society and links easily with the ideas of liberal democracy, it has only a partial fit with even, say, London today, let alone many parts of Britain and continental Europe. In some towns and cities in northern England there is not a range of groups but often just two—for example, Asian Muslims and whites. Minority individuals do not float across identities, mixing and matching, but have a strong attachment to one or few identities. Most British Muslims seem to think of themselves as 'Muslim' and/or 'British' (usually both) (Travis 2002). The fact of super-diversity is emerging alongside rather than displacing the fact of settled, especially postcolonial, communities, who have a particular historical relationship with Britain and a particular political significance. Similarly, there are communities in other European countries with their own historical significance such as Maghrebians in France and the Turks in Germany. Some groups continue to be much larger than others, and stand out as groups, in their own eyes and those of others, and are at the centre of public policy and debate, especially if they are thought to be failing to integrate. Muslims, for example, seem to be in this category across much of Western Europe, even when there are high levels of conviviality or diversity.

That is not to say that such minority identities are exclusive. Successive surveys have shown that most Muslims in Britain strongly identify with being Muslim but the majority also identify as British; indeed they are more likely to identify as 'British' and say they have trust in key British institutions than non-Muslims (Heath and Roberts 2008). Gallup (2009) found the same in Germany, but less so in France, although Pew (2006)

---

[11] British exponents of this view tend, however, to put some communal identities in a normative, privileged position. This particularly applies to political blackness and to some extent to non-cultural and non-religious political identities generally (Modood 1994).

found much higher levels of national identification in general in France than in other western European countries. Post-immigration hyphenated identities, such as British-Indian, have become as commonplace in Britain as they have been in the USA for decades. Similarly, diasporic links as described above certainly exist, and are likely to increase, but the net result is not an inevitable erosion of national citizenship—British African-Caribbeans and South Asians have families in their countries of origin and in the USA and Canada, but there is little evidence that most branches of those families do not feel British, American or Canadian. Indeed, studies show that the more multiculturalist countries achieve higher levels of national identity (Esses *et al.* 2006; Wright and Bloemraad 2012).

An important point of difference, then, between the concepts of individualist-integration and multiculturalism proper is in the understanding of what constitutes a group. In multiculturalism, the groups formed of post-immigration minorities are not of one kind but are several—a 'multi'. However, neither multiculturalism nor cosmopolitanism provides a comprehensive sociological or political model because our society includes both people whose identities are based on group membership, as Sikhs or Muslims for example, and people who are not committed to or identified by a single core identity. For the latter, one of a range of different identities may be relevant in different contexts, sometimes as a worker, or a woman, or a Londoner, or a Briton. From the multiculturalist perspective, these alternative ways of identifying with a group should be viewed as complementary (CMEB 2000; Modood and Dobbernack 2011). Moreover, while recognition of ethnic or religious groups may have a legal dimension, for the most part it will be at the level of civic consultations, political participation, institutional policies (for example, in relation to schools and hospitals), discursive representations, especially in relation to the changing discourses of societal unity or national identity, and their remaking. For these reasons both multiculturalism and cosmopolitanism can be helpful in understanding different aspects of ethnic relations in our society.

Regardless of the extent to which recognition of minority identities in this way is formal or informal, led by the state or by the semi-autonomous institutions of civil society, individual rights and the shared dimensions of citizenship are not challenged. There may, however, be genuine concern that some groups at a particular time and in some areas are becoming too inward-looking. Where the concern is primarily about a lack of positive mixing and interaction between groups at a local level, community cohesion measures, for example, a Christian school offering places to non-Christians or twinning with a non-Christian school, may be an appropriate response (Cantle 2001). Where the concern is about self-conceptions and discourses more generally, the issue will be about the national or societal identity. Whilst such inwardness has never been part of any theory or policy of multiculturalism, it is clear that it is a fundamental anxiety of the critics of multiculturalism, many of whom go as far as to define multiculturalism in terms of such separatism.[12] It is therefore important to emphasise both that accommodation of ethno-religious communities is a mode of integration, and that it, no less than hostility to minorities or other modes of integration, should be examined as a possible contributory cause of exclusion and integration (Banting and Kymlicka 2008).

Ways in which multiculturalism is not dead

This unpacking of what is meant by 'multiculturalism' is also helpful in understanding those who say that multiculturalism has failed (Weldon 1989; and see Presseurop 2010 for Angela Merkel's speech on the failure of *multikulti*) or that multiculturalism is dead (Cameron 2011). They may mean to endorse assimilation, individualistic integration or cosmopolitanism. But at the same time they are acknowledging and possibly reinforcing the social behaviour and structures of group difference because their lament is that some groups (especially Muslims) are clearly visible as distinct groups when they should not be; they attribute this fact to a separatist tendency in the groups, encouraged by allegedly multiculturalist policies. Hence, paradoxical as it may sound, fierce critics of multiculturalism are usually accepting certain assumptions of multiculturalism even

---

[12] A review of the American social science literature found that '[t]he most common conception of multiculturalism in both scholarly circles and popular discourse is a negative one, having to do with what multiculturalism is not or what it stands in opposition to. Multiculturalism in this usage represents heterogeneity as opposed to homogeneity, diversity as a counterpoint to unity' (Hartmann and Gerteis 2005: 219). They found that if they looked at exponents, as opposed to critics, of multiculturalism, such simplistic dichotomies were unsustainable and they concluded: 'multiculturalism is best understood as a critical-theoretical project, an exercise in cultivating new conceptions of solidarity in the context of dealing with the realities of pervasive and increasing diversity in contemporary societies' (221–222).

while rejecting its political implications. If they thought these groups were merely the product of stereotypes and exclusion (in the sense that 'racial' groups are a product of racism) or were primarily socioeconomic in character (perhaps a working-class 'fraction'), then that would be a sociological disagreement with the multiculturalists. The irony is, of course, that the accusatory discourse of 'some groups are not integrating' may actually be reinforcing group identities and therefore contributing to the social conditions that gives multiculturalism a sociological pertinence. On the other hand, a sociology that marginalised ethnicity in favour of say, individuals, class and gender, would have a better fit with anti-multiculturalist politics but might be unable to explain or predict the relevant social reality, resulting in a weaker basis for politics. Our normative orientation, individualist or multiculturalist, suggests to us an ideal sociology but also recommends itself to us as feasible politics because we think that our view of how groups and individuals interact in society is more accurate than not.

Moreover, it is not just at the level of sociology that anti-multiculturalists may find themselves using multiculturalist ideas; even while deploying an anti-multiculturalist discourse they may enact multiculturalist policies.[13] For example, they may continue with group consultations, representation and accommodation. The British government has found it necessary to increase the scale and level of consultations with Muslims in Britain since 9/11, and, dissatisfied with existing organisations, has sought to increase the number of organised interlocutors and the channels of communication. Avowedly anti-multiculturalist countries and governments have worked to increase corporatism in practice, for example with the creation by Nicholas Sarkozy of the Conseil Français du Culte Musulman in 2003 to represent all Muslims to the French government in matters of worship and ritual; and in the creation of the Islamkonferenz in Germany in 2005, an exploratory body, yet with an extensive political agenda. These bodies are partly top-down efforts to control Muslims or to channel them in certain directions and away from others; nevertheless, such institutional processes can only be understood as multiculturalist as they do not fall within the

[13] While the popular belief is that multiculturalism died in years following 9/11, analysis of policies in 21 countries shows that, whilst there was substantial growth of multicultural policies between 1980 and 2000, yet far from halting or retreating it continued to progress between 2000–2010, with only three countries having a lower score in 2010 than 2000 (MCP Index: http://www.queensu.ca/mcp/immigrant/table/Immigrant_Minorities_Table_2.pdf).

conceptual framework of assimilation, individualist integration or cosmo-politanism. They are normatively less than the best of multiculturalism but they clearly are deploying a multiculturalist mode of integration and their presence offers the possibility of movement towards a more egalitarian, rather than a controlled top-down, multiculturalism.

Hence, aspects of what is often understood as a backlash and denial of multiculturalism are actually forms of multiculturalism, even if highly restrictive ones, which in countries such as France and Germany are illus-trating a movement towards, not away from, multiculturalism. There is indeed a new intolerance in relation to certain Muslim practices (for example, the niqab) and this is leading to some new laws or policies in parts of Europe (though not yet in Britain). We do not yet seem to be witnessing a paradigm shift, a fundamental change in the models or inter-pretations used to explain events, for example, from pluralistic integra-tion to individualist integration. The anti-multiculturalist may not just be pointing to the visibility of groups like Muslims, but expressing the view that there is an insufficient participation of such groups into a common life or sharing of common values. My point is that some of the measures are not consistent with assimilation or individualism but acknowledge the social reality and political significance of groups. It may be thought that I am here obscuring the central difference between multiculturalism and its political critics. Namely, that the latter but not the former emphasise integration into a common life. I am, however, disputing this: the mul-ticulturalism in the writings of key theorists such as Charles Taylor, Will Kymlicka, Bhikhu Parekh and Anne Phillips, and in the relevant docu-ments, laws and policies of Canada, Australia and Britain are all aimed at integration (see Modood 2007: 14–20 for details). The difference between the pro- and anti-multiculturalists lies not in the goal of integration but, firstly, in the normative understanding of integration. I have tried to bring this out by reference to the alternative interpretations and prioritising of the normative concepts of liberty, equality and fraternity (summarised in Table 5.1). Secondly, there are different judgements about contexts and about what will deliver results and more generally how society works or what I have been calling implicit sociologies.

This analytical framework helps us also to understand those who say they welcome diversity but seem to be in agreement with critics of political multiculturalism. Critics of multiculturalism are usually pointing to the public assertion of strong group identities, by people within that group, in order to mobilise a group to achieve certain policies and/or to demand differential treatment. One response is from those who point to the success of multiculturalism in their neighbourhoods, which they describe as multi-ethnic and where people do not just live peaceably side by side but mix freely and where that mixing is valued above monoculturalism. This is, however, a weak response. For such views do not imply support for strong group identities and related policies; on the contrary, their success may be seen to be dependent on the absence of the latter.[14] While this is a reasonable response in its own terms it does not counter the above criticism of multiculturalism and in fact may share it. It is the increasingly unpopular group-based multiculturalism that is what critics have in mind and the weakness of the rebuttal is obscured by the fact that advocates of neighbourhood 'multiculturalism' are actually referring to what I call 'cosmopolitanism'.

An example of this tendency is the way in which the majority of Australians welcome multiculturalism, and indeed see it as part of the country's identity, but see it 'in terms of a mix of individuals rather than an ensemble of groups' (Brett and Moran 2011: 203; see also Fenton and Mann 2011 and Searchlight Educational Trust 2011 for related discussions in relation to England). A group-based multiculturalism is much less popular than cosmopolitanism but what we have to consider is whether the integration of all post-immigration formations can be achieved without the former. Moreover, a group-based multiculturalism, where group membership is voluntary, may be part of the future in an unintended way as it is highly compatible with Prime Minister Cameron's vision of a 'Big Society' in which civil society associations based on locality and faith, including inter-faith groups, take over some of the responsibilities currently falling to state agencies. A flagship policy of the Big Society agenda is the state funding to create new community-based non-state schools called 'free schools'. Over a quarter of these are led by religious groups; those that started in September 2011 included two Jewish, a Hindu and a Sikh school (Vasagar 2012). Of the 102 schools approved for funding in

[14] Hence the irony that anti-multiculturalists like President Sarkozy are trying to create corporate representations for Muslims in France; while pro-diversity authors call for the cessation of government meetings with Muslim community leaders (Sen 2006; Malik 2011).

July 2012 three were Jewish, one was Hindu, four were Sikh and four were Muslim (BHA 2012). It is difficult to see how the new Big Society represents a break with what is rejected as 'state multiculturalism' (Cameron 2011). The same trend is found in France, where three Muslim schools have joined the many thousands (mainly Catholic) of state-supported religious schools (Akan 2009: 246–247), and in Germany, where there are no state-funded religious schools but where Islam is increasingly joining the religions that the provincial government funds instruction in within state schools (The Local 2011; see also DIK 2009).

The analysis offered here of related ideas about society and policy paradigms, each of which consists of a model of society and normative political ideas, includes a sense of unity or fraternity. For modes of integration are not just about how society is organised, or about politics, but include ideas, however rudimentary or undeveloped, of ourselves as a social unity (as displayed at the bottom of Table 5.1). For assimilationists, this consists of a strong, homogeneous national identity. Individualist-integration emphasises the liberal and democratic character of the national polity. Cosmopolitanism is uneasy with the national, an identity that demands allegiance from all citizens, whilst creating boundaries between ourselves and the rest of the world. With multiculturalism comes a positive vision of the whole remade so as to include the previously excluded or marginalised on the basis of equality and sense of belonging. It is at this level that we may fully speak of multicultural integration or multicultural citizenship (Taylor 1994; Parekh 2000; Modood 2007). This third level of multiculturalism, incorporating the sociological fact of diversity, groupness and exclusion, but going beyond individual rights and political accommodation, is perhaps the level that has been least emphasised. That is how it seems to many whose understanding of multiculturalism, sometimes polemical but sometimes sincere, is that multiculturalism is about encouraging minority difference without a counterbalancing emphasis on cross-cutting commonalities and a vision of a greater good. This has led many commentators and politicians to talk of multiculturalism as divisive and productive of segregation.

Theorists of multiculturalism such as Taylor (1994) and Parekh (2000), related policy documents such as the report of the CMEB (2000), and enactments such as those in Canada and Australia, universally regarded as pioneers and exemplars of state multiculturalism, all appealed to and built on an idea of national citizenship. Hence, from a multiculturalist point of view, though not from that of its critics, the recent emphasis on cohesion and citizenship, sometimes called 'the civic turn' (Mouritsen 2008), is a necessary rebalancing of the political multiculturalism of the 1990s. This largely took the form of accommodation of groups while being ambivalent about national identity (Meer and Modood 2009a).[15] This does not invalidate the analysis offered here that integration without some degree of institutional accommodation is unlikely to be successful. Indeed, for multiculturalists, a renewing of national identity has to be distinctly plural and hospitable to the minority identities. It involves 'rethinking the national story' with the minorities as important characters; not obscuring difference but weaving it into a common identity in which all can see themselves, and that gives everyone a sense of belonging to each other (CMEB 2000: 54–56; Modood 2007: 145–154). Minority politics are common in the USA, but most groups, while honouring their origins, seek inclusion in the American dream. They seek to be and have come to be accepted as hyphenated Americans (for example, as Italian-Americans, or Asian-Americans). The trend is present in parts of Western Europe. While not yet fully accepted, it may be that hyphenated nationalities will become the norm here too.

What kind of integration in Europe?

The above discussion raises three important questions about what to expect as we look to the future. They are profound questions of public philosophy and policy but also require social science inquiry in relation to trends, possibilities and feasibilities, and are ranked from least to most challenging. They are questions about integration and identities; about long-term cleavages; and about religion and secularism.

Europe is a large and diverse continent, incorporating a number of different religious and cultural identities and traditions of citizenship. Here we focus on the larger and more economically dominant nations, most

---

[15] In the 1990s cosmopolitanism and multiculturalism in Britain began to be linked to a national identity and its modernisation, to, for example, 'Cool Britannia' and 'rebranding Britain' (Leonard 1997) but others welcomed globalisation as an era of the 'post-national' (Hall 1992b; Soysal 1994). For how the CMEB report (2000) confusedly tried to adopt both of these positions, see Modood forthcoming.

important among them Germany and France. Will these countries insist on assimilation, the dominant historical pattern, or allow some space for private cultural difference within a model of civic integration (the current French ideology but not comprehensive practice) or some degree of multi-cultural integration (found to some degree, for example, in the Netherlands and Sweden)? The latter was becoming influential in the English-speaking world until 9/11, but since then the perception has grown that unassimi-lated migrants, especially if Muslim, are a potential security threat. A recent European study of seven countries (but not including the Netherlands and Sweden) concluded that only Britain and to a lesser extent Belgium could be said to approximate to multiculturalism, with the others not so much retreating from multiculturalism but having never got there in the first place (Triandafyllidou *et al.* 2012).[16] Nevertheless, the theme of cultural identity is powerful, for example, in relation to sexuality and to historically squashed nationalisms (such as the Catalonian, Scottish, Flemish and so on). It is unlikely to fade in the current context of globalisation. This seems to foster identity movements in reaction to perceptions of global, currently Americanised, cultural homogeneity (Castells 1997).

Migration-based second and third generations who breathe this atmos-phere may continue to mobilise around identities of cultural difference and demand equality of respect, especially when those identities are the basis of discrimination and structural inequalities. Of course, one may wish that these minority identities were not held in such a way that they become the dominant identities of the individual and groups involved. This is not a matter that can be decided by wishful thinking. Much depends upon the pressure certain minorities feel they are under, and the extent they feel able to pursue their lives as members of a minority. If the media are constantly talking about a particular group in alarmist and stereotyping ways, and if individuals feel highly 'visible', thinking that everyone is identifying them primarily in terms of their group membership, then it is difficult to have a relaxed identity. Nevertheless, there are recent examples of how monopo-lising identities can become secure and pluralised. In the 1970s and 1980s many black Britons, especially young men, felt that society could only think of them as black and as a problem, indeed as an object of fear. Yet, as stated

[16] As stated in footnote 13 the scarcity of multiculturalism does not indicate a retreat from previous more extensive coverage. These seven countries were Britain, Germany, France, Belgium, Denmark, Spain and Greece.

above, through their participation and leadership in popular culture, black people came to be seen in the media and in social interactions as talented and entertaining, as attractive and fashionable, and as champions of the nation on the sports field, alongside if not displacing the negative representations.

A further aspect of this question concerns the level at which integration is to take place, especially in relation to identity-building: city/region or national or European? Another way of posing the question is to ask what hyphenation is on offer, or what will work? In the USA, the hyphenation always refers to America (not Texas, California and so on), but in contemporary Europe, integration policies are directed to developing a sufficiently strong sense of national citizenship. Indeed, in countries such as France and Britain a (hyphenated) national identification is quite strong amongst the second generation (and thus a basis for complaints of unequal treatment as co-nationals), but identification with Europe is much weaker than amongst white peers. European identity as a platform for equality/belonging and lever for equality/belonging at the national level may or may not be helpful in some countries. Faas (2010) argues that young Turks in Germany prefer to think of themselves as 'Europeans' and it is probably the case that ethnic minority identification with the city one lives in (for example, Liverpool or Rotterdam) may be easier than 'British' or 'Dutch' because of all the national, cultural, historical and political baggage that go with the latter. For example, one can say one is proud to be a Liverpudlian without feeling that this implicates you in the US–UK occupation of Iraq. Moreover, co-citizens may say of you 'you are not really Dutch' even if you were born in the Netherlands but are less likely to say 'you are not a Rotterdammer' if you are a long-term resident of that city. Some current social science and policy thinking stresses the importance of urban and regional identities as a way of bypassing more emotive and divisive debates about national identities (Cantle 2001; Keith 2005; Commission on Integration and Cohesion 2007). This kind of localism has actually been part of the British race relations tradition in which 'race' was regarded as too 'hot' for the national state, and funds and powers were given to local authorities in the hope that breaking the problems down would limit the scope for conflict. This kind of local identification also seems to be consonant with the idea of the Big Society favoured by the Prime Minister, Mr Cameron, even though for many young people and not just ethnic minorities, it is favoured because of alienation from a national identity.

Strong minority identities, however, especially when mobilised at a national and transnational level (as has been the case with some Muslim controversies such as the Rushdie and the Danish cartoon affairs, not to mention militant Islamism), are unlikely to be counterbalanced without sufficiently imaginative and affective strong national, inclusive narratives. Indeed it is unlikely that majority–minority relations can achieve new forms of cross-cutting alliances and solidarities without both task-oriented cooperation in a multitude of localities and the 're-thinking of the national story' (CMEB 2000: 14). Integration should be thought of as a multi-level process. It must tackle discrimination and the related issues of socioeconomic disadvantage but, at the same time, offer inclusion in an identity of which people can be proud. Respect for 'difference' is essential for many minority individuals. In order to ensure that is not divisive, minority 'difference' must be grounded in a suitably pluralised conception of equal citizenship. For most people equal citizenship is too abstract a concept unless it is part of something more experiential and imaginative. Hence, equality and 'difference' have to be expressed at different levels and woven together into a sense of commonality strong enough to encompass and counterbalance, without stigmatising, other identities.

Dividing lines

A second question is 'where will the major dividing line in Europe be in relation to post-immigration social formations?' Will it, for example, be a colour-line? In Britain we have come to approach issues to do with integration through what used to be called (in other countries the language will not always have a natural resonance) 'race relations', itself an American term. People saw the issue as primarily one of racial discrimination or colour-racism, which of course had a historical legacy through slavery, colonialism and empire. The issues to do with Muslims, which dominate the headlines today, only became a feature of majority–minority relations from the early 1990s. In Britain virtually nobody, policy-makers, the media, or academics, talked about Muslims until the late 1980s, the time of the Salman Rushdie affair. In France, where Muslims and Islam are even more central to national post-immigration debates, the first 'headscarf affair' was contemporaneous. Since then hostility to Muslims has grown considerably and Islamic symbols such as dress and mosques have become targets of populist politicians and objects of legal control across Western Europe.

In the Anglo-American or Atlantocentric version of racism, which is certainly one of the classical and enduring versions, it is the combination of genetics and social conditioning which is alleged to explain the existence of certain, mainly negative cultural traits (Miles 1989: 71–72). Yet while these racists present people of African descent as a 'race' drawing on their perceptions of African physical appearance, as, for example, strong, sensual, rhythmical and unintelligent, the racialised image of South Asians and Arabs is not so extensively linked to physical appearance. It emerged in relation to cultural motifs such as language, religion, family structures, exotic dress, cuisine and art forms (Modood 2005: 6–18 and chapter one; Meer and Modood 2009b). Such motifs are appealed to in excluding, harassing or discriminating against Asians, Arabs and Muslims, both constituting them as a group and justifying negative treatment of them. Through these motifs Muslims are currently stereotyped or 'racialised' in Europe and elsewhere. For the most part they are visually identified by a phenotype (primarily Arab or South Asian appearance) though also by dress and name and sometimes by accent. Attached to this identification, or image, are stereotypes about religious fanaticism, separatism, not wanting to integrate, lack of national feeling or even disloyalty and association with or sympathy for terrorism (Malik 2010; Sayyid and Vakil 2010).

One should perhaps also note the presence of a more general xenophobia, which can include white victims, as recent East European and South American labour migrants have discovered (Fox, Moroşanu and Szilassy 2012). There is little evidence so far that the long-term faultline will be here (perhaps because it is too early to tell). The likely candidates, therefore, are a white/non-white divide, or one based on 'cultural racism', combining 'race' and 'culture', especially in the form of an anti-Muslim racism. Or, relatedly, a Muslim/non-Muslim divide, in which amongst Muslims are included those of European phenotype, and amongst non-Muslims are Jews, Hindus, black Christians and so on. Multiple lines of division may emerge, perhaps with one predominating, as in the USA.

Religion and secularism

In most, if not all European countries there are points of symbolic, institutional, policy and fiscal linkage between the state and aspects of Christianity. Secularism has increasingly grown in power and scope, but a historically evolved and evolving compromise with religion is the defining feature of Western European secularism, rather than the absolute separation of religion and politics. Secularism today enjoys an increasing dominance in Western Europe, but it is a moderate rather than a radical secularism (Modood 2012).The presence of Muslims and Islamic claims-making upon European societies and states, however, has resulted in a perhaps temporary reversal of aspects of secularisation and the decline of collective religion. In reaction there are increased assertions of Enlightenment secularism and of (cultural) Christianity. Hence there seem to be three visible trends.

Firstly, there is the trend of institutional accommodation, in which regard the Conseil Français du Culte Musulman and the Islamkonferenz have already been mentioned. The development of a religious equality agenda, the incorporation of some Muslim schools on the same basis as schools of religions with an established presence, the inclusion of a religion question in the 2001 UK Census for the first time since its removal in 1851, and the recommendations of the Royal Commission on the Reform of the House of Lords (2000) to pluralise religious representation in that House are some British examples (for more on these European cases see Cesari 2004; Modood and Kastoryano 2006; Bowen 2010).

Secondly, there is a renewal of Christian cultural identities. For example, the voluntary religion question in the 2001 UK Census elicited a much higher 'Christian' response than most surveys. While in the British Social Attitudes (BSA) survey of 1992, 31 per cent did not profess a belief in god(s) and in the latest BSA survey 43 per cent self-identified as non-religious (indeed 59 per cent did not describe themselves as religious: Park *et al.* 2010), in the 2001 Census 72 per cent identified themselves as Christians and less than 16 per cent as without a religion.[17] It seems that the presence and salience of Muslims may have been a factor in stimulating a Christian

[17] In the 2011 Census only 59 per cent identified themselves as Christians and 25 per cent identified themselves as having no religion. It seems that for many in Britain, Christian identification is highly nominal.

identity (Voas and Bruce 2004). The emergence of a new, sometimes politi-cally assertive, cultural identification with Christianity has been noted in Denmark (Mouritsen 2006). In Germany, Chancellor Merkel has asserted that '[t]hose who don't accept [Christian values] don't have a place here' (cited in Presseurop 2010; see also Fekete 2011: 45–46). Similar sentiments were voiced in the European Union constitution debate and are apparent in the ongoing debate about Turkey as a future Union member (Casanova 2009). These assertions of Christian values are not necessarily accompa-nied by any increase in expressions of faith or church attendance, which continues to decline across Europe. Giscard d'Estaing, the former President of France, who chaired the Convention on the Future of Europe, the body which drafted the (abortive) EU constitution, expresses this assertiveness nicely: 'I never go to Church, but Europe is a Christian continent'. It has to be said, however, that such political views about Europe are held not just by cultural Christian identitarians but also by many practising Christians including members of the Catholic Church. It has been argued that Pope John Paul II 'looked at the essential cleavage in the world as being between religion and unbelief. Devout Christians, Muslims, and Buddhists had more in common with each other than with atheists' (Caldwell 2009: 151). Pope Benedict XVI, it is said, 'thinks that, within societies, believers and unbelievers exist in symbiosis. Secular Westerners, he implies, have a lot in common with their religious fellows' (ibid.: 151). The suggestion is that secularists and Christians in Europe have more in common with each other than they do with Muslims. That many secularists do not share Pope Benedict's view is evident from the fact that the proposed clause about Christianity was absent from the final draft of the abortive EU constitu-tion. While there is little sign of a Christian right in Europe of the kind that is strong in the USA, there is to some degree a reinforcing or renewing of a sense that Europe is 'secular Christian', analogous to the term 'secular Jew' to describe someone of Jewish descent who has a sense of Jewish identity but does not practise the religion and may even be an atheist.

Thirdly, besides this secular assertion of Christian identity which is to be found, although not exclusively, on the centre-right, there is also a more radical secularism which is more characteristic of the left. It is a tradi-tion that goes back to the Enlightenment (though more the French than the British or German Enlightenments) and is often anti-religious. It has been most epigrammatically captured by Karl Marx's famous 'religion is the opium of the masses' and Nietzsche's 'God is dead'. Post-9/11 has seen the emergence of a radical discourse referred to as 'the new atheism' (see Beattie (2007) who has authors such as Dawkins (2006), Harris (2004) and Hitchens (2007) in mind). Its political manifestation is found amongst intellectuals and political commentators such as A.C. Grayling, Kenan Malik and Polly Toynbee, and in organisations such as the National Secular Society and the European Humanist Association. They interpret political secularism to mean that religious beliefs and discourse should be excluded from the public sphere and/or politics and certainly from activities endorsed or funded by the state. Thus they argue, for example, for the disestablishment of the Church of England, the removal of the Anglican bishops from the House of Lords, the withdrawal of state support for faith schools, and the removal of symbols such as crucifixes from state schools (an Italian case recently having been lost in the European Court). With groups like Muslims, Sikhs and Hindus pressing to have some of these benefits extended to themselves (as to some extent has already happened in the case of the Jews), and religious groups more involved in the delivery of welfare and urban renewal, it is clear that this radical political secularism is not only a break with the inherited status quo secularism in most parts of Western Europe, with France being something of an exception (although see Bowen 2010), but is at odds with the current institutionalisation of religious pluralism.

Which of these will become dominant, or how these trends may develop and interact, is not clear. The critical issue of principle is not how but *whether* religious groups, especially those that are marginal and under-represented in public life, ought to be included. If Christians and Jews are already recognised by European states, why should this not be pluralised to include Muslims, Hindus, Sikhs and others? Similarly, if race, ethnicity and gender can be the basis of public policy and actions to redress under-representation in public institutions, why should groups who prioritise religious identity be excluded from these initiatives? The New Labour government took an inclusionary path by including 'religion and belief' as a strand within the new UK Equality and Human Rights Commission, as it is in the European Convention, on a par with all other strands in the Equality Act 2010. In the light of European historical experience of religion as a source of prejudice and conflict it is understandable that the presence of militant Muslims, not to mention networks of terrorists, is creating anxieties. It must, however,

be a matter of concern that this fear of Muslims is strengthening intolerant, exclusionary politics across Europe. The fact that some people are today
developing cultural Christianity and/or secularism as an ideology to oppose
Islam and its public recognition is a challenge both to pluralism and equality,
and thus to some of the bases of contemporary democracy. In the present
context of high levels of fear of, and hostility to, Muslims and Islam, this
threatens to create a long-term racialised-religious division in Europe.

Conclusion

It may be the case that all the attempted models of integration, especially
national models, are in crisis. They are certainly perceived as such. We can,
however, have a better sense of what the issues are and so what needs to be
done if we recognise that discourses of integration and multiculturalism are
exercises in conceptualising post-immigration difference and as such operate at three distinct levels: as an (implicit) understanding of the relationship
between individuals and groups in society; as a political response; and as
a vision of the whole in which difference is to be integrated. Depending
upon the understanding in question, certain political responses are more or
less possible. The sociological and political assumptions are thus mutually
dependent.

   In this chapter I have offered a framework in which four distinct political responses (assimilation, individualist-integration, cosmopolitanism
and multiculturalism) can be understood in terms of liberty, equality and
fraternity/unity, thereby bringing out what is of merit in each mode as well
as the ways in which it is deficient. They illuminate each other and each
successive position attempts to include what is thought to be missing from
the predecessor. Each position can in principle be attractive from different
perspectives: some ethnic minorities may wish to assimilate, some to have
the equal rights of integrated citizens, some to maintain the cultural differences of their group identities, and some to be free to choose cosmopolitan
mixed identities suiting the roles they take on in a more diverse society.
Equally, host communities may look on different groups of migrants in
all these different ways. Assimilation may be more appropriate in terms
of national language acquisition before naturalisation; individualist-
integration may provide the model for non-discrimination in the labour
market; yet multiculturalism may be the basis for supplementing electoral

representation (where minorities are underrepresented) and in creating new attitudes of inclusivity and in rethinking national identities. Each approach has a particular conception of equal citizenship but the value of each can only be realised if it is not imposed but is the preferred choice of minority individuals and groups, who, of course, being a 'multi', are bound to choose differently. Thus no singular model is likely to be suitable for all groups. To have a reasonable chance of integrating the maximum number of members of minorities, none of these political responses should be dismissed. Communitarian multiculturalism, then, has to be understood in terms of meeting the liberty, equality and unity requirements which the other modes of integration fall short on. Yet, perhaps the ultimate meaning of multiculturalism, let's call it multicultural citizenship, is not as one mode of integration but as the perspective which allows all four modes of integration their due.

Communitarian multiculturalism may currently be viewed as undesirable by European publics and policy-makers. Given how central Muslims have become to the prospects of integration on a number of fronts, it is unlikely that integration can be achieved without some element of this approach, which is being practised even by those politicians who are making anti-multiculturalist speeches. Perceptions of Muslims as groups, by themselves and by non-Muslim majorities, are hardening. The key question is whether Muslims are to be stigmatised as outsiders or recognised as integral to the polity. Finally, we must not overlook the third analytical level, which in many ways is not primarily about minorities but about the majority. The enlargement, hyphenation and internal pluralising of national identities is essential to an integration in which all citizens have not just rights but a sense of belonging to the whole, as well as to their own 'little platoon' (Burke 1982: 135).[18]

Acknowledgements

I would like to thank my colleagues in the British Academy 'New Paradigms in Public Policy' project, especially its chair, Peter Taylor-Gooby, and two anonymous referees for their comments on earlier drafts; and also to

---

[18] To be attached to the subdivision, to love the *little platoon* we belong to in ... we proceed towards a love to our country, and to mankind' (Burke 1982: 135).

Bhikhu Parekh, Albert Weale, Geoff Levey, Nasar Meer, Varun Uberoi, Jan Dobbernack and Aleksandra Lewicki for the same.

References

Akan, M. (2009) 'Laïcité and Multiculturalism: the Stasi Report in Context', *British Journal of Sociology* 60(2): 237–256.

Appiah, K.A. (1994) 'Identity, Authenticity, Survival: Multicultural Societies and Social Reproduction', in A. Gutmann (ed.) *Multiculturalism: Examining the Politics of Recognition* (Princeton, NJ: Princeton University Press), 149–164.

Bader, V. (2011) 'Associational Governance of Ethno-Religious Diversity in Europe. The Dutch Case', in R. Smith (ed.) *Citizenship, Borders, and Human Needs* (Philadelphia: Penn State University Press), 273–297.

Banting, K. and Kymlicka, W. (2008) *Multiculturalism and the Welfare State: Recognition and Redistribution in Contemporary Democracies* (Oxford: Oxford University Press).

Barry, B. (2001) *Culture and Equality: An Egalitarian Critique of Multiculturalism* (Cambridge: Polity).

Beattie, T. (2007) *The New Atheists: The Twilight of Reason and the War on Religion* (London: Darton Longman & Todd).

BHA (2012) 'BHA: Approved 2013 Free Schools Include First "Faith" Special, Alternative Provision Schools', 16 July [online], http://www.politics.co.uk/opinion-formers/bha-british-humanist-association/article/bha-approved-2013-free-schools-include-first-faith-special-a.

Bouchard, G. (2011) 'What is Interculturalism?', *McGill Law Journal* 56: 435–468.

Bouchard, G. and Taylor, C. (2008) *Building the Future: A Time for Reconciliation* (Quebec: Consultation Commission on Accommodation Practices Related to Cultural Differences).

Bowen, J.R. (2010) *Can Islam Be French? Pluralism and Pragmatism in a Secularist State* (Princeton, NJ: Princeton University Press).

Brett, J. and Moran A. (2011) 'Cosmopolitan Nationalism: Ordinary People Making Sense of Diversity', *Nations and Nationalism* 17: 188–206.

Brubaker, R. (1992) *Citizenship and Nationhood in France and Germany* (Cambridge, MA: Harvard University Press).

Burke, E. (1982) *Reflections on the Revolution in France* (Harmondsworth: Penguin).

Caldwell, C. (2009) *Reflections on the Revolution in Europe: Immigration, Islam and the West* (London: Allen Lane).

Cameron, D. (2011) *PM's Speech at Munich Security Conference* [online], http://www.number10.gov.uk/news/speeches-and-transcripts/2011/02/pms-speech-at-munich-security-conference-60293 (accessed on 29 March 2011).

Cantle, T. (2001) *Community Cohesion: A Report of the Independent Review Team* (London: Home Office).

Casanova, J. (2009) 'Immigration and the New Religious Pluralism: A European Union–United States Comparison', in G.B. Levey and T. Modood (eds) *Secularism, Religion and Multicultural Citizenship* (Cambridge: Cambridge University Press), 139–163.

Castells, M. (1997) *The Information Age: Economy, Society and Culture, Volume II: The Power of Identity* (Malden, MA and, Oxford: Blackwell).

Cesari, J. (2004) *When Islam and Democracy Meet: Muslims in Europe and in the United States* (New York and Basingstoke: Palgrave Macmillan).

Commission on Integration and Cohesion (2007) *Our Shared Future* (London: Department for Communities and Local Government).

Commission on Multi-Ethnic Britain (CMEB) (2000) *The Future of Multi-ethnic Britain: Report of the Commission the Future of Multi-Ethnic Britain* (London: Runnymede Trust).

Dale, A. (2008) 'Migration, Marriage and Employment Amongst Indian, Pakistani and Bangladeshi Residents in the UK', University of Manchester, CCSR Working Paper 2008–02.

Dawkins, R. (2006) *The God Delusion* (London: Bantam Press).

DIK (Deustsche Islam Konfrenz) (2009) 'Islamic Religious Education Trials in Schools', 16 February [online], http://www. deutsche-islam-Konferenz.de/nn_1875202/SubSites/DIK/EN/ReligionsunterrichtImame/ReligionBildung/Schulversuche/schulversuche-node.html?__nnn=true.

Emmerson, M. (2011) *Interculturalism: Europe and its Muslims, in Search of Sound Societal Models* (Brussels: Centre for European Policy Studies).

Esses, Victoria, Ulrich Wagner, Carina Wolf, Matthias Preiser and Christopher J. Wilbur (2006) 'Perceptions of National Identity and Attitudes Toward Immigrants and Immigration in Canada and Germany', *International Journal of Intercultural Relations* 30: 653–669.

Faas, D. (2010) *Negotiating Political Identities: Multiethnic Schools and Youth in Europe* (Farnham: Ashgate).

Fekete, L. (2008) *Integration, Islamophobia and Civil Rights in Europe* (London: Institute of Race Relations).

Fekete, L. (2011) 'Understanding the European-wide Assault on Multiculturalism', in H. Mahamdallie (ed.) *Defending Multiculturalism: A Guide for the Movement* (London: Bookmarks).

Fenton, S. and Mann R. (2011) '"Our Own People": Ethnic Majority Orientations to Nation and Country', in T. Modood and J. Salt (eds) *Global Migration, Ethnicity and Britishness* (Basingstoke: Palgrave Macmillan), 225–247.

Foner, N. and Alba, R. (2008) 'Immigrant Religion in the US and Western Europe: Bridge or Barrier to Inclusion?', *International Migration Review* 42: 360–392.

Fox, J. and Miller-Idriss, C. (2008) 'Everyday Nationhood', *Ethnicities* 8(4): 536–563.

Fox, J. E., Moroşanu, L. and Szilassy, E. (2012) 'The Racialization of the New European Migration to the UK', *Sociology* 46(4): 680–695.

Gallup (2009) *The Gallup Coexist Project: Muslim West Facts Project* [online], http://www.euro-islam.info/wp-content/uploads/pdfs/gallup_coexist_2009_interfaith_relations_uk_france_germany.pdf (accessed on 28 March 2011).

Gilroy, P. (2000) *Between Camps: Race, Identity and Nationalism at the End of the Colour Line* (London: Allen Lane).

Glazer, N. and Moynihan, D.P. (1963) *Beyond the Melting Pot: The Negroes, Puerto Ricans, Jews, Italians and Irish of New York City* (Cambridge, MA: The MIT Press and Harvard University Press).

Hall, S. (1992a) 'New Ethnicities', in J. Donald and A. Rattansi (eds) *'Race', Culture and Difference* (London: Sage), 252–259.

Hall, S. (1992b) 'The Question of Cultural Identity', in S. Hall and T. McGrew (eds) *Modernity and its Futures* (Cambridge: Polity Press), 218–240.

Hall, S. (1998) 'Aspiration and Attitude... Reflections on Black Britain in the Nineties', *New Formations* 33: 38–46.

Harris, S. (2004) *The End of Faith: Religion, Terror, and the Future of Reason* (New York: W.W. Norton & Company).

Hartmann, D. and Gerteis, J. (2005) 'Dealing with Diversity: Mapping Multiculturalism in Sociological Terms', *Sociological Theory* 23(2): 218–240.

Heath, A. and Roberts, J. (2008) *British Identity: Its Sources and Possible Implications for Civic Attitudes and Behaviour* [online], http://www.justice.gov.uk/docs/british-identity.pdf (accessed on 28 March 2011).

Heath, A.F. and Cheung S.Y. (2007) *Unequal Chances: Ethnic Minorities in Western Labour Markets* (Oxford: Oxford University Press for the British Academy).

Hitchens, C. (2007) *God is not Great: How Religion Poisons Everything* (New York: Twelve).

Jenkins, R. (1967) 'Racial Equality in Britain', in A. Lester (ed.) *Essays and Speeches by Roy Jenkins* (London: Collins).

Joppke, C. (2004) 'The Retreat of Multiculturalism in the Liberal State: Theory and Policy', *British Journal of Sociology* 55(2): 237–257.

Joppke, C. (2010) *Citizenship and Immigration* (Cambridge: Polity Books).

Kaufmann, E., Goujon, A., and Skirbekk, V. (2011) 'The End of Secularization in Europe? A Socio-demographic Perspective', *Sociology of Religion* 73(1): 69–91.

Keith, M. (2005) *After the Cosmopolitan? Multicultural Cities and the Future of Racism* (London and New York: Routledge).

Koopmans, R, P. Statham, M Giugni and F. Passy (2005) *Contested Citizenship: Immigration and Cultural Diversity in Europe* (Minneapolis: University of Minnesota Press).

Kymlicka, W. (1995) *Multicultural Citizenship* (Oxford: Oxford University Press).

Leonard, M. (1997) *Britain TM: Renewing Our Identity* (London: Demos).

Loury, G.C., Modood, T. and Teles, S.M. (eds) (2005) *Ethnicity, Social Mobility, and Public Policy: Comparing the USA and UK* (Cambridge: Cambridge University Press).

Lutz, W., Skirbekk, V. and Testa, M. (2007) 'The Low-fertility Trap Hypothesis: Forces That May Lead to Further Postponement and Fewer Births in Europe', *Vienna Yearbook of Population Research 2006* (Vienna: Vienna Institute of Demography), 167–192.

Malik, K. (2011) 'I Am Still a Critic of Multiculturalism, Honest', *Pandemonium* [online], http://kenanmalik.wordpress.com/2011/02/10/still-a-critic-of-multiculturalism (accessed on 30 March 2011).

Malik, M. (2010) *Anti-Muslim Prejudice: Past and Present* (London: Routledge).

McGhee, D. (2008) *The End of Multiculturalism? Terrorism, Integration and Human Rights* (Milton Keynes: Open University Press).

Meer, N. and Modood, T. (2009a) 'The Multicultural State We're In: Muslims, "Multiculture" and the "Civic re-balancing" of British Multiculturalism', *Political Studies* 57: 473–497.

Meer, N. and Modood, T. (2009b) 'Refutations of Racism in the "Muslim Question"', *Patterns of Prejudice* 43: 335–354.

Meer, N. and Modood T. (2012) 'How Does Interculturalism Contrast with Multiculturalism?', *Journal of Intercultural Studies* 33(2): 175–196.

Miles, R. (1989) *Racism* (London: Routledge).

Modood, T. (1990) 'British Asian Muslims and the Rushdie Affair', *The Poltical Quarterly* 61: 143–160.

Modood, T. (1994) 'Political Blackness and British Asians', *Sociology* 28: 859–876.

Modood, T. (1998) 'Anti-essentialism, Multiculturalism and the "Recognition" of Religious Minorities', *Journal of Political Philosophy* 6: 378–399.

Modood, T. (2005) *Multicultural Politics: Racism, Ethnicity and Muslims in Britain* (Edinburgh: Edinburgh University Press).

Modood, T. (2007) *Multiculturalism: A Civic Idea* (Cambridge: Polity).

Modood, T. (2012) 'Is There a Crisis of Secularism in Europe? 2011 Paul Hanly Furley Lecture, *Sociology of Religion* 73(2): 130–149.

Modood, T. (2013, forthcoming) 'Multiculturalism and Britishness: Provocations, Hostilities and Advances', in R. Garbaye and P. Schnapper (eds) *Managing Diversity and Multiculturalism in Britain* (Basingstoke: Palgrave).

Modood, T. and Dobbernack J. (2011) 'A Left Communitarianism? What about Multiculturalism?', *Soundings*, 48: 55–64.

Modood, T. and Kastoryano, R. (2006) 'Secularism and the Accommodation of Muslims in Europe', in T. Modood, A. Triandafyllidou and R. Zapato-Barrero (eds) *Multiculturalism, Muslims and Citizenship: A European Approach* (London: Routledge), 162–178.

Modood, T., Triandafyllidou, A. and Zapata-Barrero, R. (eds) (2006) *Multiculturalism, Muslims and Citizenship: A European Approach* (London: Routledge).

Mouritsen, P. (2006) 'The Particular Universalism of a Nordic Civic Nation: Common Values, State Religion and Islam in Danish Political Culture', in T. Modood, A. Triandafyllidou and R. Zapata-Barrero (eds) *Multiculturalism, Muslims and Citizenship: A European Approach* (London: Routledge), 70–93.

Mouritsen, P. (2008) 'Political Responses to Cultural Conflict: Reflections on the Ambiguities of the Civic Turn', in P. Mouritsen and K. E. Jørgensen (eds) *Constituting Communities: Political Solutions to Cultural Conflict* (London: Palgrave), 1–30.

Parekh, B.C. (2000) *Rethinking Multiculturalism: Cultural Diversity and Political Theory* (Cambridge, MA: Harvard University Press).

Park, A., Curtice, J., Thomson, K., Phillips, M., Clery, E. and Butt, S. (eds) (2010) *British Social Attitudes. The 26th Report* (London: Sage).

Peach, C. (2006) 'Islam, Ethnicity and South Asian Religions in the London 2001 Census', *Transactions of the Institute of British Geographers* 31: 353–370.

Peach, C. (2007) 'Muslim Population of Europe: A Brief Overview of Demographic Trends and Socioeconomic Integration, with Particular Reference to Britain', in S. Angenendt *et al.* (eds) *Muslim Integration: Challenging Conventional Wisdom in Europe and the United States* (Washington, DC: Center for Strategic and International Studies).

Pew Forum (2011) *The Future of the Global Muslim Population* [online], http://www.pewforum.org/the-future-of-the-global-muslim-population.aspx (accessed on 14 February 2013).

Pew Research Center (2006) *The Great Divide: How Westerners and Muslims View Each Other* [online], http://pewglobal.org/2006/06/22/the-great-divide-how-westerners-and-muslims-view-each-other (accessed on 28 March 2011).

Portes, A. and Zhou, M. (1993) 'The New Second Generation: Segmented Assimilation and its Variants', *The Annals of the American Academy of Political and Social Science* 530: 74–96.

Presseurop (2010) *Mutti Merkel handbags Multikulti* [online], http://www.presseurop.eu/en/content/article/364091-mutti-merkel-handbags-multikulti (accessed on 28 March 2011).

Sayyid, S. and Vakil, A. (eds) (2010) *Thinking Through Islamophobia* (London: C. Hurst & Co).

Schmitter Heisler, B. (1986) 'Immigrant Settlement and the Structure of Emergent Immigrant Communities in Western Europe', *The Annals of the American Academy of Political and Social Science* 485: 76–86.

Searchlight Educational Trust (2011) *Fear and Hope Project Report* [online], http://www.fearandhope.org.uk/project-report/ (accessed on 29 March 2011).

Sen, A. (2006) *Identity and Violence* (London: Allen Lane).

Simon, P. and Sala Pala, V. (2010) ' "We Are Not All Multiculturalists Yet": France Swings Between Hard Integration and Soft Anti-discrimination', in S. Vertovec and S. Wessendorf (eds) *The Multiculturalism Backlash: European Discourses, Policies and Practices* (Abingdon and New York, Routledge).

Soysal, Y. (1994) *Limits of Citizenship: Migrants and Post National Membership in Europe* (Chicago, Chicago University Press).

Taylor, C. (1994) 'The Politics of Recognition', in A. Gutmann (ed.) *Multiculturalism and 'the Politics of Recognition': An Essay* (Princeton, NJ: Princeton University Press), 25–73.

Taylor, C. (2009) 'Foreword: What is Secularism?', in G.B. Levey and T. Modood (eds) *Secularism, Religion and Multicultural Citizenship* (Cambridge: Cambridge University Press), xi–xxii.

The Local (2011) 'Islamic Studies Gain Foothold in State Schools', 22 December [online], http://www.thelocal.de/education/20111222-39667.html.

Triandafyllidou, A., Modood, T. and Meer, N. (eds) (2012) *European Multiculturalisms: Cultural, Religious and Ethnic Challenges* (Edinburgh: Edinburgh University Press).

The Royal Commission on Reform of the House of Lords (2000) *A House for the Future* (London, Cm 4534).

Travis, A. (2002) *The Need to Belong - But With a Strong Faith* [online] http://www.guardian.co.uk/uk/2002/jun/17/september11,religion1 (accessed on 2 June, 2011).

Vasagar, J. (2012) 'Third of New Free Schools are Religious', *The Guardian*, 13 July [online], http://www.newstatesman.com/uk-politics/2008/08/religious-state-secular.

Vertovec, S. (2007) 'Super-diversity and its Implications', *Ethnic and Racial Studies* 30: 1024–1054.

Vertovec, S. and Wessendorf, S. (eds) (2010) *The Multiculturalism Backlash: European Discourses, Policies and Practices* (Abingdon and New York: Routledge).

Voas, D. and Bruce, S. (2004) 'Research Note: The 2001 Census and Christian Identification in Britain', *Journal of Contemporary Religion* 19: 23–28.

Waldron, J. (1991) 'Minority Cultures and the Cosmopolitan Alternative', *University of Michigan Journal of Law Reform* 25: 751.

Weber, M. (1949) *The Methodology of the Social Sciences,* translated and edited by E.A. Shils and H.L. Finch (Basingstoke: Macmillan).

Weldon, F. (1989) *Sacred Cows* (London: Chatto & Windus).

Wright, M. and I. Bloemraad (2012) 'Is There a Trade-off between Multiculturalism and Socio-political Integration? Policy Regimes and Immigrant Incorporation in Comparative Perspective', *Perspectives on Politics* 10(1): 77–95.

6

Demographic futures

Addressing inequality and diversity among older people

PAT THANE

Current paradigms

The dominant paradigm in political and public discourse about the demographic future focuses on the rapid ageing of the population combined with shrinking numbers of younger people of working age due to falling fertility in the recent past. This demographic shift is said to be causing an unprecedented economic burden imposed by an apparently undifferentiated age group of 'old people' whose numbers are driving up the costs of health and social services and pensions, causing a crisis for the welfare state and, indeed, for the economy. Policy solutions to this perceived challenge include raising the universal state pension age in order to expand the workforce and cutting the costs of pensions.

There is a competing paradigm influential among social scientists and based on a substantial and growing body of research. This stresses the great diversity within an 'age group' said to extend from around age 60 to past 100, in terms of health, income, capacity for independent living, culture and experience. Its advocates assert, among other things, that the dominant paradigm overlooks this diversity, including the very considerable contributions of many older people to society and the economy, through paid and unpaid work, tax, spending and substantial gifts to younger people, which should be placed in the balance against the costs. The dominant paradigm also risks blaming ageing people for costs with other causes. For example the rising health care bill owes much to the costs of changing technology and salaries as well as to demographic change (Gill and Taylor

2012: 13); and the shrinking of private pensions is partly attributable to past management decisions and tax changes concerning pension funds, and to actuarial errors (Clark 2000).

Recent innovative research on the attitudes of older people themselves suggests that, to many of them, the second of these paradigms makes greater sense of their lives. Also that many feel alienated from a political system which persists in embracing the first paradigm, to a point at which some are even becoming reluctant to vote (despite this age group having previously been the most likely of all age groups to vote). They express exasperation at having policies preached at or imposed upon them based on abstract assumptions rather than upon assessing their actual conditions and experiences and listening to them (Bazalgette *et al.* 2011: 10[1]).

A third paradigm has recently gained some prominence, that of 'intergenerational inequity' between the so-called 'baby-boomers', born *c.*1945–*c.*1965, and younger people whose 'birthright' they are said to have 'pinched' by living too long and accumulating too many assets, especially in the value of their houses, which, it is claimed, they devote primarily to their own pleasures (Willetts 2010; Howker and Malik 2010). As we will see, this overlooks extreme socioeconomic inequalities *within* genera-tions, which are at least as great as those between generations, and also the extensive lifetime financial transfers from older to younger generations. This paradigm has produced no policy proposals clearly distinct from those arising from the first paradigm above. For a balanced assessment of the debate see Piachaud *et al.* (2009).

What is the evidence for and against the competing paradigms and what are the policy implications?

Evidence

Numbers

Between 1984 and 2009 the proportion of people aged over 65 in the UK population increased from 15 to 16 per cent according to the Office for National Statistics (ONS 2011a). This was lower than the *c.*19 per cent

[1] This is the first report of a project funded by the Economic and Social Research Council through the New Dynamics of Ageing Initiative. It was led at Brunel University by Philip Tew, Nick Hubble and Jago Morrison, who are co-authors of the report. The report is extensively referenced.

rise by 2011 projected by the Office of Population, Censuses and Surveys in 1985, for England and Wales (OPCS 1988), mainly because the birth rate rose from 2002, which was quite unforeseen in 1985 (see below). The fastest growth has been among people aged 85 and over, whose numbers more than doubled from 660,000 in 1984 to 1.4m in 2009 (ONS 2011a). The number of centenarians in UK more than quadrupled from 2,600 in 1981 to 11,600 in 2009 of whom 1,700 were males, and 9,900 females (ONS 2010a).

Life expectancy

Average life expectancy has risen steadily since official statistics of births and deaths were first comprehensively recorded in 1837 (in England and Wales, 1855 in Scotland, 1864 in Ireland). Statistics of life expectancy are often misunderstood and this can lead to overestimation of the speed and impact of demographic ageing. For example, in 2009, the Department of Health (DoH) stated in a green paper:

> In 1948 when the welfare state was founded, society looked very different. A boy born at that time could expect to live to 66; a boy born today, in 2009, can expect to live to over 78 (DoH 2009: 32).

This refers to life expectancy at birth, but death rates in the early years of life were higher in 1948 than has since become the norm. High infant death rates of course reduce average life expectancy at *birth* across the whole population. A man who reached age 65 in 1948, as very many did, could expect, on average, to live to 78 (HC Health Committee 2010: 38–39). Survivors of the hazardous early years of life tended, throughout history, to be hardy and capable of long life (Thane 2000: 19–27). The larger numbers of women who survived childhood could expect to live still longer. In most times and places through history, so far as we can tell, women have tended to outlive men (Thane 2000: 21–24).

From 1948 to 2009, male life expectancy at age 65 rose by 4.6 years, but male life expectancy at birth rose by 12 years. This was due to a more dramatic fall in deaths at earlier than at later ages, in a period of rising standards of living and of medical care. What occurred is sometimes described as a 'rectangularisation (or a 'compression') of mortality', that is, the concentration of deaths into an increasingly narrow set of older age bands (e.g. Fries 1980: 130–135; Gill and Taylor 2012). This occurred in the UK and other developed countries over the past century, especially the past 60 years, and was a major change compared with the whole of previous history when deaths were more evenly spread across the life cycle. This has obvious implications for the age distribution of health care costs.

Average life expectancy at birth in 1981 was 76 for men, 80.4 for women; in 2007–9, 77.7 for men, 81.9 for women—the highest on record and a slight narrowing of the life expectancy advantage of women. In 1984 there were 156 women aged 65 and over for every 100 men of the same age, 129/100 in 2009. Based on 2007–9 mortality rates, a man aged 65 could expect to live another 17.6 years, a woman aged 65, 20.2 years, compared with about 14 and 18 years respectively in 1980 (Pensions Commission 2004: 3).

There are significant variations in life expectancy within the UK. Life expectancy at birth in England in 2007–9 was 78 for males, 82.1 for females; in Scotland it was the lowest in the four countries, at 75.3 and 80.1 respectively. There were similar gaps in life expectancy at age 65. Within each country of the UK there were regional differences. These were closely related to socioeconomic status (see below) and to patterns of internal migration e.g., the retirement of better-off older people to seaside resorts, especially in the south of England and East Anglia and to certain rural areas (ONS 2010b: 4–5). Differences in life expectancy among ethnic groups cannot be established from national statistics because birth certificates do not record ethnicity, but differences certainly exist (see below).

The impact of increasing life expectancy since c.1945 is currently all the greater because it coincided with the rising birth rates of the period from the Second World War to the mid-1960s, the so-called 'baby boom'. Since this was followed by a 35-year birth-rate decline, it created a 'bulge' of people who are now growing older and living longer than any previous generation. These will continue to enter 'old age'—defined as from age 65—until 2030. They will be followed by a smaller 35-year cohort, the birth rate decline ('baby-bust'?) generation, born between the later 1960s and 2002. Since 2002 birth rates have risen, though there was a slight fall in 2009 (see below, ONS 2011b). It is widely assumed that life expectancy will continue to rise for the foreseeable future, though, as we will see, the rate, and indeed the certainty, of increase is debated.

Expectation of healthy or 'disability free' life

This is equally, or more, important to assess. It is often assumed that because the number of older people is growing and they are living to later ages, the numbers needing health care must grow more or less commensurately, creating a crisis for health and social care. It is clear that many more people are remaining fit and active to later ages compared with the 1940s–60s and all previous times, though comparable data over long periods is hard to find. According to the Office of National Statistics (ONS), life expectancy (LE) increased faster than healthy life expectancy (HLE, expected years of life in good, or fairly good, health) and disability free life expectancy (DFLE, expected years of life without a limiting illness or disability), between 1981 and 2006 (Table 6.1).

On average, the proportion of life spent in good health fell between 1981 and 2006, as the population aged, but only slightly. However, as ONS points out, national averages hide significant socioeconomic differences. Currently, people living in the most advantaged fifth of the population can expect to spend 10 per cent more of their lives in favourable health than the most disadvantaged fifth (ONS 2010b: 4).

A government-commissioned report, published in February 2010, chaired by the distinguished epidemiologist, Sir Michael Marmot, heading a team of experienced social and medical scientists, *Fair Society, Healthy Lives*, rigorously reviewed the available evidence on health related to social inequalities.[2] The report concluded that the poorest people in the UK die on average seven years earlier than the richest. The gap in 'disease free life expectancy' is 17 years, which the report describes as 'an

Table 6.1   LE, HLE, DFLE for males and females at birth and age 65, GB 1981 and 2006

	Year	Males			Females		
		LE	HLE	DFLE	LE	HLE	DFLE
At birth	1981	70.9	64.4	58.1	76.8	66.7	60.8
	2006	77.2	68.5	62.6	81.5	70.5	63.8
At 65	1981	13	9.9	7.6	16.9	11.99	8.5
	2006	17.2	12.8	10	19.9	14.5	10.6

Source: ONS (2010a: 3).

[2] It reviewed and cited extensively the available social science and medical evidence assisted by a large number of experts in relevant fields.

avoidable difference which is unacceptable and unfair'. Men in Kensington and Chelsea have a life expectancy at birth of 88 years; men in Tottenham can expect 71 years, and are more likely to suffer from conditions related to inadequate diets, lack of exercise, smoking, low pay and job insecurity. The gap widened in the ten years preceding the study, despite increased spending on health services, by 2 per cent among men and 11 per cent among women (Marmot 2010: 45–55).

Inequalities earlier in life, indeed from the very beginning of life, affect health standards in later life, perpetuated by continuing inequalities in income and living conditions after retirement (Glaser *et al.* 2009a and b). In the UK, average gross pensioner incomes increased by 44 per cent in real terms between 1994/5 and 2008/9, ahead of the growth in average earnings of the whole population. But the averages conceal wide variations. The highest fifth of pensioner couples in 2006–9 had median net incomes 3.8 times those in the lowest fifth; the comparable figure for single pensioners was 3.1. On average, older pensioners have lower incomes than younger, and females lower incomes than males. In 2008/9, couples where the household head was aged 75 or above had an average gross income of £469 per week compared with £602 for those under 75; single males aged 75 and over grossed on average £301 per week compared with £308 per week for those under 75; single females over 75 grossed £250 per week compared with £280 for females under 75. In 2008/9 an estimated 1.8m pensioners lived in poverty, according to the most commonly used official measure: less than 60 per cent of equivalised median income after housing costs, a decline from an estimated 2.8 million in 1999/2000 (ONS 2010b: 7–8). The decline was due mainly to the introduction of the Minimum Income Guarantee, later named the Pension Credit in 1999. This was more generous than any previous means-tested supplement to the pension. However, as with most means-tested benefits, around 20 per cent of suitably qualified pensioners have consistently failed to claim and remain in poverty (Ginn 2006: 92).

The proposed universal state pension appears likely to improve the incomes of some poorer pensioners if it is implemented at the level suggested in the Budget of March 2012—'about' £140 per week—though large inequalities will remain and it will not, apparently, apply to existing pensioners or to anyone before 2016. At the time of the 2012 Budget, the final details were still to come.

The inequalities faced by minority groups at all ages also continue into later life and increase their difficulties. The older minority ethnic population is large and growing and they are likely to be among the poorest older people. In particular, those from the Bangladeshi and Pakistani communities, who are among the poorest at all ages, will fall into this group. Members of minority groups may not qualify for full state pensions if they have not lived in the UK throughout their working lives. If they are female, they may not have been in paid employment and are likely to have low state pensions and no, or very low, occupational pensions. Members of minority ethnic groups, especially members of South Asian communities, are likely to suffer relatively poor health, often due to poverty in earlier life in their countries of birth, perpetuated by conditions in the UK. They are more likely than others to live in poor housing. English may not be their first language, especially among women, which can cause problems in accessing health and social services. Health and social care services may not recognise their different cultural and religious needs. The Policy Research Institute reported in 2005:

> Black and minority ethnic elders do not enjoy the same quality of life as their peers, continue to have many unmet needs, from care to quality of life issues, which reduce their potential for participation, have witnessed changing family structures and are growing old in a country that many of them thought they would not remain in after their 'working period'. These experiences are in addition to a lifetime where discrimination and disadvantage have often been an everyday part of their experience (ODPM 2006: 101–2; for a survey of more recent research see EHRC 2010).

I have found no information on the experience of older members of the most marginalised minority group of all: Gypsies and Travellers.

Older lesbian, gay, bisexual, transsexual and transgender (LGBT) people also report negative responses and a lack of recognition of same-sex relationships in hospitals, care homes and from home-carers. Many of them suffer weakened health in later life due to HIV infection (Ward *et al.* 2011).

Future trends in HLE and DFLE are hard to predict. They will depend on whether the multiple lifetime inequalities described above are diminished or exacerbated; on advances in medical knowledge and its application— for example, in the treatment of dementia; in the further development of preventive health education, to encourage fitness at all ages. Current high levels of obesity at all ages, and of associated diseases such as diabetes, may slow or even reverse current trends towards better health at later ages, though they may not significantly affect life expectancy. Various forms of dementia may afflict the growing numbers of people who survive other hazards to reach later life. The dementia research community is not optimistic of a cure in the next 15 years, but are hopeful that they can develop understanding and treatments which will modify and slow its effects. Opinion on all of these issues is uncertain and contested. More certainly, more people with long-term mental and physical disabilities are now living to later ages and their needs in later life must be taken into account (HC Health Committee 2010: Ev. 618[3]).

Housing

The housing conditions of older people both exemplify and reinforce inequalities. Older women are more likely than older men to live alone and the percentage increases with advancing age, due to their longer life expectancy. In 2008 in Great Britain, 30 per cent of women aged 65–74 lived alone compared with 20 per cent of men of this age group; among those aged 75 and over the proportions living alone were 63 and 35 per cent respectively. 79 per cent of people aged 50–64 lived in owner-occupied households in 2008, compared to 61 per cent of those aged 85 and over. Particularly among the older age group, homes are more likely to be in poor repair than those of younger home-owners. Sixteen per cent of 50–64 year olds and 33 per cent of people over 84 live in social rented housing (ONS 2010b: 5–6). There is urgent need for adaptation of existing housing and provision of more housing designed to enable older people to live as independently as possible while taking account of their wishes. Many of them wish not to live in older persons 'ghettoes' but in contact with people of all ages and with space to accommodate visiting relatives and friends (Bazalgette *et al.* 2011: 135–136; HAPPI 2009.)

Age discrimination

Age discrimination in the NHS and social care services—often unconscious and taken-for-granted on the part of practitioners and administrators—also undermines the health of older people in the UK. Among other evidence, a

---

[3] This report references extensively the mass of relevant research in these fields.

survey by the Royal College of Surgeons and AgeUK reported in 2012 that many older people are denied vital surgery for conditions including cancer, hernia repairs and joint replacement on grounds of chronological age without regard to their actual physical condition or 'biological age' (AgeUK and Royal College of Surgeons 2012). Such denials shortsightedly restrict the capacity of many older people to be active and independent if their health conditions were remedied, increasing their demands on costly social and health care. Women over 70 had markedly poorer access to investigation and treatment for breast cancer than younger women, though they were more likely to suffer the disease. Age discrimination in health and social care became illegal under the Equality Act 2010, implemented in 2012. The coalition government declared that this will be observed, and that 'the NHS must never discriminate based on age' (DoH 2011).

Birth rates

To understand what is happening to the UK age structure, and the implications, we need to take account of birth and migration as well as death, life and health expectancy rates. The proportion of older people in the population depends not only on survival rates to old age but also on fertility and the ratio of births to deaths and life expectancy. Older people are now a higher proportion of the population than at any time in the past, both because more people are living longer than ever before and also because the fertility rate declined from the later 1960s to the lowest level since the early 1930s, which was the lowest level then ever recorded.

The report of the Pensions Commission, chaired by Adair Turner, *Pensions: challenges and choices* (2004), assumed that the Total Fertility Rate (TFR) for England and Wales would flatline from 2000 to 2050 at the low level of 1.7/1.75, since 'no significant increase has been observed in any developed country since birth rates came down in the 1970s and 80s and the most reasonable assumption is that only a small recovery [to 1.75] will occur' (Pensions Commission 2004: 4–5). The Commission was convinced that the reversal from the 1940s of the comparable decline before the Second World War was 'unlikely' to be repeated (Pensions Commission 2004: 130). In reality, the TFR fell still further to 1.63 in 2001, then, contrary to the report's assumptions (which were widely shared), started to rise, reaching 1.96 in 2008, still below the replacement rate (that is, the rate necessary for total births to compensate for total deaths) of 2.07, but much closer. The TFR fell slightly in 2009 to 1.94, but it was still at its highest since 1973 (ONS 2010b, 2011b). Currently, fertility is rising also in some other European countries, including Sweden, France and Belgium, though at lower rates than in the UK in these three countries (HM Treasury 2009: 35–36). In the UK, the increase appears to be led by higher fertility among women in their later 30s and 40s, though births to women in their twenties also rose 2002–8, before declining slightly in 2009 (ONS 2011b). Births to immigrants have also contributed (ONS 2011a). Fertility levels are notoriously difficult to predict, as the unanticipated turnaround from 2002 (like the equally unanticipated one of the 1940s) suggests.

Patterns of migration

Immigration to UK by younger people from the late 1940s added to the post-war bulge in younger age groups. Continuing immigration helps reduce the proportion of older people in the population, at least in the short run, since most immigrants are in younger age groups. Net immigration grew in the period 1997–2007. In the past it has fallen during recessions and ONS statistics indicated a fall of 70,000 in 2008 (ONS 2009). Over the longer run, many of the first generation of immigrants are among the growing numbers of older people at present. Another important and unpredictable variable is the number of immigrants who do or do not stay in the UK for their lifetimes.

Emigration by older people, either those who immigrated when younger returning to their country of origin, or British-born people retiring abroad, also affects age structure, though statistics are elusive. Emigration of British-born people may have declined as the pound, and hence the value of their pensions overseas, has fallen relative to other currencies such as the euro. Older British émigrés tend to return to the UK at later ages to be close to family when they are widowed or become infirm (King et al. 2000).

Projections of future birth, death and migration rates are frequently quoted in discussions of demographic futures. This is unavoidable. Seeking to assess the future shape of the population is essential for planning. But population projections should always be read critically, because future patterns are uncertain, as we have seen when discussing fertility trends. As a Treasury report put it in 2009:

Some aspects of demographic change are much harder to predict than others. Future developments in life expectancy and even more in fertility and net migration are all unknown today and therefore extremely difficult to project with any certainty. In contrast, the ageing of past baby boom generations is more certain as the key events (past fluctuations in birth rates) have already taken place and the relevant people are already born. Given the uncertainties around future developments, it is important to interpret population projections with great caution, and where possible to consider a range of different outcomes that allows for variations in the underlying assumptions (HM Treasury 2009: 11).

Caution is important because failure in the recent past to recognise that births can go up as well as down led to planning failures. During the high birth-rate boom of the 1940s–60s it was assumed by politicians and their advisers that there would be no return to low birth rates, so there was no reason to remember the acute concern about the low birth rate and ageing population from the 1920s to 1940s. Consequently, also forgotten was the extensive research and debate of that period on realistic means to extend the working lives of older people in order to redress the balance of costs across age groups (Thane 1990: 283–305). Similarly, when lower birth rates did return from the late 1960s, it was wrongly assumed that this was a reversion to a long-run trend following a blip in the 'baby-boom' years which would not be reversed. The Turner report commented that:

The baby boom is not … the cause of the high dependency ratio [which the report projected] from 2030 onwards. Instead … because the baby-boom allowed us to ignore long-term realities, we must now in the next 30 years make adjustments to public policy and to private retirement and savings behaviour which we should ideally have started to make over the last several decades. (Pensions Commission 2004: 10)

This was correct, but the report went on to make the similar error of assuming that the birth rate would not rise again, and when it rose, from 2002, policy-makers were unprepared.

The ONS has learned some lessons from recent demographic history and now cautiously produces a range of population projections based on different combinations of assumptions about future developments in life expectancy, fertility and net migration (ONS 2009), though these complexities are not always picked up in public debate. The first paradigm, described above, assumes greater certainty about the demographic future than is justified by experience or by recent official statistics.

Older people's inputs to economy and society and intergenerational equity

A prominent assumption of paradigms one and three above, which is challenged by paradigm two, and by a great deal of evidence, is that 'old people' are takers from, not contributors to, society and economy; that they are dependent, costly burdens on the active, younger workforce.

To assess whether or not this is so we need, firstly, to examine how the employment patterns of older people have changed over time. Ages at retirement fell for some years but have recently risen. The average male retirement age in the UK fell from 67.2 in 1950 to 64.6 in 1980 and 63.1 in 1990. There were similar falls elsewhere in Europe (Kohli *et al.* 1991). It then rose to 63.8 in 2004 and 64.5 in 2011. The average female retirement age also rose slightly from 61.2 in 2004 to 62 in 2009, despite their state pension age remaining at 60 (though it was in process of rising for younger women). Following an historically unprecedented general shift to earlier retirement, more people are now staying at work to later ages (Pensions Commission 2004: 41–4).

In the 1950s and 1960s, the key change among men was the falling numbers in employment aged 65–69, from 48 to 30 per cent between 1952 and 1971. From the mid-1970s to the mid-1990s, employment of men aged 50–64, fell from 88 per cent in 1973 to 63 per cent in 1995. This was concentrated in two phases: the early 1980s saw a major decline in the male manufacturing workforce, many of whom, especially older men, never re-entered employment; in the early 1990s there were further manufacturing job losses but, more significantly, redundancies and early retirements in financial and other areas of white-collar employment. Older, better-paid managers were laid off with generous retirement packages from pension funds which were then in significant surplus. These are a source of popular images of prosperous golden retirees on permanent vacation in the sun (Pensions Commission 2004: 34).

By the early 2000s, the early retirement of men aged 55–59 was concentrated in the lowest and the highest wealth quintiles, with a large percentage of those in the lowest two describing themselves as sick or unemployed, that is, not reconciled to retirement but forced into it. Most of the richest were content to describe themselves as 'retired'. The picture for women aged 55–59 was similar but with higher levels of inactivity across all wealth quintiles (Pension Commission 2004: 27–55).

There was a turnaround in trends in retirement from the mid-1990s due partly to economic recovery leading to fewer redundancies and some re-entry to employment by people in their 50s. Also, companies were less willing to provide generous pension packages as the surpluses in their pension funds dwindled. Some employers began to recognise that they had lost valuable skills by paying off experienced senior workers, and that the potential shortage of younger workers due to the fall in the birth rate required them to keep older workers, even to raise retirement ages. They became somewhat more willing to employ older workers. Labour governments between 1997 and 2010 actively encouraged and advised over-50s into work because they thought it desirable in view of demographic change and as a means to cut the cost of welfare benefits. Furthermore they were under growing pressure from older people themselves, who were organising and campaigning to remain in employment, such as through the Third Age Employment Network (TAEN), now the Age and Employment Network.

The economic crisis from 2008 did not, by 2011, increase the numbers of older unemployed people as previous recessions had done. At the end of January 2011, 900,000 people over 65 were in work, the largest number since 1992. Over the previous three months, the number of over-65s in work increased by 25,000 men and 31,000 women. In 2010, 11.7 per cent of men aged 65 or over were in work compared with 10 per cent in 2008, and the rate among women of the same age grew from 12.3 to 13.5 per cent (ONS 2011c). The rise had much to do with deteriorating private sector pensions and, especially from 2008, falling interest rates on savings, combined with the, very gradual, impact of age discrimination legislation and, as suggested above, the growing recognition by some employers of the value of older workers and their need for them. Whether this trend will continue as the public sector continues to contract remains to be seen. It may be influenced by the fact that until April 2011 employers could insist on retirement at 65 (as many did) even if the worker asked to stay on (as many did). In April 2011 employers lost this right.

Older people make a growing contribution to the economy through paid work. Also important, and overlooked, are their unpaid contributions to society and the economy. A survey in 2011 revealed that people over 65 are a substantial proportion of volunteers, both formally, through voluntary organisations (about 30 per cent of over 60s volunteer regularly) and informally, by helping relatives, friends and neighbours, many of them also retired (WRVS 2011[4]). Growing numbers work with overseas charities as nurses, doctors, teachers, giving training in office skills and how to start businesses, improving water supplies, with skills and experience to offer which is vastly greater than that of many younger people. For example, the large international NGO, Voluntary Service Overseas (VSO), was set up in 1956 to provide opportunities for young people to volunteer in poorer countries for a year or so after leaving university. Now, an important resource is the growing number of fit, active retired people. In 2008 28 per cent of VSO volunteers were aged 50 or above, compared with 3 per cent twenty years before.[5]

In 2011, 65 per cent of people over 65 regularly helped elderly neighbours and they were the most likely age group to do so: 30 per cent helped neighbours aged under 65; 49 per cent looked after young children, including grandchildren. The value of their formal volunteering was estimated at £10 billion pa saved to public social services; that of informal social care at £34 billion (WRVS 2011). Increasing numbers of grandparents help younger people in employment by caring for grandchildren, sometimes retiring from paid work themselves to do so. One in 3 working mothers rely on grandparents for child care, 1 in 4 of all working families. Forty-three per cent of children under 5 whose mothers are employed are looked after by grandparents; 42 per cent aged 5–10, after school, when sick and in school holidays. The value of this child care contribution is estimated at £3.9 billion. Four in 10 parents say they are more likely to turn to grandparents for help with child care during recessions, such as that from 2008, to save money and due to the growing costs and falling numbers of nursery places, largely outcomes of government cuts in public spending from 2010. Grandparental care is most common in poorer families but not exclusive to them (Griggs 2010). Forty per cent of grandparental care is provided by grandfathers (Daycare Trust 2011; 25). Whether such care is more or less common than in the past we do not know because there are no reliable, long-run statistics. It is certainly not new.

---

[4] This survey was carried out for WRVS by independent economists, SQW. The report was peer reviewed by Professor Tom Kirkwood, Director of the Institute for Ageing and Health, Newcastle University and Robert McNabb, Professor of Economics, Cardiff Business School.

[5] Personal communication from CEO of VSO, 2010.

Far from lavishing their money on their own pleasures, as much rhetoric about 'intergenerational inequity' would have it, 31 per cent of grandparents save in order to to help grandchildren buy a home; 16 per cent in their 60s and one-third in their 70s give financial support to grandchildren and, increasingly in the recession, to their children (Grundy 2005: 233–255; GrandparentsPlus 2011). It is only when grandparents reach age 75 or older that they are more likely to receive than to give financial and practical help to younger people (Glaser *et al.*, 2010). Nor is this new: historically, older people have been givers as well as receivers of care and financial help (Thane 2000: 489–93).

Over-65s are estimated to make a net contribution to the UK economy, after deduction of the costs of pensions, welfare and health care costs, of £40 billion through tax payments, spending power, donations to charities (£10 million per annum) and volunteering (WRVS 2011). They are much less of a 'burden', dragging down the welfare state, than conventional policy paradigms would have it.

This evidence seriously challenges the 'intergenerational inequity' paradigm. There is a danger that rhetoric about generational inequality diverts attention from wider socioeconomic inequalities and their consequences. The generation now retiring has not always been so fortunate compared with younger people. Even in the 1960s fewer than 4 per cent of school-leavers went to university and a very high proportion of people left school at 15 without qualifications. University education was free, but few benefitted. Now more than 40 per cent stay in full-time education to approximately age 21, then rarely go on to lives of hard manual labour. Many, though not all, older people have gained from rising house prices in recent decades, but, as we have seen, it should not be assumed that they are all spending the gains on self-indulgence. The issues involved in the intergenerational equity debate are too many and too complex to be fully reviewed here. For a fuller, but still incomplete discussion see Piachaud *et al.* (2009).

The generations do not live in separate boxes, but in families and communities, where there is much mutual support across the generations, contrary to popular assumptions that the generations have no time for one another in the modern, runaway, mobile world. There is a widespread tendency to overestimate the extent of family support for older people in 'the past' and to underestimate it in the present (Thane 2000: 119–146,

287–307, 407–36, 480–481; McCrae 1999, esp. 199–262). There are serious problems such as the acute shortage of affordable housing for people of all ages. But these are not best tackled by blaming the older generation, who did not on the whole consciously cause, or always welcome, rising house values. Rather, successive governments failed to control house prices or to expand building of affordable housing. Demographic change is too often given the burden of blame for problems with other sources.

Occupational pensions

The debate about the cost and welfare implications of the ageing society would be helped by greater transparency about the reasons for cuts in public and private sector occupational pensions in recent years. It is often asserted that the current 'burden' of public sector pensions is due entirely to the ageing population living longer on their pensions. But it is also due to the declining investment income of pension funds. The financial crisis exacerbated this decline, but the causes go back further. Many private pension schemes were cut back in the 1990s, allegedly due to population ageing leading to increased costs. In reality, many private sector employers—and also some public sector employers—took 'pension holidays', cutting employer contributions to pension funds when investment returns were high in the 1980s. Instead they could have built up the funds against the highly predictable likelihood that shares would go down as well as up. They were encouraged at the time by the then Chancellor of the Exchequer, Nigel Lawson. The situation was made worse by persistent underestimation by actuaries of rising life expectancy. The outcome has been problematic for the pension funds. There is no space available for a detailed assessment of these complex issues, but see Clark (2000), Cutler and Waine (2010 and 2011) and the references they cite. Again, demographic ageing alone does not explain every problem in public or private welfare systems.

Policy futures

What policy implications follow from the evidence reviewed above?

Fertility

A central policy question is whether government should consider policies to stabilise the birth rate at replacement level for a sustained period.

There are environmental reasons for not seeking further to expand population size. And there are very few examples, nationally or internationally, at any time, of government policies successfully influencing fertility. Measures to encourage women to stay out of the workforce and have more children would be seriously retrogressive after decades of modest advance towards gender equality and it is highly doubtful that many women would respond positively, or that this is economically desirable if we do indeed face a shortage of younger workers. Much improved child care provision, combined with child benefits, was successful in raising the French birth rate in the twentieth century and it did not fall in the later twentieth century commensurately with that in other European countries (Quine 1996: 52–88). Improved child care, combined with extended, adequately funded, parental leave, enabling fathers as well as mothers to take a substantial role in child-rearing, could have positive effects in preventing a future decline in the birth-rate, if that is thought desirable.

Immigration
Encouraging immigration by younger people to maintain population 'balance' raises similar concerns about the environment and about taking workers from poorer countries. If it is favoured, positive measures both to assist immigration and improve reception of immigrants in the UK are possible, though they go against the grain of current government policy.

However, Treasury forecasts suggest that concerns about a shrinking younger workforce are not acute in the near future, hence there is no immediate need to consider measures to increase fertility or immigration. It stated in 2009:

> The workforce in the UK is likely to continue growing, as the number of people of working age continues to grow. In addition ... trends in labour participation will also affect total employment. For example it is likely that participation of females will continue to increase and labour participation among older workers is likely to continue increasing as healthy life expectancy improves (HM Treasury 2009: 34).

This optimistic forecast was grounded in analysis of a range of projected outcomes based on high and low fertility and high and low life expectancy scenarios to 2059. It challenges the gloomy first and third policy paradigms described above.

Extending healthy life expectancy

The Treasury forecast was partly based on the likelihood that more older people would remain at work. As discussed above, there is much to be said for evaluating more positively than at present the current and potential contributions of many older people to the economy and to society, and seeking to maximise these contributions. Also, as we have seen, more people are remaining in employment to later ages. Measures seeking to extend expectation of healthy life would be a useful first step in encouraging even more to do so. It is reasonable to expect the general trend towards staying healthy and active to later ages to continue. But, to ensure real improvement, socioeconomic, ethnic and other cultural inequalities need to be eliminated, or at least substantially reduced, along with age discrimination in health and social care. Equality legislation is making a start in reducing some inequalities and discrimination but, obviously, it must be implemented effectively from very early life, which is when inequalities originate. However there are few signs at present of effective early interventions. On the contrary, the OECD reported in April 2011 that progress in the reduction of child poverty in UK, visible under the last government, had stalled, because of cuts by the coalition government to schemes such as Child Benefit and early years services such as Sure Start (OECD 2011).

Further encouragement, training and accessible facilities can help all age groups improve their diets, increase exercise and generally promote healthier lifestyles. Past experience suggests that this can work: for example, measures to dissuade people from smoking and to persuade them to exercise and to eat with care appear to have reduced the incidence of heart disease and some other illnesses. But cuts to local authority budgets are currently reducing preventive measures already in place, such as free access for older people to swimming pools and support for exercise classes. There is also need for continued research into serious causes of ill-health at later ages—for example, Alzheimer's—and their alleviation and cure. Research into the health conditions particularly afflicting older people, like care for these conditions, was too often marginalised in the recent past (MRC 1994).

Raising pension and retirement ages

This, as the government currently plans it, can potentially reduce pension costs and increase the workforce, but is not without problems. The long-run trend of increasing Healthy Life Expectancy suggests that this is realistic, but only up to a point. Current pension/retirement ages of 60/65 became universal in UK after the Second World War. The Civil Service pension age was set at 60 in the 1850s, and then adopted elsewhere in the public and private sectors. State pension ages were set at 60 for women (currently rising to 65) in 1940 and at 65 for all men in 1946. At that time most people reaching those ages had left school at ages 13/14 and led long, often hard, working lives, often on low incomes, with no National Health Service. It was only after the Second World War that retirement at the state pension age began to be normal for most of the workforce. Previously poorer people worked until they dropped and the better-off could choose when to retire (Thane 2000, esp. 385–406). Living standards, health care and conditions of work have since been transformed, though great inequalities remain. As we have seen, average fitness at age 65 has risen significantly since the 1940s, not to mention the 1850s. The case for raising the state pension/retirement age seems clear. The current government, like its predecessor, proposes to raise the minimum state pension age, as the Pensions Commission recommended, though exactly to what age, and when, is unclear at the time of writing. A target age of 68 was proposed by the Labour government.

But already significant numbers of people are not fit to work even to 65. About 20 per cent retire for health reasons before reaching the state pension age. The major cause of economic inactivity in the age group 50–65 is ill-health or disability, primarily among men and low earners. Nearly half (47.4 per cent) of incapacity benefit claimants are in this age range (Marmot 2010; McNair, 2011; DWP 2011 Even fewer stay fit to 68. In *Fair society, healthy lives*, Sir Michael Marmot points out that 'Three-quarters of the country do not have disability-free life expectancy [at 68]' (Marmot 2010: 18). There is a real danger that if we move in the next few years from an inflexible retirement/pension age of 65 to an inflexible later age many people, mostly the poorest, will be further disadvantaged. If they lose their present right to a state pension at age 60/65, under current arrangements, they will be forced onto the alternative, discretionary Employment Support Allowance (ESA, before 2008, Incapacity Benefit). ESA is currently lower than the state pension, relatively stigmatised and recipients are required to undergo stringent fitness for work tests which can lead to reductions in benefit and considerable stress. Alternatively, older workers may feel pressured to struggle on in any employment they can find until they reach the higher pension age—a return to the common experience of poor people through the centuries, which is hardly desirable.

A fairer option, better suited to the actual needs and capacities of many older people, is a flexible retirement/pension age, which recognises the diversity of the older age group. This is not a new, or unrealistic, idea. In his influential wartime report, *Social insurance and allied services* (1942), William Beveridge recommended just this: a flexible retirement age, designed to keep the labour force in balance between younger and older workers, to be achieved by paying higher pensions to those who felt able to defer retirement. Almost 70 years ago Beveridge knew that people become physically unfit at diverse ages, but it was not a new idea even in 1942. The first state pensions in the world, introduced in Germany by Bismarck in 1889, were Disability and Old Age Pensions paid at any age, whether 50 or 80, at which the contributor was judged permanently unfit for work (Hennock 2007).

Beveridge's recommendation arose from his concern about the combination of the falling birth rate with increasing life expectancy, and its impact on the labour market. He believed that the improved pensions he proposed would avert the danger that fit older people might withdraw from the workforce, but his proposal for a flexible retirement age was accepted only minimally by the post-war Labour government. The additional pensions for late retirees were too small to have a noticeable impact and, as Beveridge foretold, retirement at the state pension age spread as never before. This is not the first, nor the last, example of politicians failing to listen to expert advice from a social scientist. If Beveridge's recommendations had been followed in full, we might already have a more flexible retirement/pension system better suited to contemporary needs, higher pensions on which people could survive without means-tested supplements and lesser income inequalities in later life, as Beveridge also intended (Beveridge, 1942; Harris 2006: 27–38). It must surely be possible in the twenty-first century to invent an adequate pension payable at flexible ages.

Enabling those who can to stay in the workforce to later ages requires the government to persuade employers and society in general that older people *can* be economically useful, are not past learning new skills, can be retrained, have valuable experience and may even be more reliable than younger workers. In addition, the working environment can be adapted to maximise the work capacities of older people. There has long been strong evidence for all of this (Munnell and Sass 2008; Myerson 2010).

The recent increase in employment in later life suggests that employers may be somewhat more willing to recognise the value of older workers than in the past. But we still need more positive efforts to combat pervasive age discrimination in the workplace and to ensure that physically and mentally fit older workers have access to training. Labour made a start on this while in government, through its New Deal 50+ programme. Their policies should be continued and further developed. Employers might also be encouraged to be more positive about part-time work for older people at all levels, since many older people express the desire to shift from full- to part-time work as they age, in place of what is often the shock of the sudden transition from full-time work to full-time leisure.

But if we want people to work longer, we need joined-up thinking about the paid and unpaid contributions of older people to the economy and society. As we have seen, older people make a major contribution to voluntary and community action and this needs to be acknowledged and valued. However, if older people are to stay longer in the workforce, fewer of them will have time for formal or informal unpaid care and support for others, such as grandchildren and people still older than themselves. These are potential losses from extending working lives, which will impose real social and economic costs.

Health and social care

For those who can no longer work, paid or unpaid, due to physical and mental frailty, we need non-discriminatory care geared to maximising the independence that surveys show is preferred by most older people. Good health care is essential. Furthermore, very many older people want to stay as long as possible in their own homes because they prefer independence; want contact with people of all age groups rather than the more restricted company of residential homes and sheltered housing; and want to maintain their social networks (Bazalgette *et al.* 2011) . There is evidence that such connections keep people active. But they often need some support. A major problem is the uncertain dividing line between 'health care' which is free of charge and 'social care' which is currently free to only 4 per cent of over 65s in the UK (compared with 25 per cent in Denmark, 13 per cent in The Netherlands and 9 per cent even in the USA (Wanless 2006), and there are signs that it is currently being cut further in the UK. The point at which support for an Alzheimer's sufferer, or someone recovering from a stroke becomes 'social' rather than health-related has long been uncertain and contentious; it remains unresolved, and the potential costs worry many older people (HC Health Committee 2010). One policy move so far is towards personal budgets for social care, 'to make sure that anyone who needs care and support can exercise choice and control to live their lives as they want' (Putting People First 2011). However, many older people are unenthusiastic about personal budgets: the costs of purchasing care are likely to be higher for individuals than for local authorities able to benefit from economies of scale, and the budgets are in danger of being cut (Bazalgette *et al.* 2011: 100–1). A government-appointed committee chaired by Andrew Dilnot has thoroughly reviewed this field (see the review for an up-to-date survey of relevant research) and has made recommendations for reform which have been widely praised. The policy response is unknown at the time of writing (Dilnot 2011).

Alternatives to state and personal provision for care in later life are proposed voluntary solutions, such as encouraging local 'good neighbour' schemes, as initiated by Labour in the 1970s and still surviving in some areas. As we have seen, such informal support is already quite extensive and it is quite unclear whether it is capable of further expansion. A variant is 'Time-Credit' schemes, pioneered in Japan, whereby people give care and accumulate credits in return for support when they need care themselves or in exchange for care given to their parents living at a distance. These are helpful to many older people, though the extent of their coverage is unclear and, as is commonly the case in voluntary situations, carers are willing to carry out certain tasks, such as shopping, cooking, socialising with a person needing care, but not the more intimate services that many people need—such as washing, helping to the toilet—that are defined as 'social care' (Hayashi 2010). Informal care by volunteers cannot substitute wholly for trained professional care, although it may complement it. There is a need for clear definition of the tasks that can reasonably be expected of either volunteers or professionals and for clarity about the real potential for the growth of voluntary and community action.

Housing

It is trite but true to say that the independent living of older people can be helped by an adequate supply of suitably designed housing. There is no shortage of designs but a shortage of implementation which requires a combination of effort by public, private and NGO sectors.

Policy priorities

Paradigm two, above, suggests that the most realistic, evidence-based policies to deal with issues around the ageing population should include:

> Listening to the opinions of older people before formulating policies and evaluating their needs carefully. Being aware of the great diversity within the age group *c*.60–100+.

> Formulating measures to reduce socioeconomic inequalities throughout life, from improved early years' services to higher pensions.

> Introducing flexible state pension/retirement ages, taking account of current real differences in healthy life expectancy.

> Improving health education to prolong healthy life.

> Ending age discrimination in health and social care, in the workplace and in society generally.

> Encouraging employers to implement measures, such as improved workplace design and access to training, to enable older people to work longer.

> Increasing research into health conditions particularly affecting older people.

> Providing adequate, affordable, support for independent living, including the provision of suitably designed housing and assistance to improve existing homes.

> Recognising the value of the inputs of older people into the economy and society, in place of labelling them as 'burdens'.

> Carefully evaluating the extent of voluntary/community action at present, the potential for future growth and which tasks are most appropriately assigned to volunteers, and which to trained professionals, as a necessary basis for 'Big Society' proposals to assist older people.

Most of these policies require the continued collaboration of central and local government with non-governmental organisations and individuals.

References

Most items below contain extensive further references to the mass of research in this broad field.

AgeUK (2011) 'Average Retirement Age on the Rise' [online], http://www.ageuk.org.uk (accessed on 17 January 2012).

AgeUK and Royal College of Surgeons, MHP Health Mandate (2012) *Access all Ages. Assessing the Impact of Age on Access to Surgical Treatment.* www.ageuk.org.uk/ Documents/EN-GB/For-professionals/Health-and-wellbeing/access_all_ages-final-web (accessed 16 October 2012).

Bazalgette, L., Holden, J., Tew, P., Hubble, N., Morrison J. (2011) *'Ageing is Not a Policy Problem to be Solved...': Coming of Age* (London: Demos).

Beveridge, W. (1942) *Social Insurance and Allied Services,* Cmd 6404 (London: HMSO).

Clark, G.L. (2000) *Pension Fund Capitalism* (Oxford: Oxford University Press).

Cutler, T. and Waine, B. (2010) *Moral Outrage and Questionable Polarities: The Attack on Public Sector Pensions* (University of Manchester, CRESC Working Paper, 80).

Cutler, T. and Waine, B. (2011) *In Defence of Public Sector Pensions: a Critique of the Independent Public Service Pensions Commission* (University of Manchester, CRESC Working Paper, 100).

Daycare Trust (2011) Jill Rutter and Ben Evans, *Listening to Grandparents.* Informal Childcare Research Paper 1 (London: Daycare Trust).

Dilnot, A. (2010) Commission on Funding of Care and Support (the Dilnot Commission) *Call for Evidence on the Future Funding of Care and Support* [Online], http://www.dilnot-commission.dh.gov.uk/files/2010/12/1.1-Call-for-Evidence-FINAL-pdf.pdf (accessed on 15 January 2012).

Dilnot, A. (2011) Commission on Funding of Care and Support (the Dilnot Commission) *Fairer Care Funding. The Report of the Commission on Funding Care and Support* [Online], www.dilnotcommission.dh.gov.uk (accessed on 15 January 2012).

DoH (Department of Health) (2009) *Shaping the Future of Care Together,* Cm 7673. [Online], http://www.doh.gov.uk (accessed on 16 January 2012).

DoH (2011) Press release 'No More Age Discrimination in the NHS'. Press Release, 3 March 2011 [Online], http://www.doh.gov.uk (accessed on 16 January 2012).

Department of Work and Pensions Information Directorate (DWP) (2011) Work and Pensions Longitudinal Study, November 2010 [Online], http://www.dwp.gov.uk/ (accessed on 16 January 2012).

EHRC (Equality and Human Rights Commission) (2010) *Just Ageing? Fairness, Equality and the Life Course. Final Report* [Online], http://www.equalityhumanrights.com/ publications/key-commission-reports/ (accessed on 19 January 2012).

Fries, J.F. (1980) 'Aging, Natural Death and the Compression of Morbidity' *The New England Journal of Medicine* 303: 130–135 [Online], http://www.nejm.org/doi/full/10.1056/ NEJM198007173030304 (accessed on 23 January 2012).

Gill, J. and Taylor, D. (2012) *Active Ageing: Live Longer and Prosper. Realizing the Benefits of Extended Healthy Life Expectancy and 'Disability Compression' in Europe* (London: UCL School of Pharmacy).

Ginn, J. (2006) 'Gender Inequalities: Sidelined in British Pensions Policy' in H. Pemberton, P. Thane and N. Whiteside (eds) *Britain's Pensions Crisis: History and Policy* (Oxford: Oxford University Press for the British Academy).

Glaser, K., Price, D., Willis, R., Stutchbury, R., Nicholls, M. (2009a) *Life Course Influences on Health and Well-being in Later Life: a Review* [Online], http://www.equalityhumanrights. com/uploaded_files/research/life_course_influences_on_health_and_well-being_in_ later_life-_a_review.pdf (accessed on 23 January 2012).

Glaser, K., Nicholls, M., Stuchbury, R., Willis, R., Gjonça, E. (2009b) *Life Course Influences on Poverty and Social Isolation in Later Life* [Online], http://www.equalityhuman-rights.com/uploaded_files/research/life_course_influences_on_poverty_and_social_ isolation_in_later_life_a_secondary_analysis.pdf (accessed on 23 January 2012).

Glaser, K. *et al.* (2010) *Grandparenting in Europe* (London: GrandParentsplus).

GrandparentsPlus (2011) 'Policy Briefing Paper 01. Statistics' [Online], http://www. grandparentsplus.org.uk (accessed on 23 January 2012).

Griggs, J. (2010) *Protect, Support, Provide: Examining the Role of Grandparents in Families at Risk of Poverty* (London: EHRC with GrandParents Plus).

Grundy, E. (2005) 'Reciprocity in Relationships: Socio-economic and Health Influences on Intergenerational Exchanges between Third Age Parents and Their Children in Great Britain', *British Journal of Sociology* 56(2): 233–255.

HAPPI (Housing Our Ageing Population: Panel for Innovation) (2009) *Report about Meeting Housing Needs of Older People* (London: Homes and Communities Agency).

Harris, J. (2006) 'The Roots of Public Pensions Provision: Social Insurance and the Beveridge Plan', in H. Pemberton, P. Thane, N. Whiteside (eds) *Britain's Pensions Crisis: History and Policy* (Oxford: Oxford University Press for the British Academy).

Hayashi, M. (2010) 'Testing the Limits of Care for Older People', *Society Guardian* 29 September 2010 [Online], http://www.guardian.co.uk/society/2010/sep/28/japan-elderly-care-mutual-support (accessed on 23 January 2012).

Hennock, E.P. (2007) *The Origin of the Welfare State in England and Germany, 1850–1914* (Cambridge: Cambridge University Press).

HM Treasury (2009) *Long-term Public Finance Report: An Analysis of Fiscal Sustainability* [Online], http://www.hm-treasury.gov.uk (accessed on 23 January 2012).

HC (House of Commons) Health Committee (2009–10) *Social Care*. Third Report of 2009–10 (London: The Stationery Office).

Howker, E. and Malik, S. (2010) *Jilted Generation: How Britain Has Bankrupted its Youth* (London: Icon Books Ltd).

King, R., Warnes, T. and Williams, A.M. (2000) *Sunset Lives: British Retirement Migration to the Mediterranean* (Oxford: Berg).

Kohli, M., Rein, M., Guillemard, A.-M., van Gunsteren, H. (1991) *Time for Retirement. Comparative Studies of Early Exit from the Labor Force* (Cambridge: Cambridge University Press).

Marmot, M. (2010) *The Marmot Review: Fair Society, Healthy Lives. Strategic Review of Health Inequalities in England* [Online], http://www.marmotreview.org (accessed on 23 January 2012).

McCrae, S. (ed.) (1999) *Changing Britain: Families and Households in the 1990s* (Oxford: Oxford University Press).

McNair, S. (2011) 'Older People and Skills in a Changing Economy', UK Commission for Employment and Skills, Briefing Paper [Online], http://www.ukces.org.uk/assets/

bispartners/ukces/docs/publications/equality-older-people.pdf (accessed on 23 January, 2012).

Medical Research Council (MRC) (1994) *The Health of the UK's Elderly People* (London: Medical Research Council).

Munnell, A. and Sass, S. (2008) *Working Longer: The Solution to the Retirement Income Challenge* (Washington, DC: Brookings Institution Press).

Myerson, J. (2010) *New Demographics, New Workspace* (London: Gower Publishing).

ODPM (Office of the Deputy Prime Minister) (2006) *A Sure Start to Later Life. Ending Inequalities for Older People. A Social Exclusion Unit Final Report* [Online], http://www.communities.gov.uk/publications/corporate/surestart (accessed on 23 January, 2012).

OECD (Organisation for Economic Cooperation and Development) (2011) *Doing Better for Families* [Online], www.oecd/social/family/doingbetter (accessed 23 January, 2012).

ONS (Office of National Statistics) (2009) '2008-based ONS Population Projections' [Online], http://www.statistics.gov.uk/hub/index.html (accessed on 23 January, 2012).

ONS (2010a) *Statistical Bulletin: Older People's Day*, 30 September 2010 [Online], http://www.ons.gov.uk/ons/rel/mortality-ageing/focus-on-older-people/older-people-s-day-2011/index.html (accessed on 23 January, 2012).

ONS (2010b) *Record Number of Centenarians in UK*. Press release, 30 September 2010: 'Centenarians. Number of Centenarians Grows' [Online], http://www.ons.gov.uk/ons/dcp171778_235000.pdf (accessed on 23 January, 2012).

ONS (2011a) 'Ageing. Fastest increase in the oldest old' April 1 2011. (Online), http://www.ons.gov.uk/ons/index.html(Accessed on 23 January, 2012).

ONS (2011b) 'Fertility: UK Fertility Remains High', 24 June 2011 [Online], http://www.ons.gov.uk/ons/index.html (accessed on 23 January, 2012).

ONS (2011c) 'Pension Trends: the Labour Market and Retirement', February 2011 [Online], http://www.ons.gov.uk/ons/index.html (accessed on 23 January, 2012).

OPCS (Office of Population, Censuses and Surveys) (1988) *Censuses of England and Wales and Mid-1985-based Population Projections for Local Authority Areas in England*, Monitor PP3, 88/1 (London: OPCS).

Piachaud, D., Macnicol, J., Lewis, J. (2009) *A Think Piece on Intergenerational Equity* [Online], http://justageing.equalityhumanrights.com/wp-content/uploads/2009/09/Intergenerational-Equality.pdf (accessed on 23 January 2012).

Pensions Commission, First Report (2004) *Pensions: Challenges and Choices* (London: The Stationery Office).

Putting People First (2011) *Transforming Adult Social Care* [Online], www.puttingpeople-first.org.uk/about (accessed on 23 January 2012).

Quine, M.S. (1996) *Population Politics in Twentieth Century Europe* (London: Routledge).

Rutter, J. and Evans, B. (2010) *Informal Childcare: Choice or Chance?* [Online], daycare trust: www.daycaretrust.org.uk (accessed on 14 January 2012).

TAEN (The Age and Employment Network) (2011) (Online), http://taen.org.uk/news. (accessed on 23 January 2012).

Thane, P. (1990) 'The Debate on the Declining Birth-rate in Britain: the "Menace" of an Ageing Population', *Continuity and Change*, Cambridge Journals 5(2): 283–305.

Thane, P. (2000) *Old Age in English History: Past Experiences, Present Issues* (Oxford: Oxford University Press).

Wanless, D. (2006) *Securing Good Care for Older People* (London: The King's Fund).

Ward, R., Pugh, S., Price, E. (2011) *Don't Look Back? Improving Health and Social Care Service Delivery for Older LGB Users* [Online], http://www.equalityhumanrights.com/uploaded_files/research/dont_look_back_improving_health_and_social_care.pdf (accessed on 23 January 2012).

Willetts, D. (2010) *The Pinch: How the Baby Boomers Took Their Children's Future—and Why They Should Give It Back* (London: Atlantic Books).

WRVS (Women's Royal Voluntary Service) (2011) 'Gold Age Pensioners: Contribution Outweighs Cost by £40 Billion' [Online], http://www.goldagepensioners.com (accessed on 23 January 2012).

7

The 'Big Society' and concentrated neighbourhood problems

ANNE POWER

Introduction: communities and state are interdependent

In a period of deep economic uncertainty and rapid social change such as now, governments and citizens search out continuities and adopt well-grounded, widely accepted solutions to problems. The 'Big Society' was introduced by David Cameron in 2009 as a way of involving ordinary citizens in active communities, tackling local problems, caring for their neighbourhoods, doing things for themselves, rather than relying on an overextended state (Cameron 2009).

The chapter argues that the state and civil society are intimately connected; the Big Society idea, if it is to help disadvantaged communities, relies on an active but light-handed state, willing to support community-level activity, while accepting responsibility for the overarching framework that community groups and social movements have sought. It also implies a less imposing, more enabling state (Osborne and Gaebler 1992). The logic of the Big Society is underpinned by evidence that within different political contexts and different social settings, community action can develop new ways of organising the small-scale local services communities need which can deliver benefits far beyond what state systems per se achieve (Tunstall et al. 2011). Most of the examples are neighbourhood-based because it is within small geographical communities that community action develops. Many of the strongest examples in this country are housing-based because housing policy has played such a powerful role in shaping neighbourhoods and communities in the twentieth century (Dunleavy 1981; Power 1987).

This chapter shows that current political debates about the Big Society, localism and community organising have their roots in the small-scale, self-help activity of low-income communities, which evolved in earlier periods of economic and social upheaval. The chapter explores the continuity between many different strands of community organisation, highlighting the particular influence of the American 'Great Society' programme of the 1960s, inspired by the civil rights movement, as paving the way for radically different state approaches to impoverished urban communities, involving communities directly in shaping their future while providing strong backing from the state (Garrow 1999; Lemann 1994).

The roots of mutual aid

The idea of the 'big society' as opposed to the 'big state' is not new. The concept has its origins in nineteenth-century conditions when co-operatives, friendly societies and mutual aid were the survival strategies of the poor, underpinning families and communities in the face of harsh social conditions and a brutally untamed factory production system (Owen 1821). The devastation of the social fabric was the dark side of these small community endeavours. *The Cambridge Social History of Britain* (Thompson 1992) explores the growth of clubs, associations, friendly societies, savings groups, and myriad less formal forms of mutual aid. It details the thousands of groups that formed in inner Birmingham, in northern textile towns and in mining areas, not just to pick up the pieces of the industrial revolution and its debris, but to provide congenial, solidaristic relief from toil (Birchall 1997). Very often access to accommodation and work depended on established social networks, while co-operative savings groups and friendly societies protected the working poor from desperation and disgrace, such as not being able to pay for shoes or a family burial. The greatest drivers and beneficiaries of these innovative forms of association were the new labourers in factories, making good the reduced power of extended family networks and traditional hierarchies as people moved into towns (White 2007; Thane 2012). Housing, work and community interacted in nineteenth century cities and towns, as long factory hours, low wages and lack of transport required workers to live close to sources of employment (Briggs 1968; Thompson 1992: vol. 2).

Rapidly industrialising and urbanising conditions that produced self-help 'caring, sharing' initiatives were so harsh that entrepreneurs at the

helm of the new factory system favoured the creation of government structures to combat the appalling consequences (Briggs 1968). As local government emerged and central government imposed stronger controls over
public health, sanitation and overcrowding, the community-based social
protection model was not immediately replaced (Thompson 1992). In fact,
the co-operative model that evolved in early industrial towns in England
encouraged comparable social movements in different countries facing
similarly difficult conditions. For example, most Danish social housing is
run today on co-operative principles under clear government regulation
(Czischke and Pittini 2007). The Grameen Bank in today's poverty-stricken
Bangladesh is a co-operatively run, member-based social enterprise that is
community based, with a majority of extremely poor women on its board,
while working within the framework of international financial regulation
(Yunus 1998, 2007). Informal settlements in Latin America, Africa and
South Asia are frequent hosts to similar, co-operatively formed associations
(Mitlin and Satterthwaite 2004).

Member-owned, member-run co-operatives offer probably the most
enduring model of 'big society' activity, based on shared resources, pooled
efforts and the fair distribution of benefits. They are founded on trust,
need and mutual interest. There are a number of important conditions
for success that have been documented, including transparency, restricted
credit and dividends, education, wider community benefits, open membership and democratic decision-making. They rarely work when they are
imposed and they require a wider legal and regulatory framework as
the well-known Scandinavian and Basque models show (Birchall 1997;
Mondragón 2010; Jones 1986).

Many explanations have been offered for the strengths of co-operative
forms of organisation. The most convincing theory for the frequent emergence of co-operation is that human beings are motivated by altruism as
well as self-interest for reasons of survival—we succeed as social animals
based on co-operation. Social structures, requiring mutually beneficial
inputs and gains, have proved a highly productive way of managing human
affairs in many challenging situations (Ridley 1996). Pooling resources for
mutual gain is fundamental to survival. For example, by members saving
small amounts each week, they accumulate capital, which is then used for
the benefit of members in turn. It would be impossible for an individual
to achieve this alone as co-operation both pools and reinforces effort,

bringing social control into play. Benefits range from the purchase of basic necessities such as flour or fuel, to a rotating fund for essential equipment such as shoes, to support for widows, orphans or family members in times of unemployment. The pattern of solidaristic mutual aid was a foundation stone of the original Rochdale Pioneers in 1844 (Holyoake 1857). The Co-operative Bank, which still operates on mutual principles, underwent a major growth spurt in the recent banking crisis and recession because in hard times people prefer to save with a trusted and sharing organisation. The Co-operative Group, still headquartered in Manchester, reveals the durability and social benefits that can derive from co-operation, embracing not only savings, banking and insurance, but consumer and producer co-operatives as well as community self-help of all kinds, including tenant co-operatives.[1]

Co-operatives flourish in countries where the legal, regulatory and financial structures are firmly in place, such as Scandinavia, Italy and Spain. Mondragón, a small Basque town in the Pyrenees, is an impressive example of every type of co-operative. The high mountain valley became home to the now world-famous worker co-operatives, funded by the local co-operative savings and loan bank, the Caja Laboral, producing many successful consumer goods, and offering machinery and high-tech engineering, training, education, jobs and social underpinning to Basque society, which was deeply harmed by the Spanish Civil War and nearly 40 years of authoritarian government. The Basque language was outlawed, and the total lack of political representation found expression, not only in nationalism and violence, which the world has heard much about, but also in forms of mutual aid, saving, insurance and investment, which helped underpin the Basque country's remarkable resilience during Spain's acute economic crisis, which began in 2007.[2] Spanish and Italian house building, predominantly in dense high blocks, is frequently organised through community-based savings co-operatives. In Italian cities, many social services are provided at community level within neighbourhoods through co-operative service organisations. There are many examples (Tunstall *et al.* 2011; Bifulco *et al.* 2008).

---

[1] For further information see http://www.co-operative.coop/.
[2] Observations supplemented by personal visit to Mondragón in June 2011.

A critical role for government

The idea of co-operation has re-emerged in the UK in recent times, deriving powerful and politically polarising rhetoric from the view that the state might end up damaging the altruistic, sharing and small-scale social relations on which society depends if state systems become too dominant and overbearing in the social life of communities. On the other hand, if private interests come to dominate, they might undermine the solidaristic ideas of the welfare state itself, as Titmuss powerfully argued in attempting to create an essential balance between the individual, society and the state (Titmuss 1970). In the present policy debates about how to compensate for essential cuts in public spending to reduce the public deficit, the aim is that the Big Society should help to create stronger communities that can do more to help themselves without first turning to the state to help them. In the Big Society, communities know how to organise local events and services, they are involved in running local schools, they raise funds for local causes and help with children, families and young people in need of friendly, caring contact and support. But there are clear limits to how far this 'localist', hands-off approach can carry wider responsibilities on behalf of society (Hills *et al.* 2002). The limitations arise from the low internal capacity of many deprived communities, the lack of local resources, and the common need for overarching frameworks in complex urban societies. Asa Briggs argued this in his important study of Victorian cities and a recently published audit of the Big Society in action suggests this too (Briggs 1968; Slocock 2012).

To grasp the implications of the Big Society, we need to understand not only the causes of dependence on state underpinning but also the interdependence between society and the state that grew up in the nineteenth century and has prevailed since then. Local social protection and social provision within communities need overarching government, both local and national, as early industrialists and co-operative thinkers recognised (Owen 1821). For example, many vital underpinnings to education derive from parental and community support, but without the physical infrastructure, training, equipment, funding, links to wider knowledge, standards and myriad other contributions by the state, our education system in poorer, lower-skilled areas, would fail, as demonstrated in many parts of the developing world and in the United States (UNICEF 2011; Economist 2011c). Community-based organisations cannot displace or act as substitutes for the overarching role of the state on which modern nations rely for key aspects of social order and harmony, although it is true that some communities can play a bigger role. Robert Sampson, the eminent Chicago sociologist, argues this forcibly in relation to crime control and neighbourhood 'efficacy'. A major role of effective communities is to activate the state and persuade it into a more, not less, proactive role (Sampson 2004). The private sector, with its profit motive, cannot play such overarching brokering roles, although it can provide some of the services and indirectly some of the resources, which both the state and citizens need. The Big Society is not about private and individual self-interest. It is essentially about the role of communities and civic responsibility, as Steven Goldsmith, Professor of Government at Harvard University, argues in his book about social innovation (Goldsmith 2010).

The co-operative instinct, meaning mutual and shared interest in achieving a common benefit, appears deeply embedded within human beings, based on social contact which engenders trust. The state evolves as broker, enforcer and framer of the very co-operation that small, local groups are best able to foster and deliver. In Scandinavian countries, admired by governments of different political hues, co-operatives of all kinds are widespread and have long historic roots. The state plays a key role in creating the legal, financial, regulatory and supervisory framework for co-operative ownership, management, production and delivery (Scott 1975; Jones 1986).

The role of social capital

It is hard to separate the evolution of co-operation from the idea that social and community networks help bind people together and form a recognisable kind of capital, termed 'social capital' on the grounds that these social networks have an asset value for the bigger society as well as the smaller, local community. The loss of social capital causes real harm particularly to families as the longitudinal study of two hundred families in low-income areas shows (Power 2007).[3] Where social and community networks exist,

---

[3] The ESRC-funded research Centre for the Analysis of Social Exclusion conducted a 10-year investigation into bringing up children in highly disadvantaged areas. See the CASE website for more information—http://sticerd.lse.ac.uk/case/.

this valuable form of capital needs investment and protection so that it survives, expands and provides real and concrete, if hard to measure, value to communities (Putnam *et al.* 1993; Halpern 2004; Baron, Field and Schuller 2000; Sampson 2004). Yet it proves remarkably hard to achieve this balance between government support and community responsibility.

Academic studies have documented a remarkable decline in social capital in America that has alarmed policy-makers on both sides of the Atlantic. But major studies by Peter Hall, Robert Putnam and others have shown that in many European countries social capital is higher (Hall, 1999; Putnam, 2000; Halpern, 2004). British society displays high levels of social capital in terms of voluntary activity, in the active role of grandparents, and in the level of cross-cultural contact, compared with the USA (Maloney, Smith and Stoker, 2004; Halpern, 2004). It is one of the puzzles of modern European societies that community cohesion, social inclusion and attempts to equalise conditions are state driven, yet heavily reliant on community involvement and generally supported by the public. It is particularly interesting that many European countries encourage, allow and directly support independent social provision in health, education, social housing and other related fields such as social insurance (Park *et al.*, 2008). These arms'-length systems often benefit from tax incentives, special savings and investment schemes and, above all, clear legal frameworks, as the study of European housing systems revealed (Power, 1993).

As populations have become more diverse and social problems more complex, so community involvement and representation have become more vital to government, but also more complicated to achieve. This mutual relationship between state and community is most transparent in Scandinavian countries, with their thousand-year-old democratic and participative traditions of government, where a strong, overarching and all-encompassing welfare state works with and supports community-based co-operatives particularly in the housing, building and agricultural sectors. Scandinavian countries have more homogeneous populations than other European countries, as well as a stronger history of co-operative organisation. This encourages community involvement within a regulated and well-funded welfare state system (Power, 1993; Esping-Andersen, 1990). It creates many of the social benefits and low-cost outcomes that the current coalition government craves for. But prevention of social problems, while cheaper than crisis intervention, is not cheap upfront and it implies higher taxes to create widespread social well-being (Wilkinson and Pickett, 2009; Early Action Task Force, 2011).

Social capital and Sampson's closely related theory of 'collective efficacy' can fail when structural economic changes, outside the control of local communities, undermine local social organisation and when governments fail to protect and reintegrate fragmented communities into the new mainstream (Sampson 2004; Wilson 1987). Collective efficacy works where communities are connected internally and externally with the wider society. Both William Julius Wilson, the eminent Harvard sociologist, and Robert Sampson of the University of Chicago, argue that harmonious and co-operative social relations are an important, even dominant, factor in achieving a low-crime, high-trust, open community, rather than a gated, guarded, exclusive community protected by high walls. Yet this kind of high-trust community may be particularly difficult to achieve in America's highly mobile and ghetto-prone cities without wider government support. It is also increasingly hard to maintain the necessary levels of social cohesion in Europe's diverse, and fast-changing cities. Therefore as a powerful counterweight to extreme polarisation across dense European cities, social integration and cohesion policies assume major political significance as community conditions deteriorate (Power, Plöger and Winkler 2010; Economist 2012). Successful urban communities rely not only on social capital but also on education, on well-cared-for environments, on preventive security measures and a reliably maintained public realm. In other words, they need supportive, community-attuned, publicly funded basic services if social capital is to be sustained (Tunstall *et al.* 2011).

Linkages: bonding and bridging

The gains that derive from the combined interests of state and community have led European governments to focus continuous effort on the integration of low-income and highly disadvantaged communities, often housing large concentrations of minorities, which are under strong negative pressures. Local people in such areas feel relatively powerless either to prevent or tackle local social problems without external support; yet these same communities also have less leverage on local government and on other agencies to secure local services in response to problems. For this reason governments frequently intervene proactively in an attempt to stem poor conditions in deprived areas (Power *et al.* 2010). Evidence from many countries shows that locally based services, closely attuned to community needs, can foster community bonds, social capital and co-operation, which produce mutually beneficial outcomes. In other words, successful community change and involvement depends on the synergy between state and community. The state needs to generate strong local support for programmes to better their community conditions (Power and Houghton 2007).

The 200 families bringing up children in low-income urban areas interviewed by the Centre for Analysis of Social Exclusion researchers between 1998 and 2008, show that parents want to be actively involved: to control their immediate surroundings; to be part of a community; and to know and trust their neighbours. But they rely on wider institutions to create the conditions for these micro-social links to flourish (Power 2007). In other words, communities depend on government to succeed as much as governments depend on communities (Power *et al.* 2011). Evidence from the New Deal for Communities, Neighbourhood Renewal and Sure Start evaluations bears out these claims (Hills *et al.*, 2009). International evidence from an in-depth study of problematic mass housing estates in Europe presents a common pattern of local-scale, but government-backed interventions, responding directly to ground-level community needs (Power 1997). The example of the Priority Estates Project in the UK, discussed below, will show how this combined or 'patchwork' approach can work to transform community conditions.

The Big Society is clearly not just about small-scale, local community action; it is about bigger, wider connections, about society as a whole, and its responsibilities. A large majority of people feel they belong to the bigger society in which they live, alongside their local affiliations (Department for Communities and Local Government 2008; Halpern 2004). These wider linkages and underpinnings of modern society, often referred to as 'bridging' social capital, are as vital to survival as close community links or 'bonding' social capital. These connections give access to essential services such as education and health, but also provide links to new jobs. Yet social networks are highly unequal between communities. This cleavage is particularly sharp in the USA where social scientists over decades have documented the impact of structural economic changes, weak government, rising inequality and racial separation on family and community stability particularly among African-American communities, isolated in ghettoes (Moynihan 1965). William Julius Wilson's detailed analysis of social breakdown in the poorest American ghettoes suggests that its major causes lie largely outside the control of local communities (Wilson 1987, 1997, 1999, 2006, 2009a, 2009b).

A powerful and detailed exploration of the link between poverty, ghetto concentrations, social breakdown, violence and joblessness, is the census-based study of US segregation along racial lines by Paul Jargowski (1997). While he finds some direct relationship between people's life outcomes and the social conditions that surround them, one of his most important findings is the extent to which physical ghettoes and ghetto conditions are entrenched, with their concomitant poverty and related problems. This thoughtful and evidence-based study supports Wilson's thesis that structural economic changes dominate urban conditions and drive extreme poverty, family breakdown, joblessness and social unravelling. Without external interventions it is hard to see how these barriers to progress can be overcome or how community empowerment and co-operative ventures can flourish. It is difficult to avoid the conclusion that the failure of public support in the US to counter the trend towards ghetto development has accentuated the decline and virtual collapse of many impoverished communities (Massey and Denton 1993). Many American commentators, including the current President Obama, argue the need for stronger government support for community (Katz 2010; Obama 2006). The US experience of acute polarisation has reinforced the idea of 'social Europe' (Power *et al.* 2010).

In UK government circles, both under New Labour and under the current coalition, theories around social capital, community and the Big Society gained a strong foothold. But debates become mired quickly in the controversial and radical policies being proposed by the new government, where the Big Society is in danger of being seen as a potential cost-saver, given the huge overall sums of money that flow through the various channels of the welfare state to vulnerable households to compensate for low earned incomes, lack of work, disability, lone parenthood, high rents, lack of affordable child care or adequate public services. An even clearer threat is posed by cuts to the voluntary organisations and community groups that have received significant and increasing government support over the last two decades to provide many of the community-based services that the Big Society wants to encourage in areas where the state cannot deliver effectively (Stott 2011; Mulgan 2010). There are indications that the withdrawal of state funding is undermining the very idea of the Big Society (Slocock 2012).

Comprehensive welfare systems were set up to overcome the 'five great evils besetting modern society' and to underpin society's attempts at creating more equal opportunities for all citizens, following the hardships of two world wars and the bleak interwar years (Beveridge 1942; Timmins, 1996). Yet the welfare state in this country is not nearly as generous as in most of northern Europe and it is increasingly means-tested, making for a dangerously wide poverty trap (Hills 1996, 2004; Hills *et al.* 2009; Wilkinson and Pickett 2009). The UK is already among the most unequal countries in Europe; shifting the burden of taxes, benefits and public service cuts so that those on the lowest incomes lose the most may not have the desired effect of pushing them towards more self-reliance or greater equality of opportunity (Browne and Levell 2010). In an initial phase, using the Big Society as a prop for public spending cuts simply unleashes pent-up frustration, particularly among young people, unless the new agenda is clearly focused on achieving real gains in hard-pressed areas—more homes, more child provision, more training, and more jobs. The events of summer 2011 suggest that this threat is real (Guardian and London School of Economics 2011).

Community organising

A flagship project of the Big Society programme is the proposal to train 5,000 community organisers to work across neighbourhoods throughout the country to identify local problems, local leaders and the scope to take local action. Amid considerable debate, the programme is being developed in association with community-based development trusts, settlements and community action centres, as a way of fostering more active citizen engagement in local problem-solving and stronger social enterprises to deliver needed local services (Locality 2011). This large and ambitious programme is thus firmly rooted in well-established, asset-owning, community-based organisations. While unleashing community organisers into every neighbourhood recognises the problem of social disorganisation, it will not in itself resolve neighbourhood problems, given the resource constraints, the complexities and controversies, the time lags and costs involved in community organising itself (Citizens UK 2011).

In order to understand the recent government interest in community organising, we need to explore its origins in the USA. Saul Alinsky, the creative American thinker behind the current vogue for community organising, cut his teeth on the major problems of industrial closures, job losses and consequent impoverishment of inner-city Chicago in the 1950s and 1960s. His work demonstrated the critical role of the state in helping communities survive and flourish. His book, *Rules for Radicals*, explains how to collect a critical mass of support around burning issues that affect communities, and how to gain access to decision-makers in order to change the social, economic and political balance of power (Alinsky 1972). The living wage movement in London, celebrating its 10th anniversary in 2011 as a successful Alinsky-modelled campaign, has shifted the balance of argument in government, such that Cameron himself has argued in favour of a living wage—an agreed rate of pay for the lowest paid significantly above the official minimum wage that low-skilled workers currently receive. This has been endorsed by the mayor of London and several local authorities as well as many big private and public agencies. Interestingly, the Living Wage Campaign, a model of co-operation among communities and between different levels of society, is significant proof of the need for wider public structures, support and enforcement. Fairness is a bigger issue than any single group or organisation in a multilayered society holds within its grasp. It requires a public framework support that governments evolved to provide (Islington Fairness Commission 2011; de Soto 2007).

There is a clear overlap between social movements such as the Living Wage Campaign, community organising and the early models of co-operation we have discussed. In the 1960s, when welfare states were at their zenith, many social movements—including anti-colonial and European students' movements, squatter occupations, and racial disturbances—emerged from the grassroots, to challenge both the power and application of state systems as well as to propose alternative ways of providing services. It is ironic that overzealous states, deciding on behalf of communities, unleashed forms of community action that have served as models of self-help, proving the need for citizen 'voice' within state systems such as health, housing, education and policing. However, the balance between state and citizen has never been easy to resolve (Department of the Environment 1977; Home Office 1977).

Community movements took much of their inspiration from the civil rights movement in the United States, which in turn derived much of its force from its links with liberation movements in Africa and the Indian subcontinent (King 1958). The Civil Rights movement coincided with many of the community-organising ideas of Alinsky's programmes, particularly in Chicago (King 1967). Radical community-oriented change came about when a grassroots protest movement grew on the back of humiliating discrimination, based solely on the grounds of colour. As recently as the early 1960s, a highly decentralised federal government system still accepted illegal exclusions from voting rights, applied to poorly educated black Americans in southern states. State governments also tolerated an explicit colour bar operating in public places (Garrow, 1999). The triggers of injustice, the marches, violence and victories are well known, but less known is the link to community organisation.

Following the assassination of John F. Kennedy in 1963, at the peak of the Civil Rights movement, Vice-President Johnson, who then ran for the presidency and won by a landslide in 1964, signed into law the Voting Rights Act. The American civil rights dream of a fairer society focused not just on racial inequality, but on the deeper causes of poverty, not just in law but also in communities (King 1967). In fact Martin Luther King moved his base from the deep South to Chicago in 1966 in order to highlight the desperate condition of ghetto slums. The 'hard economics' of industrial job losses, without the buttressing of a comprehensive welfare state in a European sense, led to a level of social breakdown in black family life that undermined the value of the newly won civil rights (Wilson 1987; Moynihan 1965).

The Great Society idea

Johnson, in the wake of radical Civil Rights legislation and under intense political pressure to change conditions in the ghettoes, launched the US Poverty Program, under the banner of the 'Great Society'. Its aim was to do within America what the Peace Corps and foreign aid were meant to do abroad, winning recognition for democracy and freedom by helping people out of poverty. Talented, committed community activists were paid as organisers, with generous federal support, to generate community change. Community development became a recognised, if indirect, arm of government. In practice the Great Society would be delivered through an army of community workers, many of them trained in 'Alinsky methods'. Citizens UK, the Alinsky-inspired organisation that leads the Living Wage Campaign and other community development activity, derives its philosophy and methods from its American counterparts (Ivereigh 2010).[4]

Martin Luther King, Jr was assassinated in 1968 while his civil rights organisation, the Southern Christian Leadership Conference, was organising a 'poor people's march' in support of Great Society ideas, intended to be the multiracial equivalent of the voting rights march on Washington five years earlier. His death provoked widespread rioting in virtually every northern city, devastating large tranches of inner-city ghettoes and highlighting the appalling slum conditions and social inequalities prevailing in the heartlands of American freedom and progress, from Washington, DC, through Chicago to Los Angeles. These urban riots put the shortcomings of American public and social policy—housing, schooling, health, welfare systems—under the international spotlight (National Advisory Commission on Civil Disorders 1968). They only served to accentuate the need for more concerted action (Kerner 1968).

Many thousands of community-based projects sprang up all over the United States in the late 1960s and early 1970s, employing community organisers, many of them coming from the ghetto communities they were paid by the government to 'organise'. They were supposed to build a sense of local ownership and belonging through churches, community centres, extra school programmes, community law firms and housing co-operatives. The whole idea was to unleash the power of the people to counterbalance the limitations of the federal American state, still overshadowed by the legacy of slavery and its consequences (Marris and Rein 1967; Malcolm X and Haley 1965). These programmes were given immense latitude because neither local nor central government had the capacity, competence or know-how to deliver, control or even monitor community-level programmes (Lemann 1991). Most of the anti-poverty programmes came to a rapid end as the initial funding ran out, and it proved difficult to show the lasting value or stabilising effect of such a disparate and politically controversial approach to change, unleashing as it did the pent-up anger of young

---

[4] For further information see http://www.citizensuk.org.

people from urban ghettoes without an effective umbrella of basic public services (Davis 1971; Malcolm X and Haley 1965). However, certain lessons survived and influenced thinking in Britain, not least the Community Development Projects of the 1970s (Home Office 1977) (see below). The most lasting and significant impact came from the Head Start programme, which by the 1990s demonstrated the long-term value of reaching children early in their childhood through progressive and high-quality pre-school education programmes. Long-run evaluations, tracking the children of Head Start and the Perry Pre-School Program, showed how much the children and their parents benefited from intense hand-holding support and an integrated, holistic approach to early learning (Department of Health and Human Services 2010; Gramlich 1986; Parks 2000). The families involved in Head Start were tracked over 10 years and strongly attest to its value. The Program survived many rounds of federal government cuts, decentralisation of decisions and budget shortages, because of its proven value and popular support (Eisenstadt 2011b; Waldfogel 2006). Sure Start, borrowing many ideas and methods from the Head Start programme, was launched in the UK in 1999 in specifically targeted areas of high deprivation, adapting many of these tried-and-tested ideas to low-income communities in this country. Moves to decentralise decisions to local governments have led to threatened closures of Sure Start programmes, as local authorities try to cope with budget cuts. However, local and national protests in defence of Sure Start suggest that the home-grown community based pre-school programme, underpinned by government support and community involvement, has won widespread recognition and support. It is too early to say whether Sure Start will survive in poorer communities in anything like the form that was originally intended. Early years programmes embody the essence of the Big Society—state support and funding alongside community backing and involvement with transformational effects on family lives and citizen engagement (Eisenstadt 2011b; Allen 2011a, 2011b).

In spite of the early ending of the 'Great Society' programme, community organising, social enterprise, community-based housing and other social initiatives grew as alternative ways of improving community conditions, with direct state support (Housing and Community Development Act 1977). Under successive American governments, community-based organisations, constituted as non-profit social enterprises, have emerged in most low-income urban communities and often become powerful Community Development Corporations (CDCs). They receive federal funds for some activities, provide housing and other services, generate revenue and plough proceeds back into the community. In spite of many disputes over their value and many local conflicts over their role, they are powerful local actors in most major US cities, working in the areas of highest poverty (American Assembly 2007; Mcgahey and Vey 2008). CDCs, as they are commonly known, have fought to defend community interests against big developers, community displacement and plans that sweep aside community interests in favour of imposed solutions to community problems (Brandes Gratz 1995; Power *et al.* 2010). The expansion plans for John Hopkins University in Baltimore offer one example of institutional interests overriding community interests, whatever the rationale. Columbia University's plans in New York offer another, even more sensitive, example because of their location on the edge of Harlem (Economist 2007, 2008). The whole philosophy of community organising and community-based initiative is thus often on a collision course with high-level decision-making, vested interests and overpowering wealth. At worst, this can generate alienation and violence as the Black Power movement of the late 1960s showed (Jackson 1971; Davis 1971, 1974). At best, it can aid more measured, more attuned outcomes, as frequently happens in European examples (see below).

The problem is that community-based organisations on their own do not have the power or the access or the know-how in most cases to change the way bigger decisions are made or in practice to deliver the scale of intervention that is necessary. Barack Obama's background in community organising, his legal training, and his political engagement, link a deeply held community perspective directly with government responsibility and law-making (Obama 1996). Now the first black president of the United States, he quickly recognised that community organising, parent protests, community school movements, local housing provision and job access need government action as well as community action (Obama 2006). This takes us almost full circle in our discussion, reinforcing the lessons from American experience, underlining the very different conditions in Europe.

European models of community organisation

A book of unexpected power and resonance, *Small is beautiful* by Fritz Schumacher (1973), whose title captures its central message that big, heavy-handed state action can be immensely damaging and that alternative, community-level approaches work better, helped to shape a whole generation of radical thinking around community values and the environment from the 1970s onwards. This community-orientated thinking was not unique to Britain, where the dominance of state control over most parts of the economy since the war drove a quiet revolution. Other parts of Europe, where there were more diverse forms of delivery, also experienced radical citizen-led initiatives, notably in Germany but also in other European countries (Czischke and Pittini 2007; Jacquier 1991). The new approach was accelerated in the UK through the establishment of the Community Development Projects of 1976 to test the need and potential for bottom-up change. This programme unleashed such pent-up hostility to the 'local state' that the programme was quickly stopped (Home Office 1977). However, the government's attempts at community-level structures of involvement and activity led not to a withdrawal, but rather to a reshaping of the role of the state in local communities. The government initiated a whole series of area-focused initiatives including the Urban Programme and its successors, which ran for many years (Robson *et al.* 2000).

The UK was particularly affected by its ever more far-reaching neighbourhood demolition and new building programmes (Dunleavy 1981). The International Monetary Fund (IMF), called to Britain to help solve the economic crisis generated by the oil crisis of 1974, encouraged smaller government, the divestment of state-owned industries and a halt to government-funded large-scale infrastructure projects. Community-based alternatives emerged most clearly in poorer neighbourhoods where much of the large-scale action was taking place. House building, for 30 years after the war, had been one of the biggest political issues, fuelling ambitions far beyond the government's capacity to deliver (Dunleavy 1981; Power 1987). As major national industries collapsed, so the mass-housing era ground to a halt, leaving a legacy of disrupted and blighted communities with intensive ethnic and social polarisation and an unmanageable legacy of estates.

The shift to refurbishment of existing homes in line with community priorities happened quite suddenly when it became clear that we could not go
on spending in heavily interventionist ways to rebuild demolished slums.
Many argued that a more incremental, community-based approach would
work better, including many in government (North Islington Housing
Rights Project 1976). Small-scale, community-based action and services
re-emerged not just in the UK, but across Europe after three decades of
large-scale government action (Crossman 1979; Wollmann 1985).

Curiously, the Big Society is in many ways a direct descendant of the
ideas that flowed from this austere period. The government has chosen
a path of extreme decentralisation or localism to reduce the power of a
strongly centralised state. The Westminster government has devolved control of many decisions affecting local communities to local authorities or
councils. The coalition government has cut regional funding, reduced local
government funding and encouraged communities to take control. The
hope is that community organisers, initially funded by government grants
and trained through government programmes, will unleash an army of
volunteers to take up the slack created by a shrinking public sector. Yet
evidence suggests that the survival and positive contribution of multitudes
of small community-based organisations depend on wider structures
(Richardson 2008; Tunstall et al. 2011; Slocock 2012).

Community organising has gained a new lease of life as European governments have faced increasingly complex challenges. Modern urban communities are developing the potential to reshape government methods.
The long-run protests in Stuttgart, Germany, known as Stuttgart 21, centre
around a plan to demolish and rebuild a large part of central Stuttgart with
exploding costs, causing major disruption over years and bringing mighty
German interest groups into direct conflict with citizens, in the richest
state in the Federal Republic. A strikingly diverse organising base, linked
to the German Green Party, displays a now common pattern of community organisation, public protest, and confrontation with the combined
power of government, developer interests, big finance and the police. The
popular, grassroots, democratic movement has led to a historic victory for
the Green Party in the state of Baden Württemberg where Stuttgart is the
capital, showing the clear links between community interests and policy-
making. The still-disputed compromise outcome is reshaping government
thinking in Germany about the relationship of citizens to decision-makers,

since a yawning gap has opened up between the interests of different parties to democracy (Kaiser and Windmann 2010; Der Spiegel 2010). What started as a local dispute became a major national controversy in 2011 and led to a change in the balance of political power in Germany (Economist 2011b). This is similar to what happened in the nineteenth century as various community-based societies grew into social movements that radically changed not only social conditions but also political structures, such as trade unions. It also mirrors in some ways the political changes brought about by the Civil Rights movement.

The example of Stuttgart shows just how complex modern government has become. In Europe, including the UK, planned outcomes are increasingly modified through protests because communities are integrated with the wider democratic system through comprehensive public services. Europe, of which the UK is an integral part, is a crowded continent, forcing communities to reach compromises and forcing governments to act in the name of cohesion. Wars and authoritarianism in the twentieth century taught civil society and governments that they were interdependent, and that neglecting conditions at the bottom of society could lead to intolerable tensions and explosions. This applies in Britain particularly, because we are so urbanised, and because two world wars made our political and welfare systems more state-driven and more centralised than elsewhere (Titmuss 1958; Timmins 1996). At the same time, an extreme fear of fascism and of revolutionary movements has led to the adoption of publicly endorsed methods of participation in decision-making to close the gap between communities and government. Thus we evolved a strange combination of an overcentralised and bureaucratic state, with a strong base of community organisation and participative methods. This applies particularly to planning, affecting transport, industry, power generation, and most building projects (Park et al. 2008; Hall 1988; Briggs 1986).

How community renewal paved the way for the Big Society

Housing policy in Britain has often spearheaded community-level action and change. The ending of slum clearance and mass housing in the 1970s led to a generously funded neighbourhood renewal programme to restore confidence in former slum areas. The Housing Action Area programme began in 1974, targeting decayed groups of streets in inner cities earmarked for the now-infamous bulldozer. Gentrification that earlier improvement programmes had encouraged was limited by grounding the programme street by street in deprived communities. Far from the grand sweep of redevelopment, each area, comprising around 500 'slum' houses in tightly packed terraced streets, would be upgraded house by house, as far as possible with existing residents in situ, using existing landlords where possible (North Islington Housing Rights Project 1976).

Housing co-operatives in inner London, Glasgow, and Liverpool, drawing on the earlier traditions we have discussed, took root in the wake of the 1970s policy shift in favour of communities and flourished because of public support for local community control following the failures of mass housing. These community-based housing organisations offer models of social organisation that are long-lasting, economically viable and state supported (Department of the Environment 1987a, 1987b; Cairncross *et al.* 2002). They also rely directly on the shift from large-scale to more sensitive, local-scale state intervention and support. The new community-led housing initiatives of the 1970s led to other developments, including adventure playgrounds, nurseries, summer play schemes, and law centres, all involved parents and other residents. These activities relied on a radical change in government style, no longer doing *to* people but *with* people, adopting an enabling, supportive and framing approach. Other European countries provide working models of more localised and community-oriented housing provision and public service delivery than is typical in the UK (Power 1993). They demonstrate how useful a diversified mix of social provision can be, not in opposition to the state, but as an alternative approach to developing communities with state support.

Providing a legal and financial framework of accountability for community-level organisations is time-consuming, but the added value of community and voluntary activities is most clearly seen in housing co-operatives and tenant management organisations, which emerged strongly in the 1970s and 1980s, because their activities have a clear funding stream and measurable performance (Newton and Tunstall 2012) (see below). Housing associations, part of this voluntary movement, had been dormant for nearly a century but took on a new lease of life (Jones 1985). Few would now argue against the shift from giant new housing developments that tore existing communities and social networks apart, to a more locally based and participative approach not only in Britain but across the developed world (Willmott and Young 1957; Power 1993; Pluntz 1995; Crowson *et al.* 2009).

Learning from neighbourhood programmes

Some larger-scale lessons about the balance between state and community derive from the Priority Estates Project of the 1980s which emerged directly from both the legacy of state housing and the legacy of community action of the 1970s (Department of the Environment 1981). As an idea it predated the wholesale attack by the Conservative government of Margaret Thatcher on local authority powers, public ownership of all kinds and council landlord systems in particular. The Priority Estates Project was a Labour-conceived idea, drawing on the tenant co-operative models of Islington, Liverpool and Glasgow, to combat the sense of anomie and loss of community in large public housing estates, and to reverse the disrepair, environmental neglect and remote management that were the hallmark of run-down council estates. There were at least 5,000 such housing estates covering at least 2 million homes in the UK. The original aim was to reverse the growing rejection of council estates under the banner of 'difficult to let' (Department of the Environment 1983). No less than one-third of the entire council housing stock was engulfed by these problems.

The Priority Estates Projects did not stop at housing management; they embraced tenant training, community provision, land reclamation and replanting, activities for children and young people, policing and security. They paved the way for widespread recognition that communities can do, and want to do, far more for themselves than state landlords had allowed. Ironically, local authorities did not want to 'lose their chains' and often resisted tenants' efforts to gain a bigger say in their own communities (Macey 1982a, 1982b). But one of the strengths of the Priority Estates Project was that it was a public sector initiative, running counter to the large-scale privatisation that was the hallmark of the Thatcher years. It was community-based, yet led directly to government backing for tenant management and community co-operatives as alternatives to council-controlled, poorly managed estates (Department of Environment 1987a, 1987b). It did not involve privatisation of estates, which was deeply unpopular, but it proved that locally based alternatives to large-scale state-run services could be more economical, more attractive and more successful (Power and Tunstall 1995; Tunstall and Coulter 2006).

Meanwhile, draconian and radical political funding changes of the early 1980s created community tensions and conflicts that erupted in serious riots in deprived areas of inner London, Manchester, Liverpool, Bristol and Birmingham, leading the government to support many targeted neighbourhood, inner-city and outer-estate rescue programmes to compensate for the harm to local communities of government cuts, very much as Lyndon Johnson's Great Society tried to compensate for racial inequalities and social upheaval (Scarman 1982).[5] Government supported many creative, community initiatives to manage and deliver local services differently, with more community involvement, more decentralised budgets and local staff, helping communities, while modifying the role of local authorities in favour of enabling. This philosophy and method worked best in rented housing estates where social need was increasingly concentrated because there was a regular income stream from rents and a regular job to be done of ensuring the viability of estates (Department of the Environment 1981). This gave local government and community representatives a shared interest in making headway.

Surprisingly, the Conservative governments of the late 1980s and early 1990s embraced not only ideas of community empowerment, but also the more radical co-operative ideals of the nineteenth and twentieth centuries in order to reshape the state and give communities the power to take over the running and even collective ownership of their homes (Glasgow District Council 1986; Hambleton and Hoggett 1987). Co-operatives, they quickly discovered, dominated housing and social programmes in countries as far apart as Sweden, Denmark, Spain and Italy (Power 1993; Jones 1985). Devolving real power through budgets and staff created community-oriented housing solutions that have worked in deprived communities for over 30 years in the UK and have a far longer history on the continent (Ambrose and Stone 2010; Power and Houghton 2007; Power 1993).

Four critical conditions underpinned the neighbourhood housing programmes that succeeded in transforming community conditions in many Labour heartlands and strongholds (Power 1989; Eldonian Community

---

[5] Lord Scarman visited the Tulse Hill Priority Estates Project in 1981 as part of his evidence-gathering for the Inquiry.

Based Housing Association 2008; Department of the Environment 1987a, 1987b; Mainwaring 1988)—community involvement, local budgets, locally based staff, and government support. These successful models worked within a legal framework, clear accountability, training and professional support. They were not stand-alone, but localised bodies operating within tried-and-tested rules, as registered co-operatives must do (Co-operative Group 2012). Channelling the pent-up energy, self-help instincts and ambitions of citizens needs skills, expertise and wider links. But it offers significant benefits (Cairncross *et al.* 2002).

Danish co-operative housing companies show that community-based services work when elected community representatives undergo training in basic organisational and community skills and responsibilities, since social housing companies by law have a majority of elected tenants on the board in Denmark. Preparation for the complex tasks of solving community problems requires a recognised system of training, backed by funding support and public investment. The Danish national tenant training centre at Haraldskaer provides this kind of support and was an inspirational model for what followed in the UK. Thus in 1991 the British government backed the establishment of the National Communities Resource Centre outside Chester to give residents and front-line staff the know-how and confidence to tackle serious community problems for themselves. The National Communities Resource Centre offers training and support to around 5,000 active community residents a year from deprived communities, mainly social housing estates, who want to solve local community problems.[6] Working in troubled urban communities reinforces the need for training community leaders and community organisers to carry the responsibilities of local decision-making and local community enterprise, as an independent evaluation of the training programme shows (Turcu 2011).

The value of community-based initiatives

Evidence supporting the value of community-based initiatives is far from comprehensive, given the small scale of most community endeavours, but

[6] For further information about the National Communities Resource Centre see http://www.traffordhall.com/.

concrete evidence of cost saving and better outcomes, particularly in rented housing, persuaded New Labour, to adopt a community-based approach towards deprived neighbourhoods (Social Exclusion Unit 1998c). The National Strategy for Neighbourhood Renewal, developed by the Prime Minister's Social Exclusion Unit, drew on the evidence from the 1980s and 1990s that we have discussed in this paper to tackle unequal conditions (Social Exclusion Unit 1998a, 1998b, 1999a–c, 2000a–m). Meanwhile the CASE Areas and Families studies provide evidence of the gains on the ground made by the shift in approach that happened through the National Strategy (Paskell and Power 2005; Power *et al.* 2011).

Thus, there is no party-political division over the value of community-based approaches to solving community problems. There is no serious disagreement over the value of social capital and the contribution that community leaders can make to local community activity and services. There is multi-party support for co-operatives, community organising, mutual aid, and the non-profit voluntary sector. Community-based services, community empowerment and co-operation are universally accepted as helpful, in countries around the globe (Birchall 1997). Yet community-level organisations, services and structures already at work in this country are currently losing vital, low-level flows of funds due to cuts by local authorities (Mulgan 2010). Passing responsibility down to local government, while imposing severe budget cuts, simply accelerates the withdrawal of support for communities, however strong the rationale for keeping support in place (Slocock 2012). Community and neighbourhood-level interventions to prevent serious breakdown demonstrate the lower costs of preventive support, compared with problem-driven remedies. The examples that have worked in the past and have been discussed here show this positive effect (Early Action Taskforce 2012).

The Islington Fairness Commission, convened after a major local election victory by Labour in 2010 against the national trend, has grappled with the dilemma of how to implement the centrally imposed cuts as fairly as possible, and simultaneously how to protect front-line and community-based services, of which Islington has been a long-standing advocate. It plans to implement its commitment to the living wage for all low-paid staff it employs, by avoiding wastage of scarce and shrinking resources within the bureaucracy of local government. This includes reducing the salary of the new chief executive and other highly paid administrators.

Interestingly, it has rediscovered the 1970s community-based model of tenant management organisations (TMOs) and tenant co-operatives which flourished on Islington's estates with council support, borrowing from nineteenth-century co-operative ideas (Power 1976). There are now 30 such tenant co-operatives in the lowest-income communities in the borough, mainly on council estates, offering a model of community-based, but largely publicly funded, housing management services giving tenants a clear say, training, significant decision-making responsibility, some budget-ary control, a route into work, many local social services, strong control over local conditions and over the decisions that affect them. These groups encourage other forms of community enterprise: support for the elderly, children's and youth activities, environmental care, community gardens and so on. Islington's TMOs outperform the local authority but operate with its support and within the framework of funding, fairness and pro-bity it lays down. Many examples of successful community provision that complement and supplement public services, but do not supplant them, illustrate this relationship (Islington Fairness Commission 2011).

Conclusion: evaluating the Big Society

There is more to the Big Society than a political smoke screen for cuts; there are historic precedents, in the recent as well as distant past, for recognising the Big Society as part of a long tradition of community organisation and social movements that have helped retain the viability of low-income com-munities in the face of damaging incursions on people's survival strategies, as new economic imperatives have undermined old ways of doing things. This surely applies today (Jackson 2009). The links between the lowest levels of community-based action and the highest levels of decision-taking with many connections in between will in the end shape the outcomes from the current sense of upheaval. If public resources and underpinning shrink too far or too fast, community support organisations will be increasingly forced to withdraw. Then serious trouble may erupt as happened in the 1980s and 1990s (Power and Tunstall 1997) and has already shown itself in several major cities in August 2011. If, on the other hand, lines of sup-port and communication are opened up, then innovative new approaches to problem solving may emerge as they have in previous economic crises (Giddens and Diamond 2005; Goldsmith 2010).

There is little evidence that the Big Society, as opposed to the 'big state', will on its own carry us through the difficult challenges we face, which are raised by the other chapters in this book, without major underpinning and an overarching public framework, which includes steady, if low-level, funding. Modern transport and mobility, the environment and energy supply, currency and finance, trade, health and education, housing, policing and security are all activities that communities depend on but cannot control or run independently; they require a steady, clear role for the state. At the same time there is every reason to seize the chance to build more social capital where it is weakest, in the poorest areas, and to support its use value for many local purposes in all communities through the broad framework of the state.

There is no way that the state can withdraw from its overarching responsibilities, or that private interests, at whatever level, can adequately fill those roles, particularly in poor communities (Timmins 1996). The tortuous American reform of health care, the sub-prime mortgage and banking crises, the euro zone crisis and steep energy price rises have shown just how vulnerable weaker members of society are, and how much we rely on co-operative action at government level as well as in communities (Economist 2011d, 2011e). The need for the modern state is clear, but a different way of doing things is also vital, as the cuts will not disappear quickly. Communities will find ways to articulate their responses, and organise new ways of coping, which will put pressure on governments to change their way of doing things too.[7]

The Big Society started out as an idea about the small scale at which communities function and organise their survival. This chapter has argued that such an approach is based on long-run evidence about how society and neighbourhoods work. However, the more closely we examine the complementary functions of state and civil society, the more interconnected they become. Major challenges such as climate change, energy shortages and skills mismatches will rely increasingly heavily on community resilience and new kinds of community capacity (Hopkins 2008). But they will rely equally on functioning states and on inter-governmental co-operation—in other words the Big Society writ large (Stern 2009, 2012).

---

[7] For further discussion see podcast of *Big Society and social policy in Britain: A panel discussion* (2011), available at: http://www2.lse.ac.uk/newsAndMedia/videoAndAudio/channels/publicLecturesAndEvents/player.aspx?id=868 *(Accessed 3 November 2011)*

Hernando de Soto's seminal work, *The Mystery of Capital* (2007), illustrates the central importance of publicly accepted legal, financial and political frameworks to allow citizens to invest in and develop solutions to their housing and livelihood challenges. The institutions of the modern state provide the basis for the workings of the economy and society itself (de Soto 2007). The Big Society idea can help address some of our biggest threats: deepening inequality and its social costs; social breakdown in many areas; the environment and climate change. Only with widespread citizen participation can these problems be tackled, yet the state has a key role in amassing and redistributing both resources and power on behalf of all citizens, who, in turn, rely on strongly organised, well-informed and democratically answerable citizen groups, willing to give time and resources for the common good. The deeply complex, intangible but invaluable phenomenon of social capital, collective efficacy, co-operation, mutual aid, is put at risk, not only by an overactive state, but also by a hands-off approach to deep-set problems. As Steven Goldsmith argues in his wide-ranging study of civic entrepreneurship, we need both community-level initiative and a supportive government (Goldsmith 2010). Community organising cannot deliver in a vacuum; communities rely on a response from powerful sections of society, most especially the state, to equalise conditions by distributing power, responsibility and resources fairly. When the gap between the top and the bottom of society grows too wide, then the response is too weak. Jared Diamond argues powerfully that this is a major factor in societal collapse and could affect modern, wealthy but highly unequal societies (Diamond 2005).

In the move towards strong communities there are three conditions for success, which form our conclusions. Firstly, the state must recognise and reinforce its long-run role as broker of different interests in favour of common justice, the rule of law, enforcement of basic conditions, and equaliser, holding together increasingly diverse and sometimes divided communities. We need to balance the power of citizens to form groups and to take collective action with the power and duty of the state to enforce openness and underpin these efforts, requiring detailed regulation, a clear, supportive legal framework and financial transparency, such as allows the Mondragón co-operatives and the Danish housing companies to thrive, even in periods of austerity.

Secondly, the state must redeploy public resources in favour of disadvantaged communities through locally responsive services devolving some decision-making to targeted community-level organisations, within a widely supported public framework of legal, regulatory and financial safeguards. Co-operatives, development trusts, non-profit mutuals and small local private enterprises, flourish with a strong framework of support, training and access to information requiring collaborative structures, as European countries demonstrate. This approach has enabled Tenant Management Organisations (TMOs) to grow in this country, making them currently the target of government interest in mutuals (Mutuals Taskforce 2011).

Thirdly, citizens, in small community-based groups, cannot tackle widespread, complex and costly problems alone. They lack the power, the technical know-how, the resources and the broad consensus of support that is necessary. They need a supportive, responsive state. There are some problems that are simply beyond what any one group or series of groups can do, and require higher-level governmental action (Stern 2012). Getting this balance right has become the art of government.

The Big Society encapsulates the core idea that we are social beings, that we relate most directly to local communities within local areas, that we need to tackle many local problems on a local scale, and that communities and individuals are capable of organising and delivering many basic forms of help within communities, without relying on the intervention of the state which is inevitably more remote, bureaucratic and insensitive to local problems than local residents. However, as individuals and members of small social groups, we are part of something bigger, called society.

Acknowledgements

I would like to thank Laura Lane for helping with the research for this chapter, Nicola Serle for proofing, editing and checking references, Cheryl Conner and Isobel Esberger for their help with amendments and Peter Taylor-Gooby for his invaluable advice, along with helpful suggestions from readers. I accept full responsibility for any errors or omissions.

References

Alayo, J. (2011) 'How Bilbao and the Basque Country are Affected by Spain's Financial Crisis', presentation at the City Reformers Group Meeting, London School of Economics, 21 March.

Alinsky, S. (1972) *Rules for Radicals: A Pragmatic Primer for Realistic Radicals* (New York: Vintage).

Allen, G. (2011a) *Early Intervention: The Next Steps. An Independent Report to Her Majesty's Government* (London: Cabinet Office).

Allen, G. (2011b) *Early Intervention: Smart Investment, Massive Savings. The Second Independent Report to Her Majesty's Government* (London: Cabinet Office).

Ambrose, P. and Stone, J. (2010) *Happiness, Heaven and Hell in Paddington: A Comparative Study of the Empowering Housing Management Practises of WECH (Walterton and Elgin Community Homes)* (London: Walterton and Elgin Community Homes).

American Assembly (2007) *Retooling for Growth: Building a Twenty-first Century Economy in America's Older Industrial Areas* (New York: Columbia University).

Axelrod, R. (1984) *The Evolution of Co-operation* (New York: Basic Books).

Baron, S., Field, J. and Schuller, T. (eds) (2000) *Social Capital: Critical Perspectives* (Oxford: Oxford University Press).

Beveridge, W. (1942) *Social Insurance and Allied Services* (London: HMSO).

Bifulco, L., Bricocoli, M. and Monteleone, R. (2008) 'Activation and Local Welfare in Italy: Trends and Issues', *Social Policy and Administration* 42(2): 143–159.

Birchall, J. (1997) *The International Co-operative Movement* (Manchester: Manchester University Press).

Blond, P. (2010) *Red Tory: How Left and Right Have Broken Britain and How We Can Fix It* (London: Faber and Faber).

Brandes Gratz, R. (1995) *The Living City: How America's Cities Are Being Revitalized by Thinking Small in a Big Way* (San Francisco: Wiley).

Briggs, A. (1968) *Victorian Cities* (Harmondsworth: Penguin Books).

Briggs, A. (1986) *A Social History of England* (London: Penguin Books).

Browne, J. and Levell, P. (2010) *The Distributional Effect of Tax and Benefit Reforms to be Introduced Between June 2010 and April 2014: A Revised Assessment* (London: Institute for Fiscal Studies).

Cairncross, L., Morrell, C., Darke, J. and Brownhill, S. (2002) *Tenants Managing: An evaluation of Tenant Management Organisations in England*, Office of the Deputy Prime Minister [online], http://www.communities.gov.uk/documents/housing/pdf/138919.pdf (accessed on 1 November 2011).

Cameron, D. (2009) *The Big Society*, 10 November [online], http://www.conservatives.com/News/Speeches/2009/11/David_Cameron_The_Big_Society.aspx (Accessed 1 November 2011).

Cameron, D. (2006) 'We Stand for Social Responsibility', 1 October [online], http://www.conservatives.com/News/Speeches/2006/10/Cameron_We_stand_for_social_responsibility.aspx (accessed 14 May 2012).

Cameron, D. (2012a) 'Launch of Big Society Capital', 4 April [online], http://www.number10.gov.uk/news/prime-minsiter-unveils-big-society-capital (accessed 9 May 2012).

Cameron, D. (2012b) *Co-operatives Bill to Help Build a Fairer Economy*, Speech on January 19 [online] http://www.conservatives.com/News/Speeches/2012/01/Co_operatives_Bill. aspx (accessed 14 May 2012).

Cantle, T. (2001) *Community cohesion: A report of the independent review team*, Home Office [online], http://resources.cohesioninstitute.org.uk/Publications/Documents/Document/ DownloadDocumentsFile.aspx?recordId=96&file=PDFversion (accessed on 1 November 2011).

Centre for Social Justice (CSJ) (2007) *Breakthrough Britain: Ending the Costs of Social Breakdown* (London: CSJ).

Citizens UK (2011) *Living Wage Campaign* [online], http://www.citizensuk.org/category/ living-wage-campaign/ (accessed on 1 November 2011).

Co-operative Group: About Us (2012) [online], http://www.co-operative.coop/corporate/ aboutus/ (accessed 14 May 2012).

Crook, F., Lewis, D., Stewart, R., Wilding, K. and Le Grand, J.(2011) *Big Society and Social Policy in Britain: A Panel Discussion*, podcast of public lecture, Department of Social Policy and STICERD, London School of Economics, 27 January [online], http://www2. lse.ac.uk/newsAndMedia/videoAndAudio/channels/publicLecturesAndEvents/player. aspx?id=868 (accessed 3 November 2011).

Crossman, R. (1979) *The Crossman Diaries: Selections from the Diaries of a Cabinet Minister 1964–1970*, condensed edition (Worthing: Littlehampton Book Services Ltd).

Crowson, N., Hilton, M. and McKay, J. (eds) (2009) *NGOs in Contemporary Britain: Non-state Actors in Society and Politics since 1945* (Basingstoke: Palgrave Macmillan).

Czischke, D. and Pittini, A. (eds) (2007) *Housing Europe 2007: Review of Social, Co-operative and Public Housing in the 27 EU Member States* (Brussels: CECODHAS European Social Housing Observatory).

Davis, A. (1971) *If They Come in the Morning: Voices of Resistance* (London: Orbach and Chambers Ltd).

Davis, A. (1974) *Angela Davis: An Autobiography* (New York: International Publishers).

de Soto, H. (2007) *The Mystery of Capital: Why Capitalism Triumphs in the West and Fails Everywhere Else*, reprint edition (London: Basic Books).

Department for Communities and Local Government (2008) *Citizenship Survey, 2007–8* (London: DCLG).

Department of Health and Human Services (2010) *Head Start Impact Study. Final Report* (Washington DC: Office of Planning, Research and Evaluation, Administration for Children and Families, U.S. Department of Health and Human Services).

Department of the Environment (1981) *Priority Estates Project 1981: Improving Problem Council Estates* (London: HMSO).

Department of the Environment (1977) *Inner Area Studies: Liverpool, Birmingham and Lambeth. Summaries of Consultants' Final Reports* (London: HMSO).

Department of the Environment (1983) *Investigation of Difficult to Let Estates* (London: HMSO).

Department of the Environment (1987a) *Right to Manage* (London: HMSO).

Department of the Environment (1987b) *Tenants in the Lead: The Housing Co-operatives Review* (London: HMSO).

Der Spiegel (2010) 'Debate over train station turns ugly: Stuttgart protesters storm construction site', 26 August [online], http://www.spiegel.de/international/germany/ 0,1518,713913,00.html (accessed on 1 November 2011).

Diamond, J. (2005) *Collapse: How Societies Choose to Fail or Succeed* (New York: Penguin Books).

Dryzek, J. and Dunleavy, P. (2009) *Theories of the Democratic State* (Basingstoke and New York: Palgrave Macmillan).

Dunleavy, P. (1981) *The Politics of Mass Housing in Britain 1945–1975: A Study of Corporate Power and Professional Influence in the Welfare State* (Oxford: Oxford University Press).

Early Action Task Force (2011) *The Triple Dividend: Thriving Lives. Costing Less. Contributing More* (London: Community Links).

Economist (2007) 'Handicapping Harlem', 1 October.

Economist (2008) 'Harlem Reborn: A dream is No Longer Deferred', 13 March.

Economist (2011a) 'A Not Very Happy Birthday: What Will Become of Barack Obama's Health Reforms', 17 March.

Economist (2011b) 'Germany's Victorious Greens: A Greener Future?', 31 March.

Economist (2011c) 'Atlanta's Public Schools', 15 July.

Economist (2011d) 'Bazooka or Peashooter? Greece's New Bail-out Helps, But Should Have Gone Further', 30 July.

Economist (2011e) 'Staring into the Abyss: Europe and its Currency', Special Report, 12 November.

Economist (2012) 'There Are all Too many Alternatives: The Euro Crisis', Briefing, 12 May.

Eisenstadt, N. (2011a) *Early Years, Poverty and Parenting*, presentation at the Obstacles and Opportunities workshop, Trafford Hall, Chester, March 2011 [online], http://sticerd.lse. ac.uk/textonly/LSEHousing/Events/Obstacles_and_Opportunities/Naomi_Eisenstadt. pdf (accessed 9 May 2012).

Eisenstadt, N. (2011b). *Providing a Sure Start: How Government Discovered Early Childhood* (Bristol: Policy Press).

Eldonian Community Based Housing Association (2008) *Annual Report 2007: The Rebirth of Liverpool … the Eldonian Way*, [online], http://www.eldonians.org.uk/podium/eld/ ces_docstore.nsf/wpg/3B746F27903B270F802573A8002F0ACB/$file/ELDONIAN%20 CBHA%20ANNUAL%20REPORT%202007.pdf (accessed 3 November 2011).

Esping-Andersen, G. (1990) *The Three Worlds of Welfare Capitalism* (Princeton, NJ: Princeton University Press).

Esping-Andersen, G., Gallie, D., Hemerijck, A. and Myles, J. (2003) *Why We Need a New Welfare State* (Oxford: Oxford University Press).

Etzioni, A. (1997) *The New Golden Rule: Community and Morality in a Democratic Society* (London: Profile).

Freire, P. (1996) *Pedagogy of the Oppressed* (London: Penguin).

Garrow, D.J. (1999) *Bearing the Cross: Martin Luther King, Jr. and the Southern Christian Leadership Conference, 1955–1968* (New York: Harper Collins).

Giddens, A. and Diamond, P. (2005) *The New Egalitarianism* (Cambridge: Polity).

Glasgow District Council (1986) *Inquiry into Housing in Glasgow* (Glasgow: Glasgow District Council).

Goldsmith, S. (2010) *The Power of Social Innovation: How Civic Entrepreneurs Ignite Community Networks for Good* (San Francisco, CA: Wiley).

Gramlich, E. (1986) 'Evaluation of Education Projects: the Case of the Perry Preschool Program', *Economics of Education Review* 5(1): 17–24.

Guardian and London School of Economics (2011) *Reading the Riots: Investigating England's Summer of Disorder* (London: The Guardian).

Hall, P. (1988) *Cities of Tomorrow: An Intellectual History of Urban Planning and Design in the Twentieth Century* (Oxford: Basil Blackwell).

Hall, P. (1999) 'Social Capital in Britain', *British Journal of Politics* 29: 417–461.

Halpern, D. (2004) *Social Capital* (Cambridge: Polity Press).

Hambleton, R. and Hoggett, P. (eds) (1987) *The Politics of Decentralisation: Theory and Practice of a Radical Local Government Initiative*, Working paper 46 (Bristol: School for Advanced Urban Studies, University of Bristol).

Harloe, M. (1995) *The People's Home? Social Rented Housing in Europe and America* (Oxford, UK and Cambridge, MA: Blackwell.

Hills, J. *et al.* (2004) *One Hundred Years of Poverty and Policy* (York: Joseph Rowntree Foundation).

Hills, J. (ed.) (1996) *New Inequalities: The Changing Distribution of Income and Wealth in the UK* (Cambridge: Cambridge University Press).

Hills, J. (2004) *Inequality and the State* (Oxford: Oxford University Press).

Hills, J., Le Grand, J. and Piachaud, D. (eds) (2002) *Understanding Social Exclusion* (Oxford: Oxford University Press).

Hills, J., Sefton, T. and Stewart, K. (2009) *Towards a More Equal Society? Poverty, Inequality and Policy since 1997* (Bristol: Policy Press).

HM Treasury (1998) *Comprehensive Spending Review: Cross-Departmental Review of Provision for Young Children, Supporting Papers, Volumes 1 and 2, July* (London: TSO).

Holyoake, G.J. (1857) *Self-help by the People: The History of the Rochdale Pioneers* (London: George Allen & Unwin).

Home Office (1977) *Gilding the Ghetto: The State and the Poverty Experiments* (London: Community Development Project inter-project editorial team).

Hones, M. (2010) *Reviving Britain's Terraces: Life after Pathfinder* (London: Save Britain's Heritage).

Hopkins, R. (2008) *The Transition Handbook: From Oil Dependency to Local Resilience* (London: Green Books).

US Department of Housing and Urban Development (1977) *Housing and Community Development Act* (Washington, DC: US Department of Housing and Urban Development).

Illich, I. (1971) *Deschooling Society* (London: Calder and Boyars).

Islington Fairness Commission (2011) *Closing the Gap: The Final Report of the Islington Fairness Commission* (London: Islington Fairness Commission).

Ivereigh, A. (2010) *Faithful Citizens* (London: Darton, Longman and Todd).

Jackson, G. (1971) *Soledad Brother: The Prison Letters of George Jackson* (London: Cape).

Jackson, T. (2009) *Prosperity Without Growth? The Transition to a Sustainable Economy* (London: Routledge).

Jacquier, C. (1991) *Voyage dans dix quartiers Européens en crise* (Paris: l'Harmattan).

Jargowski, P. (1997) *Poverty and Place: Ghettos, Barrios, and the American City* (New York: Russell Sage).

Jones, P. (ed.) (1985) *National Federation of Housing Associations' Jubilee Album 1935–1985* (London: National Housing Federation).

Jones, W.G. (1986) *Denmark: A Modern History* (London: Croom Helm).

Kaiser, S. and Windmann, A. (2010) 'The "Stuttgart 21" revolt: Protests against mega project grow', *Spiegel Online*, 24 August [online], http://www.spiegel.de/international/germany/0,1518,713375,00.html (accessed on 1 November 2011).

Kasmir, S. (1996) *The Myth of Mondragón: Cooperatives, Politics and Working-class Life in a Basque Town* (Albany: State University of New York Press).

Katz, B. (2010) 'New Ideas from a Changed USA: The Future of Cities in Obama's America'. Presentation given at *Phoenix Cities—Surviving Financial, Social and Environmental Turmoil in Europe and the US*. LSE Housing and Communities, LSE Cities and Joseph Rowntree Foundation public discussion. London School of Economics, 16 March.

Kerner, O. (1968) *Kerner Report: The 1968 Report of the National Advisory Commission on Civil Disorder* (New York: Bantam Books).

King, Jr., M.L. (1958) *Stride Towards Freedom* (New York: Harper).

King, Jr., M.L. (1967) *Chaos or Community* (New York: Harper and Row).

Lemann, N. (1991) *The Promised Land: The Great Migration and How it Changed America* (London: Macmillan).

Lemann, N. (1994) 'The Myth of Community Development', *The New York Times* 9 January.

Locality (2011) *The Community Organisers Programme* [online], http://locality.org.uk/projects/community-organisers/ (accessed on 19 August 2011).

Macey, J. (1982a) *Housing Management*, fourth edition (London: Estates Gazette).

Macey, J. (1982b) Personal Communication with the Author.

Mainwaring, R. (1988) *The Walsall Experience: A Study of the Decentralisation of Walsall's Housing Service* (London: HMSO).

Malcolm, X and Haley, A. (1965) *The Autobiography of Malcolm X* (Harmondsworth: Penguin Books).

Maloney, W., Smith, G. and Stoker, G. (2001) 'Social Capital and the City', in B. Edwards, M. Foley and M. Diani (eds) *Beyond Tocqueville. Civil Society and the Social Capital Debate in Comparative Perspective* (Hanover, NH: University Press of New England).

Maloney, W., Smith, G. and Stoker, G. (2004) 'Voluntary Organisations and the Generation of Social Capital in City Politics', in M. Boddy and M. Parkinson (eds) *City Mmatters: Competitiveness, Cohesion and Urban Governance* Bristol: Policy Press).

Marris, P. and Rein, M. (1967) *Dilemmas of Social Reform: Poverty and Community Action in the United States.* (London: Routledge and Kegan Paul).

Massey, D. and Denton, N. (1993) *American Apartheid: Segregation and the Making of the Underclass* (Cambridge, MA: Harvard University Press).

Mayo, E. (1999) '*Brave New Economy*', speech delivered at the NEF Cooperative conference, June 2011 (Birmingham: NEF).

Mcgahey, R. and Vey, J. (2008) *Retooling for Growth: Building a 21st Century Economy in America's Older Industrial Areas* (American Assembly) (Washington, DC: Brookings Institution).

Miliband, D. (2011) *Joint Statement on Role of Community Organising in Reinvigorating Politics from the Grassroots* (Liverpool: Labour Conference).

Mitlin, D. and Satterthwaite D. (2004) *Empowering Squatter Citizen: Local Government, Civil Society and Urban Poverty Reduction* (London: Earthscan).

Mondragon Corporation (2010) *La Experienca co-operativa de Mondragon 1956–2008* [online], http://www.mcc.es/LinkClick.aspx?fileticket=8DgFa4sIOs0%3d&tabid=406 (accessed 13 January 2012).

Morenoff, J. , Sampson, R.J. and Raudenbush, S. (2001) 'Neighbourhood Inequality, Collective Efficacy, and the Spatial Dynamics of Urban Violence', *Criminology* 39: 517–560.

Moynihan, D.P. (1965) *The Negro Family: The Case for National Action* (Washington, DC: Office of Policy Planning and Research United States Department of Labor).

Mulgan, G. (2010) *Investing in Social Growth: Can the Big Society be More Than a Slogan?* (London: The Young Foundation).

Mumford, K. and Power, A. (2003) *East Enders: Family and Community in East London* (Bristol: The Policy Press).

Mutuals Taskforce (2011) *Our Mutual Friends: Making the Case for Public Service Mutuals* (London: Cabinet Office).

National Advisory Commission on Civil Disorders (1968) *Report of the National Advisory Commission on Civil Disorders* (Washington, DC: Government Printing Office).

National Communities Resource Centre (2011) *Trafford Hall: Home of the National Communities Resource Centre* [online] http://www.traffordhall.com/ (accessed on 3 November 2011).

Newton, R. and Tunstall, R. (2012) *Lessons for Localism: Tenant Self-management* (London: Urban Forum).

North Islington Housing Rights Project (1976) *Street by Street* (London: Shelter).

North Islington Housing Rights Project (1976) *Street by Street: Improvement & Tenant Control in Islington* (London: Shelter).

Obama, B. (1996) *Dreams from My Father: A Story of Race and Inheritance* (New York: Three Rivers Press).

Obama, B. (2006) *The Audacity of Hope: Thoughts on Reclaiming the American Dream* (New York: Crown Publishing).

Office of the Deputy Prime Minister (ODPM) (2006) *Neighbourhood Management—at the Turning Point?* Research report no 23, Programme Review 2005–06 (London: ODPM).

Osborne, D. and Gaebler, T. (1992) *Reinventing Government: How the Entrepreneurial Spirit is Transforming the Public Sector* (New York: Penguin Books).

Owen, R. (1821) *Report to the County of Lanark of a Plan for Relieving Public Distress* (Glasgow: Glasgow University Press).

Park, A. *et al.* (eds) (2008) *British Social Attitudes: The 24th Report* (London: Sage).

Park, A. *et al.* (eds) (2010) *British Social Attitudes: The 27th Report* (London: Sage).

Park, A. *et al.* (eds) (2011) *British Social Attitudes: The 28th Report* (London: Sage).

Parks, G. (2000) *The High/Scope Perry Preschool Project.* Juvenile Justice Program US Department of Justice, Office of Justice Programs, Office of Juvenile Justice and Delinquency Prevention [online], https://www.ncjrs.gov/pdffiles1/ojjdp/181725.pdf (accessed 14 May 2012).

Paskell, C. and Power, A. (2005) *The Future's Changed: Local Impacts of Housing, Environment and Regeneration Policy since 1997.* CASE report 29 (London: Centre for Analysis of Social Exclusion).

Pluntz, R. (1995) *A History of Housing in New York City: Dwelling Type and Social Change in the American Metropolis* (New York: Columbia University).

Power, A. and Houghton, J. (2007) *Jigsaw Cities: Big Places, Small Spaces* (Bristol: Policy Press).

Power, A. and Tunstall, R. (1995) *Swimming Against the Tide: Polarisation or Progress on 20 Unpopular Council Estates, 1980–1995* (York: Joseph Rowntree Foundation).

Power, A. and Tunstall, R. (1997) *Dangerous Disorder: Riots and Violent Disturbances in Thirteen Areas of Britain.* (York: Joseph Rowntree Foundation).

Power, A. (1976) *Holloway Tenant Co-operative Five Years On* (London: Shelter).

Power, A. (1979) *Tenant Co-operatives or Tenant Management Corporations in the USA* (London: North Islington Housing Right Project).

Power, A. (1987) *Property Before People: The Management of Twentieth Century Council Housing* (London: Allen & Unwin).

Power, A. (1989) *Guide to Local Housing Management* (London: Longman).

Power, A. (1993) *Hovels to High Rise: State Housing in Europe since 1850* (London: Routledge).

Power, A. (1997) *Estates on the Edge: The Social Consequences of Mass Housing in Northern Europe* (London: Palgrave Macmillan).

Power, A. (2007) *City Survivors: Bringing Up Children in Disadvantaged Neighbourhoods* (Bristol: Policy Press).

Power, A. (2009) *What Does Previous Experience Tell Us About the Impact of Downturns in the Economy on Low Income Areas and Communities,* Think piece for the Department for Communities and Local Government (Liverpool: Liverpool John Moores University).

Power, A. (2011) 'Research Visit to the Mondragón Corporation Headquarters', 10 and 11 June.

Power, A., Plöger, J. and Winkler, A. (2010) *Phoenix Cities: The Fall and Rise of Great Industrial Cities* (Bristol: Policy Press).

Power, A., Serle, N. and Willmot, H. (2011) *Obstacles and Opportunities: Today's Children, Tomorrow's Families,* CASE report 66 (London: Centre for Analysis of Social Exclusion).

Power, A., Willmot, H. and Davidson, R. (2011) *Family Futures: Poverty and Childhood in Urban Neighbourhoods* (Bristol: Policy Press).

Putnam, R. (2000) *Bowling Alone: The Collapse and Revival of American Community* (New York: Simon & Schuster).

Putnam, R., Leonardi, R. and Nanetti, R.Y. (1993) *Making Democracy Work: Civic Traditions in Modern Italy* (Princeton, NJ: Princeton University Press).

Richardson, L. (2008) *DIY Community Action: Neighbourhood Problems and Community Self-help* (Bristol: Policy Press).

Ridley, M. (1996) *The Origins of Virtue: Human Instincts and the Evolution of Co-operation* (London: Penguin Books).

Robson, B., Parkinson, M., Boddy M. and Maclennan, D. (2000) *The State of English Cities* (London: Department of the Environment, Transport and the Regions).

Sampson, R. J. (2004) 'Neighborhood and Community: Collective Efficacy and Community Safety', *New Economy* 11: 106–113.

Scarman, L. (1982) *The Scarman Report: the Brixton Disorders, 10–12 April 1981. Report of an Inquiry* (Harmondsworth: Penguin).

Schumacher, E.F. (1973) *Small is Beautiful: A Study of Economics as if People Mattered* (London: Blond and Briggs).

Scott, F.D. (1975) *Scandinavia* (Cambridge, MA: Harvard University Press).

Slocock, C. (2012) *The Big Society Audit 2102* (London: Civil Exchange).

Social Exclusion Unit (1998a) *Bringing Britain Together: A National Strategy for Neighbourhood Renewal.* (London: HMSO).

Social Exclusion Unit (1998b) *National Strategy for Neighbourhood Renewal: Report of Policy Action Team 7—Unpopular Housing* (London: HMSO).

Social Exclusion Unit (1998c) *National Strategy for Neighbourhood Renewal: Report of Policy Action Team 10—the Contribution of Sports and the Arts* (London: HMSO).

Social Exclusion Unit (1999a) *National Strategy for Neighbourhood Renewal: Report of Policy Action Team 3 - Enterprise and Social Exclusion* (London: HM Treasury).

Social Exclusion Unit (1999b) *National Strategy for Neighbourhood Renewal: Report of Policy Action Team 11—Schools Plus* (London: DFEE).

Social Exclusion Unit (1999) *National Strategy for Neighbourhood Renewal: Report of Policy Action Team 14—Access to Financial Services* (London: HM Treasury).

Social Exclusion Unit (2000a) *National Strategy for Neighbourhood Renewal: Report of Policy Action Team 1—Jobs for All* (London: DFEE).

Social Exclusion Unit (2000b) *National Strategy for Neighbourhood Renewal: Report of Policy Action Team 2—Skills* (London: DFEE).

Social Exclusion Unit (2000c) *National Strategy for Neighbourhood Renewal: Report of Policy Action Team 4—Neighbourhood Management* (London: HMSO).

Social Exclusion Unit (2000d) *National Strategy for Neighbourhood Renewal: Report of Policy Action Team 5—Housing Management* (London: HMSO).

Social Exclusion Unit (2000e) *National Strategy for Neighbourhood Renewal: Report of Policy Action Team 8—Anti-Social Behaviour* (London: HMSO).

Social Exclusion Unit (2000f) *National Strategy for Neighbourhood Renewal: Report of Policy Action Team 9—Community Self-Help* (London: HMSO).

Social Exclusion Unit (2000g) *National Strategy for Neighbourhood Renewal: Report of Policy Action Team 12—Young People* (London: DFEE).

Social Exclusion Unit (2000h) *National Strategy for Neighbourhood Renewal: Report of Policy Action Team 13—Shops* (London: HMSO).

Social Exclusion Unit (2000i) *National Strategy for Neighbourhood Renewal: Report of Policy Action Team 15—Closing the Digital Divide: Information and Communication Technologies in Deprived Areas* (London: HMSO).

Social Exclusion Unit (2000j) *National Strategy for Neighbourhood Renewal: Report of Policy Action Team 16—Learning Lessons* (London: HMSO).

Social Exclusion Unit (2000k) *National Strategy for Neighbourhood Renewal: Report of Policy Action Team 17—Joining It Up Locally* (London: HMSO).

Social Exclusion Unit (2000l) *National Strategy for Neighbourhood Renewal: Report of Policy Action Team 18—Better Information* (London: HMSO).

Social Exclusion Unit (2000m) *National Strategy for Neighbourhood Renewal: Report of Policy Action Team 6—Neighbourhood Wardens* (London: HMSO).

Social Exclusion Unit (2000n) *National Strategy for Neighbourhood Renewal: Report of Policy Action Team 17: Joining It Up Locally* (London: HMSO).

Stern, N. (2009) *A Blueprint for a Safer Planet: How to Manage Climate Change and Create a New Era of Progress and Prosperity* (London: Bodley Head).

Stern, N. (2012) *Climate Change and the New Industrial Revolution.* Lionel Robbins Memorial Lectures 2012 21–3 February 2012. London: LSE [online] , http://www2.lse.ac.uk/

asiaResearchCentre/events/individual/2012/120221-23-Stern.aspx (accessed 11 May 2012).

Stott, M. (ed.) (2011) *The Big Society Challenge* (Thetford: Keystone Development Trust).

Tenant Empowerment Programme (2008–2011) Tenant Services Authority, [online] http://www.tenantservicesauthority.org/server/show/nav.14619 (Accessed at 3 August 2010).

Thane, P. (2012) *The Ben Pimlott Memorial Lecture 2011: The 'Big Society' and the 'Big State': Creative Tension or Crowding Out.* London: Twentieth Century British History.

Thompson, F.M.L. (1992) *The Cambridge Social History of Britain, 1750–1950* Vols 1, 2, 3 (Cambridge: Cambridge University Press).

Timmins, N. (1996) *The Five Giants: A Biography of the Welfare State* (London: Fontana Press).

Titmuss, R.M. (1958) *Essays in the Welfare State* (London: Allen & Unwin).

Titmuss, R.M. (1970) *The Gift Relationship: From Human Blood to Social Policy* (Glasgow: HarperCollins).

Tunstall, R. (2011) *An Example of the Six Principles in Action: Learning from Tenant Management Organisations*, presentation at Department of Communities and Local Government seminar on neighbourhoods and localism, 10 February.

Tunstall, R. and Coulter, A. (2006) *Twenty-five Years on Twenty Estates: Turning the Tide?* (York: Joseph Rowntree Foundation).

Tunstall, R., Lupton, R., Power, A. and Richardson, L. (2011) *Building the Big Society.* CASE report 67 (London: Centre for Analysis of Social Exclusion).

Turcu, C. (2011) *Evaluations of the National Tenant Training Programme* (London: LSE Housing and Communities).

UNICEF (2011) *State of the World's Children: Adolescence; an Age of Opportunity* (New York: UNICEF).

Waldfogel, J. (2006) *What Children Need* (Cambridge, MA: Harvard University Press).

White, J. (2007) *London in the Nineteenth Century* (London: Jonathan Cape).

Whyte, W. and Whyte K.K. (1991) *Making Mondragón: The Growth and Dynamics of the Worker Cooperative Complex* (Ithaca: International Industrial and Labour Relations Press).

Wilkinson, R. and Pickett, K. (2009) *The Spirit Level: Why More Equal Societies Almost Always Do Better* (London: Allen Lane).

Willmott, P. and Young, M. (1957) *Family and Kinship in East London* (London: Routledge & Kegan Paul).

Wilson, W.J. (1987) *The Truly Disadvantaged: Inner City, the Underclass and Public Policy* (Chicago, IL: University of Chicago Press).

Wilson, W.J. (1997) *When Work Disappears: The World of the New Urban Poor* (New York: Vintage Books).

Wilson, W.J. (1999) *The Bridge Over the Racial Divide: Rising Inequality and Coalition Politics* (Berkeley CA: University of California Press).

Wilson, W.J. (2006) *There Goes the Neighbourhood: Racial, Ethnic and Class Tensions in Four Chicago Neighbourhoods and Their Meaning for America* (New York: Knopf).

Wilson, W.J. (2009a) *More Than Just Race: Being Black and Poor in the Inner City* (New York: W.W. Norton and Company).

Wilson, W.J. (2009b) 'Toward a Framework for Understanding Forces That Contribute to or Reinforce Racial Inequality', *Race and Social Problems* 1: 3–11.

Wollmann, H. (1985) 'Housing Policy: Between State Intervention and the Market', in K. Von Beyme and M. Schmidt (eds) *Policy and Politics in the FRG* (London: Gower).

Yunus, M. (1998) *Banker to the Poor: Micro-lending and the Battle Against World Poverty* (London: Arum Press).

Yunus, M. (2007) *Creating a World Without Poverty: Social Business and the Future of Capitalism* (New York: Public Affairs).

Zander, M. (1980) *The Law Making Process* (London: Weidenfeld & Nicolson).

8

Building a new politics?

GERRY STOKER

Introduction

If the social and economic challenges faced by Britain are going to be met—challenges outlined in the chapters in this book—it might reasonably be thought that citizens would need to believe that they lived in a country with an effective system of democratic governance and a vibrant politics. There are considerable doubts as to whether such a situation pertains at the beginning of the twenty-first century. We are helped to come to that judgement through findings from the Hansard Society's *Audit of Political Engagement* series which have been published annually since 2004.[1] There is substantial anti-political sentiment in Britain expressed through attitudes that indicate a lack of trust and faith in the politicians and the political system and behaviour which indicates that large numbers of British citizens have little engagement at all with formal politics. Moreover there is strong evidence that political alienation and disengagement is not evenly spread among all sections of society and indeed appears to be concentrating among some of the most disadvantaged in society. While denying there was a previous golden age of politics—looking back fifty years earlier—we can note that despite rising education levels, expanded media coverage of politics, and evidence that citizens are more confident in their own abilities, the sense that citizens can influence politics and governing decisions appears to have declined and the numbers not turning out to vote has increased. This evidence is explored in more depth in the first section of this chapter.

[1] For further information visit www.hansardsociety.org.uk.

The middle section of the chapter asks: does it matter that some citizens are alienated from politics? Broadly, we can look at the disaffection with politics through two understandings of the workings of liberal democracy labelled as protective and developmental perspectives. The protective perspective focuses on the working of democracy as a protection for individual freedom. It does not necessarily expect large-scale citizen participation in politics but rather just enough engagement to grant the system legitimacy. From this perspective it is important not to overreact to evidence of anti-politics but, given the scale of concern over the issue, to devise interventions that help to restore faith in politics. The developmental perspective, in contrast, seeks greater citizen participation both as a fuller expression of individual humanity and as a way of achieving better decision-making that is more effective in tackling collective problems. From this perspective, the negativity that surrounds politics tends to be seen as evidence that citizens have not been provided with a rich or deep enough democratic experience and, as such, should spark a major set of interventions to change how politics is done. Both perspectives, then, are paradigms that take a particular line on 'what is' happening but are also imbued with assumptions about 'what should be'. We explore the arguments of the advocates of both paradigms and test the quality of the evidence they offer. We conclude that both have something to offer when it comes to diagnosing the problems confronting British politics and thinking about solutions. Moreover, although our polity has learnt to live with a substantial degree of political disenchantment over decades, it is clear that disenchantment costs the quality of policy-making and democracy. Given the scale of policy challenges we face, leaving the issue alone is not an option.

The last section of the chapter turns to the issue of how to design solutions. It contrasts the approach of political engineers with that of democratic designers. Political engineers are guided more by insights from the protective perspective and try to use changes in electoral, party and intergovernmental systems to help representative democracy work more effectively; meanwhile, democratic designers are guided more by the developmental perspective and focus on new forms of citizen-based activism and citizen-oriented participation. In conclusion, we ask what further work social scientists might contribute to understanding and exploring the challenge of building a new politics.

The disappointed citizen and political disengagement

We should not assume that there was some prior golden age of vibrant politics in Britain. Here are some key findings from a survey about British attitudes to politics:

> Three in ten claim 'to never follow' accounts of political and governmental affairs.
>
> Two in ten can name no party leader or any government ministry.
>
> Three in ten 'never' talk about politics with friends and acquaintances.
>
> Only two in one hundred would regard involvement in politics as a preferred non-work activity.
>
> Eight in ten are doubtful of the promises made by candidates in elections.

These figures may not be surprising, until it is noted that the survey from which they are taken was conducted, not in 2011, but in 1959. Indeed, it was the first major academic study that looked in depth at public attitudes to politics. Its findings were published in 1963 in a comparative study of democracies by two American academics, Gabriel Almond and Sidney Verba, although the final finding was not included in the book itself but was reported later by Dennis Kavanagh (Almond and Verba 1963: 89, 96, 116, 263; Kavanagh 1980: 145). These findings suggest that disengagement from formal politics and cynicism about politicians are not recent phenomena.

Looking at the evidence about citizens' attitudes towards and engagement with politics in Britain at the beginning of the twenty-first century it is clear there is substantial anti-political sentiment expressed in negative attitudes towards politics and disengagement from it formal operations. It is difficult to argue that we have suddenly reached a crisis point, but the problems do appear to be deep-seated. What eight annual surveys from the Hansard Society (first undertaken in December 2003) tell us is that the average citizen in Britain could today be described as disappointed and disengaged by politics: disappointed by the practitioners, practice and outcomes of politics, and not actively engaged in the regular processes of politics. The scandal over MPs' expenses in 2009 did not create that disenchantment, but simply confirmed it.

The picture painted of the beginning of the twenty-first century by Table 8.1 suggests the overall pattern is relatively stable but negative in terms of the story it tells, providing a less than ringing endorsement of the British political system. Norris (2011) is right to claim that in Britain and in other advanced democracies there has been no collapse in faith in democracy but is mistaken in not recognising the scale of disenchantment and disengagement from politics, at least in Britain (Stoker 2006; Hay 2007). There is no great trend towards decline to point to rather signs of a stable and stubborn alienation. Citizens remain convinced by the benefits of democracy but are unconvinced by the role of politics in delivering that democracy. The annual Hansard survey results tells us that at the beginning of the twenty-first century in Britain, consistently, two-thirds believe the system of governing Britain needs a great deal or a lot of improvement. It would appear that seven in ten of us have little or no trust in politicians in general. Few of us have a strong sense of political efficacy, with only a third agreeing with the statement 'when people like me get involved in politics, they really can change the way that the UK is run'. When it comes to the UK Parliament, perhaps reflecting the impact of the expenses row, the number of those satisfied with it has dropped from just over a third to just over a quarter since the Hansard survey was first undertaken in 2003. About half of citizens say they are interested in politics and about half claim a respectable level of knowledge about it. But less than two in ten could be described as an activist in terms of undertaking a modest range of political actions.

What people do as opposed to what they think about politics is explored more fully in Table 8.2. Most citizens are not regularly politically engaged when measured by acts aimed at the formal processes of politics. The most popular political acts offered by citizens who were asked to remember what they had done over the last two or three years have an individual flavour and involve relatively little effort, such as voting, signing a petition or boycotting a product. Collective political action, such as going to a meeting, appears to be something that few citizens can remember undertaking. Online political engagement, which is seen by some as a driver of new opportunities for politics (Gibson 2009), is only undertaken by less than one in ten; and protests and demonstrations engage relatively few despite the media coverage that such action can attract. Indeed, according to the

2011 Hansard Society audit, over half of all citizens in 2010 engaged in no political activity in the previous two or three years, as measured against a rather modest range of political actions beyond the act of voting.

Table 8.1 Political attitudes and public engagement, 2003–10

	Year							
% Citizens	2003	2004	2005	2006	2007	2008	2009	2010
Great deal or fair amount of knowledge claimed about politics	42	45	39	49	44	48	51	53
Perceived sense personal political efficacy	37	37	33	33	31	31	37	30
Generally trust politicians not much or not at all	70			70			73	
Interested in politics	50	53	56	54	51	52	53	58
Satisfied with UK Parliament	36			36			33	27
Believe governing system needs improving quite a lot or a great deal	60	63	62	61	62	64	69	64
Activist (three or more political acts)					12	11	16	13

Source: Developed from data in the Hansard Society's *Audit of Political Engagement 8: The 2011 Report* and *Audit of Political Engagement 7: The 2010 report*.[2]

[2] For the 2011 report Ipsos MORI interviewed a representative quota sample of 1,197 adults in Great Britain aged 18 or over, face-to-face, at home, between 3 and 9 December 2010. For the 2010 report Ipsos MORI interviewed a representative quota sample of 1,156 adults in Great Britain aged 18 or over, face-to-face, at home, between 3 and 9 December 2010.

Table 8.2 Political activity, 2003–10

% Respondents	2003	2004	2005	2006	2007	2008	2009	2010
				Year				
A Voted in the last local council election	51	50	55	53	50	47	49	58
B Discussed politics or political news with someone else	38	38	39	41	41	40	41	42
C Signed a petition	39	44	45	47	40	37	40	36
D Donated money or paid a membership fee to a charity or campaigning organisation	41	45	45	39	37	37	42	39
E Done voluntary work	23	28	22	27	23	22	29	25
F Boycotted certain products for political, ethical or environmental reasons	19	21	18	21	19	18	19	16
G Expressed my political opinions online	n/a	n/a	n/a	n/a	10	8	9	8
H Been to any political meeting	5	6	6	9	6	4	8	6
I Donated money or paid a membership fee to a political party	5	6	6	5	4	3	5	3
J Taken part in a demonstration, picket or march	5	6	5	5	4	3	4**	4
None of these	17	16	17	19	20	20	23	19
Don't know	–	*	*	1	2	1	*	1

* Please note that the list of activities is different in Audits 1–4, and therefore comparisons with Audits 5–8 should be seen as indicative only
** APE 7 wording for half the sample '… march or strike'.
Source: Developed from data in the Hansard Society's *Audit of Political Engagement 8: The 2011 Report*. Methodology as above (fn 2). Respondents were asked which of these activities they had done in the last two or three years.

Does Table 8.2 present a fair portrait of Britain's political activity? After all, this is a Britain that has seen large-scale demonstrations in recent years involving many young citizens over many issues, such as the Iraq war in 2003 and plans to increase students' fees in 2010. Marsh *et al.* (2006), using non-survey techniques, claim young people are interested in politics but just turned off by the way that formal politics works. In these growing protests and social movements, others see the seeds for an alternative politics (Dryzek 2000; della Porta *et al.* 2006; Stoker *et al.* 2011: 51–70[3]). Yet as Marsh and colleagues admit, their young respondents might have talked in a way that could be defined as political but few were actively engaged in formal politics or active protest. Evidence about whether the amount and extent of protest is increasing needs to be treated with caution as the survey data use different questions, and sometimes fail to distinguish between lifetime and more recent political acts (for a further analysis see chapter three in Stoker *et al.* 2011). Protest remains an act for a very small minority of citizens. Surveys are good at capturing in broad terms how a representative sample of citizens behaves, but we should remain open to the idea that, under different circumstances, their behaviour might change.

Survey evidence also confirms that alienation from politics is not equally spread throughout all social groups. Given that socioeconomic factors are widely seen as a key driver in participation (see Verba *et al.* (1995) for the classic statement), this is not surprising. Those with higher income, education and status in their employment are much more likely to participate in politics (see Stoker 2006: 93–99 for an analysis). In British politics there are noteworthy differences to be observed among diverse social groups in terms of their political engagement and attitudes, along lines of gender, ethnic background and socioeconomic status (see Table 8.3).

Men and women appear equally likely to vote and be in the political activist category. Similar proportions have a sense of political efficacy. The larger differences emerge when it comes to claims about political knowledge and interest, with men being more certain about their knowledge and more categorical about their interest. Responses to knowledge questions,

[3] The lead author for Chapter 3 in Stoker *et al.*, (2011) is my former Southampton colleague Clare Saunders. The book is a combined effort from colleagues at the Centre for Citizenship, Globalisation and Governance at the University of Southampton (www.southampton.ac.uk/c2g2).

Table 8.3   Subgroup analysis of political engagement and attitudes, 2010

Political factor % of	Social class comparison		Gender comparison		Ethnicity comparison	
	Social grade AB	Social grade DE	Men	Women	White	BME
Interest	77	36***	63	53***	60	41***
Knowledge[4]	73	29***	63	43***	54	39***
Activist[5]	25	5***	12	15 ns.	14	5***
Voting	72	43***	57	59 ns.	60	44***
Efficacy[6]	31	30 ns.	31	29 ns.	29	38***
Number of respondents interviewed	265	296	591	600	968	225

Chi-square test undertaken for social class, gender and ethnicity comparisons where ***p≤0.001 **p≤0.01 *p≤0.05 and ns. not significant (see Appendix A for a further analysis).
Source: Developed from data in the Hansard Society's *Audit of Political Engagement 8: The 2011 Report*.[7]

however, may be gender-linked and reflect assumptions of confidence rather than major differences in knowledge (Dolan 2011). Differences between the white groups and black and minority ethnic (BME) groups emerge when it comes to political engagement. The latter are much less likely to vote, engage in multiple political activities or express an interest in, or knowledge about, politics. Only when it comes to felt personal political efficacy does the response from the BME group match and go beyond that of the white group.

It is the divide based on social class and occupation that is the starkest. The figures for those in professional and managerial jobs (social grade AB) compared to those in less-skilled work or without a permanent job (social grade DE) are startling in many ways. The former are twice as likely as

[4] This is claimed knowledge. There is, however, evidence that women view political knowledge differently from men (see Dolan 2011).
[5] Measured by engagement in three or more political acts as detailed in Table 8.2.
[6] A claimed sense that you could influence decisions.
[7] Methodology as before. In order to make comparisons between the white and BME populations more statistically reliable additional booster interviews were conducted with BME adults giving a total of 225 BME interviews. My thanks to colleagues from the University Iceland where I was a visiting professor in September 2011, as part of their University centenary celebrations, for help with this analysis.

the latter to express an interest in politics and claim knowledge of political issues and almost twice as likely to be certain to vote. Social grade AB has five times as many in the political activist category as social grade DE. Only when it comes to felt sense of political efficacy do the groups match up. On the surface this last finding is difficult to explain but it may be that citizens from social grade DE may still hold that they could act politically in a range of ways even if they do not do so currently.

The evidence points, then, to extensive disengagement from politics and its concentration in certain subsections of society and these differences are reflected in attitudes to the political system. According to the Hansard Society Survey conducted in December 2010 (2011: 22, 37–39), a third of social grade AB are satisfied with the way Parliament works compared to only one in five of social grade DE. In response to the statement 'the UK Parliament is working for you and me' 40 per cent of Social Grade AB agree and only 31 per cent disagree. For all other social grades those that disagree outweigh those that agree. For Social Grade DE only 21 per cent agree and 51 per cent disagree. Just over one-third of social grade AB think the governing system works well or needs only small improvements whereas only one in five of social grade DE hold that view. Some 69 per cent of social grade DE think that the system is in need of substantial improvement.

When comparing white groups with BME groups a similar proportion say the current system of government works well (30 per cent of white people and 37 per cent of BMEs) and white people and BMEs are similarly satisfied with the way Parliament works (27 per cent and 30 per cent respectively). Differences in attitudes to the political system emerge between men and women. More men are satisfied with the working of Parliament than women (30 per cent to 24 per cent respectively) and men are more likely than women to think the present system of government works well (39 per cent to 23 per cent respectively).

To conclude: our review reveals that anti-political sentiment and disengagement from political activity is widespread among British citizens at the beginning of the twenty-first century. Consistently seven in ten do not trust politicians, six in ten want major reform of the political system and at best only two in ten engage in a modest range of political activity regularly and only three in ten think it would make a difference if they got involved. Is this situation worse than in the past? The answer is that it is difficult to say with certainty because the data we have are thin, and making comparisons between one point in time and another point is fraught with difficulties. Table 8.4 presents the findings from a careful study by John *et al.* (2010: 17–18) that concludes that British citizens as a whole 'show increasing political interest, but falling efficacy' when the Almond and Verba survey data of 1959 are compared with that of 2004. Within the population they note an improved position for women, but also that education continues to influence figures: its absence does not necessarily block access to politics, but its presence drives the likelihood of engagement. A review by Stoker (2010: 55) came to a similar judgement and concludes that 'the picture of confident British citizens at ease with their democratic polity—which may have been slightly exaggerated in the account provided by Almond and Verba—is no more'. We also know the turnout in general elections has fallen. Typically, a fifth of citizens failed to vote in the 1950s (Stoker 2010: 53), but in 2010 over a third failed to vote in a tightly-contested and high-profile election which had been given an additional boost in public attention by the first ever televised leadership debates. What evidence we can muster suggests then that the standing of politics has declined over the last fifty years and when it comes to the beginning of the twenty-first century the position is clear: many citizens are disaffected with and disengaged from politics. The situation for some subgroups of society is worse than it is for others. Those who could be considered the most disadvantaged in society are also those with the least

Table 8.4   Changing political attitudes over time

Question[8]	1959	2004	Difference***
Talking about public affairs/politics[9]	23.0	45.1	+22.1***
Belief in own ability to change a law	16.5	18.0	+1.5
Feeling of having a say in government	41.1	32.5	−8.6***
Likelihood one would attempt to change a law[10]	42.7	40.7	−2.0

*p<0.05; **p<0.01; ***p<0.001
Source: Adapted from data in John *et al.* (2010).

[8] Full question wording available in John *et al.* (2010), Appendix 1.
[9] The cells report regular talk about politics.
[10] The cells present all 'likely' responses.

positive attitudes towards the political system and who are least likely to engage in political activity.

Exploring anti-politics: the perspectives of two paradigms

It is helpful to think about political disaffection by differentiating between two broad paradigms that have been fundamental in driving the analysis of politics for a long time: the protective vision of democracy and the developmental vision of democracy (Held 2006). Like other paradigms reviewed in this book, there is a normative element underlying each perspective but there is also a contrasting focus on evidence as it is seen through two different lenses. The protective paradigm does not necessarily look to large-scale engagement by citizens in politics and sees the key to effective democracy as having accountable and trusted elites, whereas the developmental paradigm would regard greater direct involvement in politics and decision-making as essential to making a viable democracy for the twenty-first century.

Both paradigms have evolved over a number of decades to provide complex and sophisticated understandings but they can also provide useful catch-all frameworks for reflecting on anti-politics. We offer only the sketchiest of reviews here. On the basis of the empirical evidence we have, it is difficult to judge which of the perspectives offers the better diagnosis of disaffection with politics in the UK—in part because of a lot of the more detailed recent empirical work has been done in the United States rather than in the United Kingdom. Crucially, neither perspective would be sanguine about the state of British politics. For the protective perspective, the lack of faith in the operations of elite politics might not make the case for participative reforms but it does argue for a cleaning-up and potentially radical reform of representative politics, in order to build greater faith. From the developmental perspective, new measures are required to give citizens a real sense that they can influence political decisions; for it is exclusion from influence, above all, that explains why they are turned off politics.

A protective paradigm

A protective vision depicts democracy as a mechanism for choosing and replacing leaders where the role of citizens between elections is expected to be one of 'democratic self-control' (Schumpeter, 1976). Its modern founding form is provided by Schumpeter (1976) in a book first published in the Second World War amid fears about how mass democracy might in turn stimulate intolerant and illiberal politics. Democracy is not defended as a means to mass participation but is instead promoted as a system where competitive groups of leaders vie for electoral support in the context of broader respect for individual freedoms and liberties. Such a position allows politicians to get on with their role, avoids excessive criticism of that role and recognises the need to tolerate differences of opinion. A variant of this argument stresses less fear about ordinary citizens' involvement and more admiration for their rationality in staying relatively unengaged since there is little that their individual intervention could do. Citizens need to be able only to read the cues from those that are involved and know just enough about who to back or oppose (Goodin 2005; Conover and Feldman 1989).

For success, the protective model requires a broad social consensus to underlie its workings, a civic culture that combined elements of activism and deference (Almond and Verba 1963; see also Stoker 2010 and Chapter 1 in Stoker *et al.* 2011 for further discussion). It is crucial that politicians are perceived to be of high calibre, that there is a bureaucracy that is viewed to be effective and of good standing, and that there is a political competition that is limited within the bounds of reasonable conflict, and not subject to deeply driven divisions in interest or ideology. Political inequality is a complex issue from a protective perspective since citizens may simply be uninterested, focused on other matters than the multiple political decisions taken each day, rather than disempowered in some way. Given the diverse interests of citizens, and therefore their differential willingness to participate over any one issue, it is difficult, as Verba *et al.* (1995: 14) put it, 'to specify what political equality would look like' since it would be absurd to expect that all citizens would participate all the time. Rather, what we should expect is participation according to intensity of preference.

The idea of intensity of preference has emerged strongly in a pluralist perspective on democracy that allows for greater group participation to complement the role of elected political leadership. Citizens' diverse interests would best find expression through a varied and complex set of organised lobby and pressure groups that would both articulate their demands and push government to respond, so that liberties and rights would be more directly protected. By the 1950s, pluralism had become the dominant paradigm. In its classical form it viewed the government processes as a site of group conflict and as a positive democratic practice (Smith 2006). Groups were relatively free to compete with one another to influence policy. Power as such was dispersed, which led to a government that was responsive to the organised wishes of its citizens and able to predict what demands from the unorganised might be in order to create in practice a working democracy. Later variations took a more jaundiced view and expressed concern about the capture of the state by vested networks, the uneven competition between different interests, and the potential dominant position of business.

The recent account of democracy offered by Hibbing and Theiss-Morse (2001, 2002) remains within the protective vision of democracy, but criticises the classic pluralist vision. They describe a 'stealth democracy', where the main cause of citizens' disenchantment with politics is the fear that government will be captured by vested interests. Hibbing and Theiss-Morse argue, from evidence in the United States, that what citizens want is a democracy that does not require them to be actively engaged or even to actively monitor most decisions made by the political system. However, they feel forced to participate and engage because they see too cosy a relationship between elected leaders and a range of special organised interests. The goal of stealth democracy is 'for decisions to be made efficiently, objectively, and without commotion and disagreement' (Hibbing and Theiss-Morse 2002: 143). What citizens want is not necessarily more direct involvement in decision-making but latent representation; an assurance that decisions are taken on grounds of general interest and not at the behest of specialist interests. Generally citizens are uneasy about over-involvement in politics (Theiss-Morse and Hibbing 2005). Some fear the conflict that is inherent to political decision-making. Crucially on the majority of issues citizens have no opinion and no particular desire to make a decision. However, they are concerned about being taken for fools. Those responsible for making decisions need to be seen to do so in the public interest and not with any obvious self-interest at stake.

Interestingly, research by Birch and Allen (2009) suggests that the British public believe MPs should be more ethical than the general public, with nearly two in three citizens arguing that politicians should be held to higher standards than ordinary members of the public. As this suggests, anti-political sentiment may in part be a result of the (perhaps unrealistic) expectations about fairness, ethical veracity and support for the common good that are loaded on to politicians by citizens. The issue of a concern about special interests also appears to have a resonance in Britain. In the backwash created about concern over former Defence Secretary Liam Fox's connections to lobbyists David Cameron has been reminded that when in opposition he predicted that 'secret corporate lobbying, like the expenses scandal, goes to the heart of why people are so fed up with politics... It is the next big scandal waiting to happen' (Cameron 2010).

Hibbing and Theiss-Morse (2002) are clear about what not to do about anti-political sentiment. Given that most citizens do not care to engage in politics on a regular basis then the last reform that is appropriate is to demand more participation. It would be worse still if it were to be offered in the form of half-hearted consultation that delivers no real increased say over the decisions that do matter to citizens (Theiss-Morse and Hibbing 2005). Even calls for greater transparency, freedom of information and sunshine laws may not be getting to the heart of issue—valuable as one could argue they might be—because they play to the attention-rich world of special interest groups rather than to the inattentive, average citizen. To be told that one is going to have to work harder still to track political decision-making is not the offer most citizens want. They want to see decisions made in the public interest, not at the behest of special interests. Hibbing and Theiss-Morse (2002: 216–228) offer two suggestions about what could be done. The first proposes a range of measures to reduce opportunities for politicians to be self-serving by reducing their salaries and perks, limiting finances provided to the political system by special interests, and curtailing the activities of lobbyists. The second idea is to promote better citizenship education so that citizens recognise that conflict is inherent to politics and the endless bickering they seem to despise reflects the real choices and differences of interest that ultimately stem from them. However, Theiss-Morse and Hibbing appear doubtful these reforms will work. Even if the reforms could be made to stick, it would be an uphill struggle to convince citizens who do not want to be engaged in politics that those who are engaged and making decisions are doing so for the right reasons.

What would a UK reform programme look like from a protective democracy perspective? Many might share Hibbing and Theiss-Morse's scepticism about the naïve expansion of ill-judged and half-hearted public consultation and participation schemes as a response to anti-political sentiment, and almost all would support their plans for a clean-up of politics and better citizenship education but still judge a radical reform of representative politics to be necessary as well. Although its programme is broad and diverse this thinking appears to be at the heart of the Power Inquiry (2006) which does advocate innovations in democratic engagement but concentrates on a radical overhaul of the way representative politics works in response to anti-political sentiment in the UK. It calls for a reformed electoral system; a substantially elected rather than appointed House of Lords; more power for Parliament and less for the Executive; less power for central government and more power to local and devolved government; the capping of donations to political parties; and, in general, greater transparency and more freedom of information about how decisions are made. From the protective perspective, the evidence presented in this chapter about political disenchantment and disengagement among large sections of the population should not be viewed as making the case for a more participative democracy which would demand even more from citizens. The direction of reform should rather be about supporting a renewal of faith in a system where representation and leadership are the dominant features over active citizen engagement. Those reforms might stretch from measures to clean up politics, to a more radical restructuring of representative processes and institutions.

The developmental paradigm

The developmental understanding of politics rests on the view that, for democracy to be sustainable, it needs to engage citizens on an active basis. Engagement will not only protect their freedoms but lead to a higher expression of citizenship, based on informed and tolerant exchange between people. This perspective can be traced through the writings of J. S. Mill in the nineteenth century and onwards to the case for a participatory democracy that was extended in the 1970s (Pateman 1970; Macpherson 1973). The 1980s witnessed an emphasis on the importance of deliberation, so that participation was informed and based on reason-giving and concerns about the public or general interest, rather than on a narrow and debilitating focus on defending immediate self-interest (Saward 2003; Goodin 2005; Dryzek 2000). A range of writers began to identify ways in which citizen participation could be advanced through institutional innovations (Fung and Wright 2003; Smith 2009).

This perspective requires opportunities for all citizens to engage, to learn and to grow into the practices of politics. This would achieve not just a more open and engaging political system, but also a more equal society that addresses gender and class inequalities in access to politics. Free sharing of information would be essential, as would multiple opportunities for political engagement. This developmental perspective is built on a faith that ordinary citizens could engage if they were given the knowledge and opportunity to do so. Through that engagement they would grow as individuals and in their capacity to find solutions to the collective problems of society.

The defining explanation of political alienation from a developmental perspective is that citizens have been made to feel powerless. As Neblo *et al.* (2010: 568) argue, this perspective, especially in its deliberative form, holds that 'a significant amount of citizen apathy is actually a *consequence* of frustration with and disempowerment in the current system'. There is a number of different versions of the empowerment argument. Some place greater emphasis on individual empowerment and on liberating the individual from unnecessary state interference, whilst others concentrate more on greater opportunities for collective engagement in decision-making. Some favour more popular or direct forms of citizen engagement such as petitions or referenda, and others prefer forums in which citizens are encouraged to become better informed and to debate, deliberate and judge what is in the common good.

A further concern from a developmental perspective is the issue of differential access to politics. This concern is shared with some from a protective perspective, notably the more critical pluralists. Keaney and Rogers (2006: 9) argue that the issue is worthy of attention in Britain on the back of empirical work showing that while electoral turnout in Britain has dropped across the board, it appears to have dropped more among the most disadvantaged groups:

> We have seen, in other words, not just a fall in voter turnout, but also a rise in turnout inequality. An across-the-board fall in electoral turnout would have been a troubling phenomenon even without this added dimension. If nothing else, democratically elected governments depend for their legitimacy on voters turning out to vote for them. Low turnout is likely to undermine public support for the political system and governmental effectiveness. But a rise in turnout inequality is arguably much more troubling. It suggests that, for whatever reason, certain parts of the electorate do not feel

that they have a stake in their democracy—a good indication that society is not treating those groups fairly. Worse still, it threatens to give those who do vote unfair influence over the political system.

The political system is failing to deliver equal access to all groups and that failure is both a driver for anti-politics and one of its worst impacts.

The developmental perspective offers, then, a diagnosis of anti-politics that shares some ground with the protective democracy perspective, but it has a much more robust concern with non-participation, which is seen as a problem in itself, undermining the legitimacy of, and potential for, collective choice. Whereas within the protective perspective the assumption is that citizens are relatively unwilling participants in politics, the argument from the developmental perspective is that given the right opportunities, and a sense that the political system was open to influence, citizens would be willing to engage to a much higher degree. Apathy among the most disadvantaged reflects not so much an active choice on their part but a choice structured by a sense of powerlessness. The problem that accompanies political disenchantment and disengagement is that some interests always tend to dominate over others, and some citizens may find their concerns systematically ignored by the political system. In Britain mobilising institutions such as parties, trade unions or churches were once able to address some aspects of that bias—hence the relatively positive political culture identified in Almond and Verba's (1963) study. However, as the influence of these forces has declined, so our political system has become more unequal in terms of those engaged and feeling the system works for them. The solution is to construct new ways for citizens to engage in politics which give them a sense of influence and opportunities to share ideas and experiences with fellow citizens and to construct, through deliberation and learning, solutions to shared collective challenges.

Judging what to do: learning from both perspectives

If we take the evidence and argument presented so far in this chapter it might be possible to still react by arguing neither the evidence of decline nor its potential impact is sufficiently strong to lead to the view that anti-political sentiment threatens Britain's democracy. Given that we know some alienation towards politics and disengagement from political activity has been a central feature for decades, it would appear that British democracy has survived and could continue to survive. But such a position, while plausible, needs to be weighed against the potential hidden costs of political alienation. As Hibbing and Theiss-Morse (2002: 211) comment: 'the polity will not crumble in the face of public distaste for politics but this not mean the consequences of such distaste are harmless'. These authors—congruent generally with a protective perspective on democracy—go on to identify three negative issues created by political disenchantment. First, sensitivity to their lack of legitimacy may discourage policy-makers from tackling difficult issues. Second, the opprobrium heaped on politics may limit the range of citizens willing to stand for elected office to the detriment of the quality of leadership available. Third, if the processes of decision-making are viewed as illegitimate then citizens may be less inclined to follow laws or support reform plans.

One might question each of these concerns, but given the focus of this collection of chapters on the scale of the policy challenges faced by Britain—global warming, financial meltdown, future housing needs and so on—it would appear that if political disenchantment weakens the system's capacity to make good policies and make them stick, then it should be a cause for concern. If, as the other chapters in this book and the tenor of recent discussion (2020 Public Services Commission 2010) suggest, the future of our public services—driven by funding pressures and the achievement of more subtle goals about enabling citizens to achieve their full capabilities—require in turn a shift of responsibility from the state to the individual, then a political system that can engage becomes less of a luxury item and more an essential requirement.

From the developmental and deliberative perception of politics, the case for doing something could be even clearer cut: citizens do not engage because they have not been offered a democracy worthy of the name. Moreover, given that the most disadvantaged are those most likely to be frustrated and disengaged, then issues about the equality of individuals at the heart of enlightenment and democratic thought are at stake if practice diverges too far from principle. If you believe in democracy, at least as understood from a developmental perspective, then the case for reform is made because the current form and practice of politics actively alienates and discourages far too many citizens, and certainly, to an unacceptable degree, deters citizens from the most disadvantaged backgrounds in society from becoming engaged with politics.

Both protective and developmental perspectives lead to recognition that anti-political sentiment and political disengagement should be a cause for concern. Where they disagree is over the diagnosis of the problem and the potential solution. From a protective viewpoint the issue is not that citizens want to participate more, but rather that they want to be able to trust political leaders to make decisions in the public interest. If they could trust them they could leave them to get on with it. From the developmental perspective, the argument is that citizens do want to be more involved, both in giving direction to their elected representatives, and in political decision-making more generally, if given the right kind of opportunities and if they can believe that the system is not rigged. One line of reform in tune with the protective perspective would push towards cleaning and improving representative democracy. The other from a developmental perspective would push towards new forms of participation.

Searching for solutions: redesigning democracy

Paradigms such as those outlined in the previous section can give reformers a broad sense of direction but what is also required is an understanding of how to design better governance. Having a goal to aim for is valuable; knowing how to achieve it is another thing. It would be fair to say that among political elites there is an increased recognition of the need for political reforms, however, their response has been modest and fragmented given the scale of the critique that emerges from either a protective or developmental perspective. The search for solutions could be aided by a greater awareness of the design approaches that are emerging in the social science literature.

Drawing on but developing the framing of the discussion in terms of protective and developmental paradigms there is a way that social science can help in exploring the redesign debate. One literature comes from those that style themselves as political or constitutional engineers (Sartori 1994; Norris 2008; Reynolds 2010). Political engineers generally set themselves the goal of designing political systems to achieve stable and inclusive democratic governance. They embrace a protective view of democracy and look at how that can be promoted. Another perspective comes from those described as the democratic designers (Fishkin 1995; Fishkin *et al.* 2010; Fung and Wright 2004; Smith 2009) who take a more developmental perspective on democracy and explore in depth the institutions that might help deliver democratic renewal and more citizen participation. Table 8.5 sets out the two perspectives that will be explored in more depth in this section of the chapter.

The response from political elites to anti-politics?

All the main parties offered substantial programmes of reform in the 2010 election to respond to the 'crisis' in our politics and political culture. It was a strong theme, for example, in the televised debates in the 2010 election campaign. The immediate framing of the issue by political elites was at least in part in terms of the context set by damaging revelations about MPs' expenses in the spring of 2009 but the option of various constitutional reforms has been part of thinking of all parties for some time. Labour when in power acted on those concerns with its devolution and other constitutional reforms and returned to them afresh again in the Brown premiership (see McLean 2010 for a critical analysis). The two coalition parties also have shown a sense that they need to reconnect governors and citizens in a different way. The title of the Conservative Party 2010 manifesto was *An invitation to join the government of Britain*. The coalition government has placed the issue of anti-politics firmly on its agenda with Liberal Democrat leader Nick Clegg, as deputy prime minster, choosing the theme of political reform for his first solo speech and declaring that the new government

Table 8.5　Political engineering and democratic design perspectives

Perspective/feature	Political engineering	Democratic design
Design goal	Stable and inclusive representative governance	Democratic renewal through citizen participation
Weapons of reform	Electoral systems, party organisation and power-sharing arrangements	Civic activism and innovations in public engagement
Favoured mechanism	Organisational incentives to change elites' behaviour	Institutional and cultural reform to reframe responses from citizens
Understanding of democracy	Protective	Developmental

'is going to persuade you to put your faith in politics once again' (Clegg 2010).

The reform agenda favoured by the coalition government is extensive (HM Government 2010). Acts have already been passed that will reduce the number of MPs in the House of Commons from 650 to 600, change the way the UK is divided into parliamentary constituencies and lead to more equally-sized constituencies, and provide for five-year fixed-term Parliaments. A referendum has been held and lost on changing the voting system for general elections, pitting Alternative Vote against the established system, in May 2011. A website has been established to collect e-petitions which can be on any subject chosen by members of the public and if they reach the target of 100,000 signatures will force a debate in Parliament (http://epetitions.direct.gov.uk/). Other reforms are also in the offing, including plans to move towards an elected upper chamber, opportunities for primaries to help in the selection of party candidates in national elections, and moves to increase transparency over lobby practices. Implementation problems, it should be noted, have bedevilled the Government's reform programme.

Given the analysis presented in this chapter it would appear that the reform package, as it stands, is unlikely to resolve the issue of public disenchantment and disengagement from politics. From the perspective of protective democracy the reform strategy makes some worthwhile steps to clean up politics but it does not focus enough on a reinvigoration of representative politics and misses out reform to the more powerful mechanisms of change. Amongst constitutional engineers the classic weapons of reform to advance representative democracy are changes to the electoral system, shifts in the formation of parties (broad-based or narrower), or various forms of power-sharing among political institutions, such as changes to the legislative-executive balance or devolution and decentralisation. The coalition proposals have failed on the first front, are silent on the second and weak in the third. A few modest powers for backbench MPs or citizens, reforms to institutions that are not a strong focus of public attention—such as the House of Lords—are an unlikely answer to anti-politics, although they may be worthwhile reforms for other reasons. Doubts about the coalition programme would also emerge from the perspective of a developmental understanding of democracy because the level of proposed empowerment for most citizens is modest and there is no attempt to grapple with the issues of unequal access to politics. Citizens have access to some very modest new powers to raise issues with their political masters, or involve themselves in the selection of candidates, but few new capacities to make a difference to decisions or politics.

So neither political engineers nor democratic designers would be convinced by the reform on the table, but can social science go beyond criticism to offering positive alternatives, and if so what would those be?

Political engineering

From an engineering perspective the key to meeting the challenge of anti-politics is to take forward more seriously, and without allowing the vested interests of political parties to stand in the way, a programme to reinvigorate representative democracy. That programme would fundamentally shift the incentives for performance among elites through a set of technical changes in the election system, through the creation of a more open party system and by facilitating a more devolved sharing of power across the country. Engineering involves changing the incentive structures for elites so that they conduct politics in a way that is perceived as legitimate by citizens. For example, a proportional representative voting system, all other things being equal, usually provides incentives for party fragmentation (because votes more closely match seats allocated to parties), so citizens are provided with a more plural and diverse set of parties with which to identify and engage.

The underlying goal of political engineers is to create a sense among citizens that they are included in the political system. This objective could be pursued in a variety of ways but following Lijphart (1977) the dominant preference among political engineers (for example Norris 2008) is for electoral systems that favour proportional representation; party systems that allow for the representation of a wide range of interests and identities; and constitutional power-sharing arrangements that facilitate the spread of decision-making centres. There are constitutional engineers (for example Reilly 2006) who point to other ways in which inclusion could be achieved through election systems that consolidate support around a few parties and by constructing party systems that make it more difficult for outlier minority parties. At the heart of the political engineering literature there is a debate about how to deal with difference. Lijphart (1977) and followers favour mechanisms that create multiple opportunities for diverse interests to be included or even veto decisions, and others argue for mechanisms that force citizens to recognise their shared or joint interests, and join together in wider coalitions. There is also a powerful arm of the political engineers' manifesto that examines how to ensure gender equality in access to representative institutions and influence on policy-making (Squires 2007).

Most of the practice of political engineers has taken place in developing democracies (Reynolds 2010) but there is no reason in principle that the practice could not be applied to an established democracy such as Britain. In a full-scale treatment of a country, the political engineer would need to spend time diagnosing what had ailed democracy in a country and then look to shifts in the election system, party arrangements and power-sharing to prescribe the changes necessary to reinvigorate representative democracy. The evidence presented so far in this chapter would be sifted, with a potential focus on indications that traditional partisan loyalties have broken down; on a sense that the parties, as they stand, are failing to attract sufficient membership and citizen engagement; and suggestions that power is too centralised around the decision-making of Westminster and Whitehall.

What would a political engineer propose for Britain? Norris (2008) shows how in the case of the devolved arrangements in Scotland one can already see the playing out of a different politics. A proportional election system has delivered a greater choice to voters and a wider representation of parties all adding up, according to Norris, to a healthier political system. Moreover, as the survey findings reported in Table 8.6 suggest, British citizens appear to be willing to give more credence to their local MP and devolved institutions such as the Scottish Parliament or the Welsh Assembly. So we may be witnessing not so much a rejection of politics as a rejection of a particular form of politics that has developed around the 'Westminster village'. The implication of this is that devolving power to more local and regional institutions, for example, might create a politics with which citizens would be more comfortable and which they might see as more legitimate. Despite the rhetoric of localism from the coalition government, its decentralisation plans are weak (see Stoker (2011) for an analysis). Paradoxically, the unintended consequences of devolution in Scotland, Wales and Northern Ireland under the previous Labour government, and the rise to power of the Scottish National Party in Scotland, may

Table 8.6 Trust and satisfaction in politicians and institutions beyond Westminster

	% Public that trust	
Year	Local MP	MPs in general
2004	47	27
2006	48	30
2009	40	20

	% Public	
	Satisfied	Dissatisfied
With Scottish Parliament		
2001	54	21
2009	49	35
With National Assembly for Wales		
2001	39	29
2009	70	26

Source: Data from IPSOS/MORI survey (2009).

have more effect in pushing reforms to our political system in the right direction than the reform programme agreed by the coalition and promoted by Nick Clegg. The crucial thing would be to extend the principles of electoral reform, wider party representation and devolved government to England.

What would a programme of reform for England look like from the perspective of political engineers? It would probably not be focused on creating a parliament for England but rather a more sustained commitment to devolution—either to existing local government institutions or to more city- or region-based institutions. If five million citizens in Scotland can have significant decision-making authority given to them, then why not give similar capacity to five million citizens around greater Birmingham, stretching into the West Midlands? A shift to proportional elections for in local government would support a wider pluralisation of representation and give more scope to a wider range of parties. The basics of a reform plan can at least be imagined.

Democratic designers

The second strand of thought outlined in Table 8.5 provides a rather different take on how to redesign democratic politics. While not rejecting the goals of stability or inclusion, it would add one more as a key focus:

the more active engagement of citizens in governing themselves. This perspective might support the electoral and other reforms of political engineers, aimed at elites, but it would add a focus on reforms that supported citizen activism and created new opportunities for citizen participation. Like political engineers, democratic designers take institutional design as central to their work but frame it in terms of looking at incentives, as well as the broader normative or cultural underpinnings that institutions can provide by, for example, encouraging deliberation or focusing on the general interest in collective decisions. Actors are socialised and influenced in their behaviour not only by incentives but also by ideas, social norms and moral imperatives supported or enabled by institutional rules. Institutions do more than structure choices: they can provide identities, values and indeed even define interests. Above all, institutions—formal and informal—give us rules by which to live (Mahoney and Thelen 2010).

Within the democratic design group a distinction can be drawn between those who celebrate civil society and self-organisation (Dryzek 2000) and those who argue that the state can have a role in designing democratic innovations (Smith 2009). From the former perspective the new politics is most likely to develop away from formal politics, government and established institutions. The internet, for example, is often seen as a potential carrier of a new politics (Gibson 2009), the seeds of which are emerging in at least three ways. First, the narrow agenda-setting of the media is being challenged by the rise of the internet. Second, the control and manipulation of information, statistics and analysis by governments and their experts is giving way to a world of multiple gatekeepers in which informed citizens can increasingly and effectively hold government agencies to account. So people are becoming informed, better educated and, with the arrival of interactive internet exchange, on the cusp of a new politics. Third, the old politics with its technologies of formal organisation and mass media are giving way to a new politics of blogs, social networking and video-sharing sites that lower the costs of campaigning and radically pluralise the political process by providing multiple options for the expression of interests and ideas.

There are grounds for caution even among those who see the potential of the internet to heal our anti-politics culture. Context matters, as Gibson (2009) notes, and technology without better political content perhaps would make no difference. The internet and these new forms of campaigning do appear to be attracting a wider range of participants—especially younger people—but there is still concern that there is a digital divide. The internet may not be an attractive tool for all, so it may reinforce problem of political inequality rather than offer a solution. Moreover, it may not support the collective civic culture favoured by the developmental perspective. Sunstein (2007) argues against the over-personalised approach to information and politics that the internet can encourage. An effective democracy, he argues, requires that people encounter some new information or experience without pre-selection or choice on their part. These haphazard encounters are vital to divert citizens from simply talking to like-minded people who reinforce each other's views, creating more fragmentation and extremism. Careful research does indeed suggest that that construction of online deliberation is challenging and difficult (John *et al.* 2011). Furthermore, all democracies require some shared common experiences and, although the internet can deliver on that to some degree, it runs the risk of creating a series of specialised ghettos where citizens live in separate worlds divorced from each other. Politics is inescapably an act of collective decision-making (Stoker 2006; Crick 2000; Flinders 2010). The internet does not offer a magic solution, although it may have a part to play in lowering the barriers of entry for ordinary citizens into politics.

The second strand of democratic designers see the emergence of a new politics as something that can be grafted onto existing political institutions providing that the commitment to innovation is deeply enough held among policy-makers and the design for engagement is radical and able to create a combination of institutional incentives and broader cultural framing. The key point emphasised by these authors is the extent and depth of experiments and practice that is already happening and the need to learn lessons about what works from that experience. It is not possible to capture the full range of innovation but the *Participedia* web site aims to do so.[11] Let us briefly focus on two innovations. First, there has been considerable experience in Europe, North America and even in China of using deliberative polling on the design lines developed by Fishkin (1995; Fishkin *et al.* 2010). Participants are randomly chosen from within the population to reflect on an issue with others, and in the light of evidence and informa-

---

[11] For further information visit: http://www.participedia.net/wiki/Welcome_to_Participedia.

tion. The development of participatory budgeting, which began in Brazil (Smith 2009) but has spread around the world, has in some cases proved a very powerful tool for getting those who are relatively disadvantaged to make a difference to decisions about the allocation of public funds.

These various innovations on public engagement, as Graham Smith (2009) argues, show how a more participative form of governance could work. This shift requires the right mix of institutional framing to not only give incentives to citizens but also to frame discussion in a way that encourages people to regard others. Various myths about the limitations of participation are nailed. Firstly, there is a variety of mechanisms for overcoming inequalities in participation; secondly, design can support an orientation to the common good; thirdly, innovation can be designed so that when citizens intervene they do so with real impact; and fourthly, if the design is right then citizens are willing to bear the burden of participation. As Stoker *et al.* (2011: 46) argue:

> Our analysis suggests that we can design political citizenship, in the sense that new opportunities to increase and deepen citizen involvement in political decision-making can be embedded effectively. But there is a caveat. Rhetoric is not enough: institutional design matters. Public authorities need to exhibit the willingness and imagination necessary to invest in democratic innovations. These emerging democratic practices offer actually-existing examples of how the relationship between governed and those who govern can be recast. Democratic innovations can be part of the strategy for reinvigorating political citizenship—and potentially re-imagining democracy itself.

The point the democratic designers would make is that although they may be only at the beginnings of their endeavours, there is enough evidence to suggest that if the design is right then better outcomes can be achieved. Democratic renewal is therefore not some utopian ambition but a combination of political will matched by learning the effective lessons about designs that work.

Concluding note

Anti-politics in culture and behaviour in Britain threatens the practice of democracy, not so much in the sense that the polity will crumble but more because a breakdown in the relationship between governors and governed undermines the capacity to make the right policy choices and develop new practices and programmes that will be needed to meet the challenges of the future. Those who study politics, therefore, have a pressing need not only to understand its causes but also to help design solutions that could support better systems of democratic governance, or ones that at least will be more engaging for a wider range of citizens (Stoker 2010). The framing of the issue, in terms of protective or developmental understandings of politics and democracy as provided in this chapter, illuminates competing ways of approaching the phenomenon. It indicates different reform trajectories and provides templates against which to assess what progress is being made but it does not provide detailed and positive guidance in the search for solutions.

To move from understanding the problem to finding a solution requires a social science that is better at analysing how to turn existing conditions into preferred ones; in short it needs a design arm. In the present discussion we contrast the design dynamics of political engineers and democratic designers. The engineers focus on changing electoral, party and power systems to make them more legitimate to citizens. The democracy designers engage in the search for innovations in democratic practice coming from the bottom-up in terms of emerging practices in civil society or, alternatively, coming from public authorities taking the issue of public engagement seriously. For the political engineer the issues are straightforward. Does the combination of election system, party organisation and power-sharing deliver the best capacity for the emergence of a stable democracy? Are the incentives sufficiently strong and aligned to get the system to the preferred destination so that it does not matter if other processes or dynamics are also driving the outcomes? Democratic designers frame the challenge in a more complex way. To push institutional reform in the circumstances of already established institutions hints at a process of change that is more ambiguous, involving the layering of some practices on top of those that are established, or displacing some practices rather than directly overthrowing them (Mahoney and Thelen 2010). Political engineers tend towards replacing one system with another; the processes of democratic design are more about gradual institutional change, as new practices of citizen engagement and participation become embedded and established.

So engineers focus on changing the core features of political system—elections, parties and power-sharing—and democratic designers spotlight the need to innovate and create new and meaningful ways for citizens to engage. It would seem possible to combine their two sets of insights to steer Britain away from the malaise of anti-politics that threatens to undermine its capacity to have the collective discussions and make the collective choices that to meet the challenges outlined in the other chapters of this book. But it is important to recognise that the play of power remains a constraining feature when designing democratic reform. It would be naive to overlook the possibility that powerful interests or forces may block reforms or lead to the neglect of evidence and analysis. Equally it is clear there are gaps and a need for further work from the world of social science.

We need to understand reform options in all their variety and intricacy. The complexity of the context in which design interventions take place limits the effectiveness of those interventions. There may be areas of politics where we lack the understanding to offer effective solutions. At the very least we need to understand more about why citizens think so negatively about politics. Good design begins with a plausible representation of the problem (Simon 1996). We know a fair amount about what kinds of political activity people engage in and what factors drive that activity. But political science and social science, in general, is less good at understanding and explaining what politics means to citizens at the beginning of the twenty-first century. We need to spend more empirical effort in trying to find out what our fellow citizens understand by the practice of politics. We also need to know more about the kinds of politics that citizens might hypothetically embrace if they were offered. A survey conducted in 2000 asks not only about political acts undertaken but also what potential acts citizens in Britain would undertake to influence rules, laws or politics (Pattie *et al.* 2004: 78). Looking at questions matching those asked in Table 8.2, we find that 42 per cent had signed a petition in the previous year but 76 per cent said they would be willing to do so; 5 per cent had attended a political meeting but 26 per cent indicated they would be willing to do so; 13 per cent had contacted a politician but 53 per cent said they might; and, finally, 5 per cent had taken part in a public demonstration but 34 per cent indicate they would be willing to do so. Moreover further analysis suggests that the gain from actual to potential political activity is consistently a greater multiple for those one the lowest income compared to those on the highest income. Pent-up demand may be out there if the offer of engagement is right. An intriguing study (Neblo *et al.* 2010) of hypothetical prospects for citizen engagement in the United States indicates that many citizens might be attracted to political decision-making, especially in deliberative non-partisan forms, and many of those who are attracted are precisely those who do not engage in traditional politics to the same degree and are drawn in by institutional offerings that provide a partial alternative to politics as usual. Indeed the study followed up its survey work with a field experiment to trial if engagement could be delivered in practice by offering a deliberative discussion with members of Congress. Again, it achieved positive results. We need many more examples of this kind of political science.

This chapter aims to challenge the relative reluctance of political and other social scientists to take on the design challenge: to move from inquisitive to purposive inquiry. Of course, that reluctance is not entirely misplaced. In addition to the technical challenges of doing design there is an entirely appropriate set of concerns about the normative implications and claims of design. Who decides what constitutes 'better politics'? Where do the goals, purposes and objectives of design come from? How can one balance claims from designers for technical expertise with the demands of modern democracy for all to have an equal say? What does design imply in terms of not only a new orientation from social scientists but also a new outlook from elected politicians, the media, citizens and stakeholders? These are important questions but it is better they are addressed than neglected. We need social scientists to contribute to debate about change not as normative advocates or activists but as scientists who take seriously the issue of design and how to get to an intended goal—a better experience of democratic politics for more of our fellow citizens.

Appendix A: Subgroup analysis—confidence intervals

	Social grade AB	95% CI	Social grade DE	95% CI
Interest	77	5.1%	36	5.5%
Knowledge	73	5.3%	29	5.2%
Activist	25	5.2%	5	2.5%
Voting	72	5.4%	43	5.6%
Efficacy	31	5.6%	30	5.2%
	265		296	
	Men	95% CI	**Women**	95% CI
Interest	63	3.9%	53	4.0%
Knowledge	63	3.9%	43	4.0%
Activist	12	2.6%	15	2.9%
Voting	57	4.0%	59	3.9%
Efficacy	31	3.7%	29	3.6%
	591		600	
	White	95% CI	**BME**	95% CI
Interest	60	3.1%	41	6.4%
Knowledge	54	3.1%	39	6.4%
Activist	14	2.2%	5	2.8%
Voting	60	3.1%	44	6.5%
Efficacy	29	2.9%	38	6.3%
	968		225	

If two confidence intervals overlap there is not a significant difference between groups.

Example: The confidence interval for white activists is between 11.8 per cent and 16.2 per cent (14±2.2 per cent) and for BME activists it is between 2.2 per cent and 7.8 per cent (5±2.8 per cent). These intervals do not overlap hence there is a significant difference between the groups.

Acknowledgements

The arguments presented here have been helped greatly by comments from co-authors involved in the broader British Academy project. They also reflect thinking from colleagues involved in the ESRC funded project: RES-000-22-4441 *Anti-politics: Characterising and Accounting for Political Disaffection*.

References

Almond, G. and Verba, S. (1963) *The Civic Culture: Political Attitudes and Democracy in Five Nations* (Princeton, NJ: Princeton University Press).

Birch, S. and Allen, N. (2009), 'How Honest Do Politicians need to Be?', *The Political Quarterly* 81: 49–56.

Cameron, D (2010) *Rebuilding trust in politics* Speech delivered February 8 2010. Available at http://www.conservatives.com/News/Speeches/2010/02/David_Cameron_Rebuilding_trust_in_politics.aspx Downloaded 17/10/11.

Clegg, N. (2010), 'Full Text: Clegg Reform Speech', *BBC News*, 19 May 2010 [online], http://www.news.bbc.co.uk/1/hi/uk_politics/8691753.stm (accessed on 19 May 2010).

Conover, P.J. and Feldman, S. (1989) 'Candidate Perception in an Ambiguous World: Campaigns, Cues, and Inference', *American Journal of Political Science* 33: 912–940.

Conservative Party (2010) *The Conservative Manifesto 2010* [online], http://www.conservatives.com/Policy/Manisfesto.aspx (accessed on 5 August 2011).

Crick, B. (2000) *In Defence of Politics*, fifth edition (London: Continuum).

della Porta, D., Andretta, M., Mosca, L. and Reiter, H. (2006) *Globalization from Below: Transnational Activists and Protest Networks* (Minneapolis, MN: University of Minnesota Press).

Dolan, K. (2011), 'Do Women and Men Know Different Things? Measuring Gender Differences in Political Knowledge', *The Journal of Politics* 73: 97–107.

Dryzek, J. (2000) *Deliberative Democracy and Beyond: Liberals, Critics, Contestations* (Oxford: Oxford University Press).

Flinders, M. (2010) 'In Defence of Politics', *The Political Quarterly* 81: 309–326.

Fishkin, J. S. (1997) *The Voice of the People: Public Opinion and Democracy* (New Haven, CT: Yale University Press).

Fishkin, J. S., He, B., Luskin, R. C. and Siu, A. (2010) 'Deliberative Democracy in an Unlikely Place: Deliberative Polling in China', *British Journal of Political Science* 40: 435–448.

Fung, A. and Wright, E.O. (2004), *Deepening Democracy: Institutional Innovations in Empowered Participatory Governance* (London: Verso).

Gibson, R. (2009) 'New Media and the Revitalisation of Politics', *Representation* 45: 289–300.

Goodin, R. (2005) *Reflective Democracy* (Oxford: Oxford University Press).

Hansard Society (2010) *Audit of Political Engagement 7: The 2010 Report* (London: Hansard Society).

Hansard Society (2011) *Audit of Political Engagement 8: The 2011 Report* (London: Hansard Society).

Hay, C. (2007) *Why We Hate Politics* (Cambridge: Polity).

Held, D. (2006) *Models of Democracy*, third edition (Cambridge: Polity).

Hibbing, J. and Theiss-Morse, E. (2001) 'The Means is the End', in J. Hibbing and E. Theiss-Morse (eds) *What is it About Government That Americans Dislike?* (Cambridge: Cambridge University Press), 243–250.

Hibbing, J. and Theiss-Morse, E. (2002) *Stealth Democracy: Americans' Beliefs about How Government Should Work* (New York: Cambridge University Press).

HM Government (2010) *The Coalition: Our Programme for Government* [online], http://webarchive.nationalarchives.gov.uk/20100623141734/http://programmeforgovernment.hmg.gov.uk (accessed on 25 August 2011).

Ipsos MORI (2009), *Expenses Poll for the BBC, J26434* [online], http://www.ipsos-mori.com/researchpublications/researcharchive/poll.aspx?oItemId=2349 (accessed on 25 August 2011).

John, P., Liu, H. and Fieldhouse, E. (2010) *The Civic Culture in Britain and America Fifty Years On*, working paper from the Institute for Social Change, University of Manchester available at http://www.humanities.manchester.ac.uk/socialchange/publications/working/documents/TheCivicCultureinBritianandAmerica.pdf.

John, P., Cotterill, S., Liu, H., Richardson, L., Moseley, A., Nomura, H., Smith, G., Stoker, G. and Wales, C. (2011) *Nudge, Nudge, Think, Think: Using Experiments to Change Civic Behaviour* (London: Bloomsbury Academic).

Kavanagh, D. (1980) 'Political Culture in Great Britain: The Decline of the Civic Culture', in G. Almond and S. Verba (eds) *The Civic Culture Revisited* (Boston, MA: Little, Brown and Company), 124–176.

Keaney, E. and Rogers, B. (2006) *A Citizen's Duty: Voter Inequality and the Case for Compulsory Turnout*, London, Institute of Public Policy Research [online], http://www.ippr.org/ecomm/files/a_citizen's_duty.pdf (accessed on 25 August 2011).

Lijphart, A. (1977) *Democracy in Plural Societies: A Comparative Exploration* (New Haven, CT: Yale University Press).

Macpherson, C. B. (1973) *Democratic Theory: Essays in Retrieval* (Oxford: Oxford University Press).

Mahoney, J. and Thelen, K. (2010) 'A Theory of Gradual Institutional Change', in J. Mahoney and K. Thelen (eds) *Explaining Institutional Change* (Cambridge: Cambridge University Press), 1–38.

Marsh, D., O'Toole, M. and Jones, S. (2006) *Young People and Politics in the UK: Apathy or Alienation* (Basingstoke: Palgrave Macmillan).

McLean, I. (2010) *What's Wrong with the British Constitution?* (Oxford: Oxford University Press).

Neblo, M., Esterling, K., Kennedy, R., Lazer, D. and Sokhey, A. (2010) 'Who Wants to Deliberate—And Why?', *American Political Science Review* 104(3): 566–583

Norris, P. (2008) *Driving Democracy: Do Power-sharing Institutions Work?* (Cambridge: Cambridge University Press).

Norris, P. (2011) *Democratic Deficit: Critical Citizens Revisited* (Cambridge: Cambridge University Press).

Pateman, C. (1970) *Participation and Democratic Theory* (Cambridge: Cambridge University Press).

Pattie, C., Seyd, P. and Whiteley, P. (2004) *Citizenship in Britain: Values, Participation and Democracy* (Cambridge: Cambridge University Press).

Power Inquiry (2006) *The Report of Power: An Independent Inquiry into Britain's Democracy* [online], http://www.powerinquiry.org/report/documents/PowertothePeople_002.pdf (accessed on 19 June 2010).

Reilly, B. (2006) *Democracy and Diversity: Political Engineering in the Asia-Pacific* (Oxford: Oxford University Press).

Reynolds, A. (2010) *Designing Democracy in a Dangerous World* (Oxford: Oxford University Press).

Sartori, G. (1994) *Comparative Constitutional Engineering: An Inquiry into Structures, Incentives, and Outcomes* (London: Macmillan).

Saward, M. (2003) *Democracy* (London: Wiley-Blackwell).

Schumpeter, J. (1976) *Capitalism, Socialism and Democracy* (London: George Allen & Unwin).

Simon, H. (1996) *The Sciences of the Artificial*, third edition (Cambridge, MA: MIT Press).

Smith, G. (2009) *Democratic Innovations: Designing Institutions for Citizen Participation* (Cambridge: Cambridge University Press).

Smith, M. (2006) 'Pluralism', in C. Hay. M. Lister and D. Marsh (eds) *The State: Theories and Issues* (Basingstoke: Palgrave Macmillan).

Squires, J. (2007) *The New Politics of Gender Equality* (Basingstoke: Palgrave Macmillan).

Stoker, G. (2006) *Why Politics Matters: Making Democracy Work* (Basingstoke: Palgrave Macmillan).

Stoker, G. (2010) 'The Rise of Political Disenchantment', in C. Hay (ed.) *New Directions in Political Science* (Basingstoke: Palgrave Macmillan), 43–63.

Stoker, G. (2011) 'If Town Halls Don't Pay the Piper They Can't Call the Tune', *Parliamentary Brief Online* 17 January 2011 [online], http://www.parliamentarybrief.com/2011/01/if-town-halls-dont-pay-the-piper-then-the-cant (accessed on 5 June 2011).

Stoker, G., Mason, A., McGrew, A., Armstrong, C., Owen, D., Smith, G., Banya, M., Saunders, C. and McGhee, D. (2011) *Prospects for Citizenship* (London: Bloomsbury Academic Press).

Sunstein, C. R. (2007) *Republic.com 2.0* (Princeton, NJ: Princeton University Press).

Theiss-Morse, E. and Hibbing, J. (2005) 'Citizenship and Civic Engagement', *Annual Review of Political Science* 8: 227–249.

Verba, S., Schlozman, K. and Brady, H. (1995) *Voice and Equality* (Cambridge, MA: Harvard University Press).

How social science can contribute to public policy

The case for a 'design arm'

GERRY STOKER AND PETER TAYLOR-GOOBY

This concluding chapter returns to the issues raised earlier about the relationship between social science and public policy. In chapter 1 we argued that, as Peter Hall points out, policy-thinking tends to be dominated by a particular paradigm. This is an intellectual framework that combines three elements: 'the goals of policy, the kind of instruments that can be used to attain them, but also the very nature of the problems they are meant to be addressing' (Hall 1993: 279). Paradigms integrate normative, analytic and direct mainstream thinking in the policy community. They also tend to foreground some of the material available from social science (research findings, analyses, appropriate disciplinary approaches), and to divert attention from other potential contributions. The outcome is that policy debate tends to take place within unargued constraints established by the dominant approach.

This issue can in principle be addressed through a number of measures: broadening recruitment to senior positions, strengthening arrangements for all academics and policy-makers to exchange roles through internship and placement schemes, supporting social scientists in expressing their findings in accessible terms and making them available outside the academic heartland. Changes in all these areas are taking place, not least in the promotion of the impact agenda across social sciences (HEFCE 2011), in the concern with 'public sociology' (Clawson *et al.* 2007; *British Journal of Sociology* 2004) and in developments in leading academic organisations, such as the British Academy Policy Centre (British Academy 2011). These shifts are unlikely to be sufficiently far-reaching to reverse the current situation.

We also argued for a broader interdisciplinary approach. This is again recognised by funding bodies such as the Economic and Social Research Council (ESRC 2011) and in the cross-disciplinary academic structure of a small number of universities following the example of Melbourne (Davies and Devlin 2007). It remains the case that the vast majority of research funding, of research assessment and of intellectual activity takes place within disciplinary boundaries.

Corresponding to interdisciplinarity is the need for interlinking between government agencies. The substantive chapters of the book show how the various issues cut across departmental, central–local and, in some cases, international boundaries, and require an appropriate response. Reorganisations in government take place regularly, sometimes combining, sometimes dividing ministries. Bodies such as the Cabinet Office Strategy Unit promote co-ordinated approaches to policy. The move to 'one-stop' shops in benefits and in local government services takes this further. New technologies combined with flatter hierarchies and the decentralisation that competitive managerial reforms impose offers opportunities to join up government across different areas (Gibson 2009).

Two factors limit the scope for developments in loosening the hold of the leading paradigm, promoting interdisciplinarity and developing more joined-up government. On the academic side the professional organisation of social science is very largely disciplinary, by departments, academic journals, grant assessment and awarding, funding council evaluation and training. People normally make their careers within disciplines, and disciplines tend to reward academic rather than practical policy-oriented contributions (Nye 2009). One outcome is that policy-focused cross-disciplinary fields of study (for example, Public Administration, Social Policy, Educational Policy, Criminal Justice Studies) have tended to develop as subsidiary activities.

On the policy side, the activities of the policy community are largely (and correctly) directed by two considerations: the concerns of politicians, whose interests are for the most part responsive to those of citizens, and the immediate issues of government which limit the time available to study possible overarching frameworks. Any change in this would be difficult and undesirable. In this chapter we go on to consider how social science engagement with policy-making may be further advanced, without damaging the core areas of professionally directed research and scholarship. This leads to consideration of how social science might contribute to policy design.

Social science and relevance

The idea that social science should be relevant is not a new one. As Gerring argues, 'no serious person... would adopt the thesis of *social science for social science's sake. Social science is science for society's sake*' (2001: 250–251, emphasis as in original). Social science does not have to have immediate policy relevance but its subject matter is inherently connected to pressing issues of concern in our world. It is the study of society for society. Embodied in the emerging idea of social science throughout the twentieth century was a clear sense that research was going to be of bene-fit as a means to support social and economic reform (Featherman and Vinovskis 2001). In a broad sense social scientists have consistently had something to say about the societies they live in. Moreover what counts as relevance can vary according to time and circumstance, and the stand-point of the observer.

The issue of relevance becomes trickier, however, when the focus moves to the question of 'What should society do'? Describing and explaining an issue, event or context is at the centre of much academic work. A more specific diagnosis of a problem or policy challenge may follow from this. Problems arise when it comes to the next stages in the potential exchange between academics and the world of relevance. The issue of relevance becomes critical and problematic when social science engages in predic-tion, prescription or evaluation. It is when moving towards these activities that doubts about the soundness of the intellectual case for relevance begin to surface and hold back engagement.

The difficulties experienced in offering solutions in part reflect the grow-ing divide in the discipline between normative theory that discusses how social and political arrangements should be constructed and empirically-based research that seeks to explain how politics and policy-making works in practice (Smith 2009; Shapiro 2003). Normative theorists can offer general schema but may lack a practical sense of what to do. Empirically-oriented social scientists might have knowledge relevant to the challenge of design but are often unsure about stepping into that territory. The two sides of our disciplines are often uninformed about each other's positions.

This outcome is doubly unfortunate: 'speculation about what ought to be is likely to be more useful when informed by relevant knowledge and ... because explanatory theory too easily becomes banal and method driven when isolated from the pressing normative concerns' (Shapiro 2003: 2).

One response has been to call for social science to develop a more problem-oriented focus in order to unify and share insights from various parts of the discipline, including both normative and empirical theories. Social science should not as part of its vocation seek to pursue an agenda driven by its own theories or methods as if it was in a separate world, sealed off from the concern of its fellow citizens. As Shapiro (2004: 40) puts it, the problems addressed by the profession need to be 'theoretically illuminating and convincingly intelligible to outsiders'.

There remains, however, much doubt about the capacity of the profession to deliver solutions. Few studies are able to successfully grapple in depth, with a clear sense of how to achieve delivery, with the question of what should be done. Even if the bar is lowered to identify appropriate trade-offs and options, social science fails to offer much in the way of solutions to some of the most pressing problems we face (for an analysis of the failings of political science see Peters *et al.* 2010). This failure to address and score highly on the solution-oriented side of the relevance challenge is, it could be argued, a reflection of a lack of design-thinking within the discipline of social science.

Policy design and scientific thinking

To move beyond the identification of problematic issues and address the question of finding solutions to them, social science needs to develop a design arm. Designing solutions is more than simply applied social science. It requires a shift in our discipline of thinking, as illustrated in Table 9.1. The crucial insight here is provided by Herbert Simon (1996), who argued that academics who examine the realm of the artificial, understood as things that are created by human beings, have attempted to follow models of investigation better suited to examining natural creations. They fail to take account of the point that artificial things have functions, goals and the capacity for adaptation. They exist for a purpose, while natural things simply exist.

Table 9.1   Two modes of thinking: science and design

Attributes	Science	Design
Focus:	On the natural	On the artificial
Mode of thinking:	Analytical	Synthesising
Empirical–normative thought:	Separated: excluding the normative	Integrated: empirical pursuit of normative goals
Form of rationality:	Comprehensive	Bounded
Key reasoning tools:	Categories	Placements
Form of conclusion:	Descriptive, causal	Means to an end

The classic approaches of science are suited to exploring the world of nature and arguably to some extent the world of the social. Leaving aside the wider debates about the appositeness of a natural science approach to the study of society, which can itself be understood as a human construct, the key point to be emphasised here is that the world of solution-seeking is the world of design. As Simon (1996: 111) puts it: 'everyone designs who devises courses of action aimed at changing existing situations into the preferred ones'. The classic focus of science is on the arrangements that currently are in place, whether or not they are stable. The classic focus of design thinking is on intentional change.

Science tends to proceed by analytical division but design rests on bringing a range of knowledge together to achieve a purpose. As Simon (1996: 4) writes,

> we speak of engineering as concerned with 'synthesis' whereas science is concerned with 'analysis'. Synthetic or artificial objects, and more specifically prospective artificial objects having desired properties, are the central objectives of engineering activity and skill. The engineer, and more generally the designer, is concerned with how things ought to be, how they ought to be to attain goals and to function.

Social scientists may often act as if they were studying a natural rather than an artificial world and focus on the problems of establishing mechanisms and causes. These concerns are of importance, but it is also worthwhile to examine goals and purposes and how they can be achieved. The first approach generally receives more attention, and its practice is valued as primary research, while the latter may be seen as a subsidiary rather than a complementary activity.

The designer addresses the issue of the relationship between normative and empirical theory. While the classic response of the scientist is to separate and exclude the normative, the designer embraces normative thinking but retains a commitment to theorising that is rigorous and empirically supported once the goal has been established. The designer is not required (and may not wish) to endorse the goal in question. Goals and the means to achieve them may both contain normative elements. In any case, it is unlikely that many political scientists would want to design means to achieve ends that they thought undesirable. Underlying Lasswell's vision of a science of democracy (1956) or Dryzek's (1989) call for a science of participatory democracy (see chapter 7) there is a sense that the overarching framework for design in social science is set within a commitment to open democratic debate and the presence of a real politics of open deliberation and exchange. The designer is committed to support democratic politics, but not necessarily every outcome of democracy in practice.

Design-thinking proceeds with a modified form of rationality compared to that which tends to dominate in scientific exchange. To make an inference in scientific debate is to make a claim about the cause of an event that excludes rival explanations to the one offered. The procedure of the scientist is in theory at least one of comprehensive rationality. This involves defining the situation, identifying all possible explanations, testing to find the key cause or causes while excluding all others, continuing the process until all options are exhausted and then stating the findings in a general and parsimonious manner. The procedure of the designer reflects much more the processes of bounded rationality. The first stage establishes a representation of the design problem that is not so much formally correct as clear and intelligible to all those involved. The process is one whereby the designer interacts with the participants in a process of iterative reflection. This may involve quantitative or qualitative research but in the end 'numbers are not the name of this game but rather representational structures that permit functional reasoning' (Simon 1996: 146). Decision-making is conditioned by the cognitive limitations of the human mind. Designers reason, but not in the heroic and comprehensive style of classical science.

When faced with a decision designers do not necessarily review every available option; they are more likely to think in terms of rules of thumb. Social science methodologies that give feedback on the effect of an intervention, such as randomised controlled experiments or action-research trials, are of particular value in policy-making. Building in feedback or learning mechanisms is central to design-thinking (Stoker and John 2009; Stoker 2010). This feature is particularly useful for designers because many of the problems they face are initially ill-formulated, information about them can be missing or contradictory, the protagonists of change may hold opposing views on objectives and means to attain them, and the ramifications of any one change may be difficult to judge. The result is that there is 'a fundamental indeterminacy in all but the most trivial design problems' (Buchanan 1992: 15–16).

Classical scientific thinking tends to use relatively stable, fixed categories in its analyses. The design approach is likely to be more flexible. Buchanan captures this in a distinction between a 'category' and a 'placement': 'categories have fixed meanings that are accepted within the framework of a theory or a philosophy, and serve as the basis for analysing what already exists. Placements have boundaries to shape and constrain meaning, but are not rigidly fixed and determinate' (1992: 13–14). 'Placements' serve to orient thinking but can stimulate new perceptions when applied in a specific context and generate new ideas and possibilities.

In contrast to the scientist (Sartori 1991), the designer actively engages in 'concept-stretching' to see if a solution that is understood to work in one setting can be made to fit a problem in another. A 'placement' offers a way of responding to a design challenge, a solution, but the implications can be adjusted to fit the situation at hand. One example would be the transfer of market logic and theories about competition and cost-efficiency into the state sector in recent years. Classical agent–principal and consumer theories are modified to include assumptions about information flows and quality control; choice is delimited and often carried out by proxies.

The end goal of the designer is to offer an effective and acceptable solution, while that of the scientist is to offer an explanation. The contrast offered here between design thinking and that dominant in scientific work should not be exaggerated. They are two forms of rational thought that in practice are more often closely connected than the ideal typical presentation suggested above would allow. If social science wishes to focus more strongly on its relevance to practical matters and to delivery, it also needs to take on the challenges of design thinking.

Conclusion: contributing to policy

Earlier chapters in this book have examined some of the major issues that confront public policy. They have focused on the actual and potential contribution of social science to understanding these issues and to devising new policies to tackle them. They show how in the various areas, from climate change to democratisation, from managing diversity to planning the recovery, from coping with neighbourhood problems to demographic change, the various perspectives available across social science cover a far broader range and offer greater scope for innovative policy-making than do the approaches that tend to dominate in policy-thinking.

In the first chapter we contended that policy-making tends to be dominated by particular paradigms that focus but also limit the viewpoint of government. Paradigms link together understandings of social issues, the goals that should be pursued and the appropriate instruments in an overarching and broadly accepted framework. Problems arise if policy-makers operate within the assumptive world of a particular framework of ideas that precludes alternative ways of thinking about the issues. We argued that in many of the areas we examined, including future economic policy, balancing constrained resources and escalating demand for public services, curbing carbon emissions and developing sustainable climate policies, addressing shifts in population structure and maximising the contribution of activities at the level of the community, the paradigms that shape government programmes limit policy in fundamental ways. Most importantly, the emphasis is on a model that sees state, private actors in the market and neighbourhood energies as separate and alternative, locked in a zero-sum game.

This approach fails to do justice to the opportunities for government intervention to support growth by leading investment, to set the stage for the management of spending issues by engaging people in a serious democratic debate, to control emissions through regulation to maximise the contribution of older people, and to facilitate and support community activities. Instead, it directs energies to the construction of an apparatus of incentives and public spending restraint that treats all those involved simply as rational market actors. Government intervention is understood as crowding out individual enterprise, community initiatives and the contributions of private market actors, and (perhaps more importantly) as incapable of complementing them. One objective of academic work should be to make the alternative paradigms available and to examine their implications in practical policy terms.

We also argued in that chapter for greater attention to the opportunities to join together insights from the various disciplinary traditions in dealing with issues that cut across the concerns of different government departments. More attention to interlinking government agencies and devising methods to co-ordinate policies across them would also be helpful. However, the dominance of disciplinary structures within academe and the exigencies of practical government impose severe limitations.

Policy-making is heavily constrained, by the immediacy of current priorities, by the exigencies of political support and now by all the pressures of the financial crisis. If changes are to take place in the relationship between academics and policy-makers, they are most likely to occur on the academic side, in the way academics think about policy issues. This requires consideration of the potential range of paradigms that can help in addressing current problems and of how they might contribute to new directions in policy. It also requires self-conscious attention to the practical issues of policy design, and a move towards a more synthetic and goal-centred approach. The development of a design arm does not diminish the capacity of academic work to pursue the theory-driven research at which it excels. It offers an additional and more practically driven way of working, to help ensure that the policy-making community gives the contribution of social science the attention it merits.

References

British Academy (2011) *British Academy Policy Centre* [online], http://www.britac.ac.uk/policy/index.cfm (accessed 10 January 2013).

British Journal of Sociology (2004) *Debate on Public Sociology* [online], http://www2.lse.ac.uk/newsAndMedia/news/archives/2004/BJSSociology_Debate.aspx (accessed 10 January 2013).

Buchanan, R. (1992) 'Wicked Problems in Design Thinking', *Design Issues* 8(2): 5–21.

Clawson, D. and 15 others (2007) *Public Sociology* (Berkeley: University of California Press).

Davies, M. and Devlin, M. (2007) *Interdisciplinary Higher Education and the Melbourne Model*, Philosophy of Education Society of Australasia, Deakin University [online], http://www.deakin.edu.au/dro/view/DU:30006786 (accessed 10 January 2013).

Dryzek, J. (1989) 'Policy Sciences of Democracy', *Polity* 22(1): 97–118.

Economic and Social Research Council (ESRC) (2011) *Impact, Innovation and Interdisciplinary Expectations* [online], http://www.esrc.ac.uk/funding-and-guidance/ guidance/applicants/iii.aspx.

Featherman, D. and Vinovskis, M. (2001) *Social Science and Policy-Making: A Search for Relevance in the Twentieth Century* (Ann Arbor: University of Michigan Press).

Gerring, J. (2001) *Social Science Methodology: A Critical Framework* (Cambridge: Cambridge University Press).

Gibson, R. (2009) 'New Media and the Revitalisation of Politics', *Representation* 45(9): 288–289.

Higher Education Funding Council for England (HEFCE) (2011) *Research Excellence Framework Impact Assessment* [online], http://www.hefce.ac.uk/research/ref/impact/.

Lasswell, H. (1956) 'The Political Science of Science: An Inquiry into the Possible Reconciliation of Mastery and Freedom', *American Political Science Review* 50: 961–979.

Nye, J. (2009) 'The Question of Relevance', in G. King, L. Schlozman, N. Kay and H. Norman (eds) *The Future of Political Science: 100 Perspectives* (New York: Routledge), 252–254.

Peters, G., Pierre, J and Stoker, G. (2010) 'The Relevance of Political Science' in D. Marsh and G. Stoker (eds) *Theories and Methods in Political Science* (Basingstoke: Palgrave Macmillan), 325–342.

Sartori, G. (1991) 'Comparing and Miscomparing', *Journal of Theoretical Politics* 3: 243–257.

Shapiro, I. (2003) *The State of Democratic Theory* (Princeton, NJ: Princeton University Press).

Shapiro, I. (2004) 'Problems, Methods, and Theories, or: What's Wrong with Political Science and What To Do About it', in I. Shapiro, R. Smith and T. Masood (eds) *Problems and Methods in the Study of Political Science* (Cambridge: Cambridge University Press), 9–41.

Simon, H. (1996) *The Sciences of the Artificial*, third edition (Cambridge, MA: The MIT Press).

Smith, G. (2009) *Democratic Innovations* (Cambridge: Cambridge University Press).

Stoker, G. and John, P. (2009) 'Design Experiments: Engaging Policy Makers in the Search for Evidence about What Works', *Political Studies*, 57: 356–373.

Stoker, G. (2010) 'Exploring the Promise of Experimentation in Political Science: Micro-foundational Insights and Policy Relevance?', *Political Studies* 58(2): 300–319.

Index